INTERNET
TECHNOLOGIES
STAGE I AWARD FOR OCR

Making the Internet work for you

**NORTH EAST
INSTITUTE
OF FURTHER AND HIGHER
EDUCATION**

MAGHERAFELT CAMPUS
22 Moneymore Road, Magherafelt,
Co. Londonderry, Northern Ireland, BT45 6AE.
Tel. (01648) 32462 Fax (01648) 33501

INTERNET
TECHNOLOGIES
STAGE I AWARD FOR OCR

Making the Internet work for you

ANNE-MARIE BRADLEY

Heinemann Educational Publishers
Halley Court, Jordan Hill, Oxford OX2 8EJ
A Division of Reed Educational & Professional Publishing Limited

Heinemann is a registered trademark of Reed Educational & Professional Publishing Limited

OXFORD   MELBOURNE   AUCKLAND   JOHANNESBURG   BLANTYRE   GABORONE
IBADAN   PORTSMOUTH (NH) USA   CHICAGO

First published 2002
2006 2005 2004 2003 2002
10 9 8 7 6 5 4 3 2 1

A catalogue record for this book is available from the British Library on request.

ISBN 0 435 45084 0

Designed by Artistix, Thame, Oxon

Typeset by Techset Ltd, Gateshead

Printed and bound in Great Britain by Thomson Litho Ltd, East Kilbride, Scotland

Acknowledgements

I would first like to thank Pen Gresford, Gillian Burrell and the team at Heinemann for their support and hard work. I would also like to thank my students who worked through the tasks in this book and provided valuable comments and feedback. Sincere thanks must also go to my husband John and my children, Jacqueline, Kelly-Anne, Anne-Marie and John Jnr for their unrelenting support and encouragement. I would also like to mention my grandchildren, Rhianna Jade and Callum for keeping me sane at times. For sorting out my computer's tantrums, I would like to thank Rob, John C, John R, and Peter in particular. Last but not least, to my late brother Johnny, thank you for your support, encouragement and faith in this and other ventures.

Screenshots reprinted with permission from Netscape Communication Corporation © 2001, Microsoft Corporation, www.virgin.net, © Crown, Met Office and Jodrell Bank Observatory.

The author and publisher would also like to thank Yahoo! Inc, Alta Vista, NASA, Sierra and OCR.

Every effort has been made to contact copyright holders of material published in this book. We would be glad to hear from unacknowledged sources at the first opportunity.

Websites

Examples of websites are suggested in this book. Although these were up to date at the time of writing, we recommend that tutors preview these sites before using them with students to ensure that the URL is still accurate and that the content is suitable for your needs.

Contents

Element 3: Publish information on a website

Introduction

About this book

This book has been designed to take you step by step through the basic skills you will need to use the Internet. It has been carefully structured to be suitable for use in a classroom situation, open learning workshop, or for self study at home.

Completion of the tasks and assignments will provide you with the skills and underpinning knowledge necessary to work towards the OCR Internet Technologies Stage 1 qualification. OCR has divided the qualification into three distinct elements: using email, online research and publishing information on a website.

This book follows a similar structure and, for easy reference, syllabus matching charts are included on pages 6, 81 and 122. This will help you match the syllabus (what you are required to do for the qualification) with the tasks you will complete throughout the book.

There is an ever-increasing choice of email providers, software packages, browsers, etc. and it is not within the scope of this book to cover every option. Therefore, the book concentrates on the Microsoft applications: Microsoft® Outlook 2000, Microsoft® Internet Explorer 5, Microsoft® Word 2000 and Microsoft® Front Page 2000. In each section, however, a matching guide is provided with instructions for performing the tasks in some other common applications (Yahoo! Mail, Hotmail, Netscape® Navigator and Netscape® Composer). In addition, the CD-ROM accompanying the book contains full step-by-step instructions for some of these additional applications (Yahoo! Mail and Netscape® Composer).

Accessing the CD-ROM

To access the CD-ROM contents:

1 Insert the CD-ROM into your CD-ROM drive.

2 From the Windows desktop **Start** menu, Select: **Run**.

3 Key in the name of your CD-ROM drive – e.g. **D:**

4 Click on: **OK**.

5 The CD-ROM contents will be displayed.

6 Double-click on the folder or file that you want to access.

How to use this book

This book is divided into three sections. Within each section there is a short introduction and then a series of tasks. Each task begins with a set of objectives showing what you will have achieved on completion of the task. At the end of each section there is a full practice assignment designed to consolidate what you have learnt in the section.

Element 1: Use electronic mail for business communication

Classroom situation

Your tutor will probably already have set up an email account for you and sent the two email messages needed to complete the tasks. If so, ignore the preparation section on setting up email accounts.

Self-study home user

If you are using the book to study at home you may already have an Internet email account. If so, ignore the section on how to set up a free Yahoo! email account. Before you begin work on the tasks you will need to send two email messages to yourself. Instructions to do this are provided in the email preparation instructions on page 2.

Element 2: Use the Internet for online research

The tasks in this section have been completed using the Internet Explorer browser application. A matching guide is provided to show the commands to use if you are using Netscape Navigator. You will also find tasks on the CD-ROM that use the Netscape Navigator browser.

Element 3: Publish information on a website

Classroom situation

If you are working in a classroom situation your tutor will have prepared tasks for you to complete.

Self-study home user

For self-study users, the material needed to carry out the tasks has been provided on the CD-ROM that accompanies this book. Instructions for accessing the material are provided on page ix.

Self-assessment procedures

Classroom situation

In many schools and colleges it is now a requirement for learners to take some responsibility for the assessment of their own learning. To promote this, a worked copy of each task is included to allow you to check your own work. It is a good idea to get into the habit of doing this. Check your work carefully against the worked copy and make necessary amendments before giving it to your tutor for marking.

Self-study home user

If you are using this book to study at home, then the assessment process is still important; checking your tasks against the worked copies will show you whether you are on the right track and will also be useful should you decide to enrol at college for further study.

About the qualification

To gain the OCR Internet Technologies award you must successfully complete the objectives for each element (see syllabus matching charts, pages 6, 81 and 122).

In a classroom situation

When you have completed the tasks in this book, there are further options available to enhance your new skills and help you to gain the award.

OCR has produced practice assignments relevant to each element of the award. To work towards the award you can either:

- work through the tasks in a particular section, work on the OCR practice assignments and complete the live assignment or:

- complete all sections, work through the practice assignments, then work on the three live assignments at the end.

Your tutor will inform you of the procedures relevant to the institution where you study.

The live assignment is conducted during class time and your tutor will inform you of the procedures to follow while working on it.

Your tutor will check the assignment. In some institutions a double-marking system is in place, which means that another tutor will also check the assignment.

Your tutor will give you appropriate feedback. If you have not completed the objectives successfully you may be allowed a second attempt at the live assignment. Your tutor will inform you of the procedures for this.

What is the Internet?

The Internet consists of millions of computers around the world that are connected together. If you are a home user, you will connect to the Internet when you want. Companies, hospitals, schools, and colleges may be permanently connected to the Internet using a network system. Computers connected to a network can share resources like software and printers.

There are many things available on the Internet, including email programs, that allow you to send messages electronically and chat rooms, where you can communicate online with other Internet users by keying in text.

There are three things that you need before you can connect to the Internet: a modem, an Internet Service Provider (ISP) and a phone line.

Modem

A modem is a hardware device (see Glossary, page 243) that allows a computer to connect to the Internet via a phone line.

Standard phone lines carry analogue data. The modem converts the digital information from the computer to analogue data and sends this down telephone lines to other modems.

Almost all computers sold these days have a modem already installed – either an internal modem, which is located inside the computer, or an external modem, which is a small box-like device connected to and stored outside of the computer.

ISP

To access the Internet you must connect to an ISP. An Internet Service Provider is a commerical organisation that allows access to the Internet via the use of software. When you connect to the Internet you are in fact connecting to the ISP's modem, which is permanently connected to the Internet – this is also known as a 'server' (see Glossary, page 243).

There are numerous ISPs to choose from, most of which now offer free Internet access – the only money you pay is to the telephone company for the time spent 'online' (connected to the Internet through your phone line). Always remember that you pay your telephone company for the time you spend on the Internet, so look into the cost of your calls and find out when the cheaper rates are available – e.g. weekends, after six, etc. Some ISPs offer services whereby you pay a monthly charge and then can access the Internet without paying any call charges. Some of these services allow you to connect without call charges only during the evening and at weekends, while others (usually for a higher monthly charge) offer 24-hour call-charge-free access. If you are going to be spending a lot of time using the Internet, then it is worth looking into some of these services.

An important point to remember is that, although some ISPs provide a free service, phoning their help lines can sometimes be very expensive. You should therefore always check the rates carefully before signing up. The ISP you choose is very much a matter of personal preference. There are too many ISPs to name them all but a few are listed below:

- AOL
- BT Internet
- Demon
- Freeserve
- Tesco
- Virgin.

When you buy a computer, it is normally pre-loaded with ISP software (although, frequently, this is for ISPs that charge you monthly fees, so always check before you sign up to them). Alternatively, you can keep a look out for free ISP CD-ROMs that come with computer magazines or in petrol stations and supermarkets.

For home users, it may be worth noting that you can use more than one ISP. You may have heard the expression 'the server is down': this means that the ISP's modem (which allows you Internet access) is experiencing problems. During this time you will not be able to connect to the Internet. If you work from home or need to access the Internet frequently, it may be useful for you to be able to connect using another ISP if necessary.

Most ISPs offer free email addresses. Some may also include free web space, which allows you to create your own web page, which will then be accessible through the Internet. Check with your ISP to find out which of these facilities it offers.

World wide web

Often referred to as **www**, this is actually only a small part of the Internet. It is made up of the web pages that you see when connected to the Internet. All web pages you visit on the Internet will have an address prefixed by **www**.

Browser application

The browser is the software that allows you to view websites. The two most popular are Internet Explorer and Netscape Navigator. The tasks and screen shots in this book have been produced using Internet Explorer. You can also find tasks on the CD-ROM using Netscape Navigator if this is the browser that you use.

Use electronic mail for business communication

Introduction

What is email?

Email stands for electronic mail, which is the process of sending messages electronically from one computer to another (using an Internet connection). Email is easy to use and messages are received almost immediately. Distance is no object since you can send an email to someone on the other side of the world as easily as you can to someone just across the street. Therefore differences in time zones are not a problem since recipients will receive their message as soon as they access their email account. There are many Internet Service Providers (ISPs) offering free email facilities. A small selection of these is listed below, however, there are many more.

 Virgin

 Freeserve

 BT

 AOL.

The tasks in this section provide instructions for using Microsoft Outlook 2000. Microsoft Outlook is supplied with Microsoft Office 2000 and is a widely used and popular email application. The advantage of using Outlook is that you can compose email messages while offline (not connected to the Internet) and then send and receive messages when you are online (connected to the Internet). This means that you only pay call charges when you send and receive messages, not while you are composing or reading them.

There are also many free Internet-based email providers (you will need to be online to use these). By following their sign-up procedures you can obtain a free email account simply and quickly.

Yahoo! Mail is another free Internet-based email package, which is accessed via the Internet in the same way as Hotmail. Yahoo! Mail is very user friendly and has an excellent Help facility. If you wish to carry out the tasks for this element using Yahoo! Mail, then you will find different versions of the tasks on the accompanying CD-ROM, which take you through the steps using Yahoo! Mail rather than Outlook.

Classroom situation

If you are working in a classroom situation you may find the school or college is permanently connected to the Internet, so you do not need to worry about call charges.

Self-study home user

It would be a good idea to find out the peak and off-peak rates of your telephone company. For example, some telephone companies offer cheaper rates after 6 pm and at weekends, or there may be special Internet offers available. It is worthwhile finding out. Limit yourself to a certain amount of time and keep the rates in mind while working online.

It is possible, with some software packages, such as Outlook, to prepare email messages when you are offline (not connected to the Internet). The message is stored on your computer until you connect to the Internet and can then be sent while you are working online.

For this procedure to work, the application must be set up to connect to your **external** email provider, otherwise your message will not be sent. To find out more about this, you will need to access your external email provider's help facility. Be careful if you telephone a helpline, as this can be expensive – find out what the charge is first.

Email message preparation

Classroom situation

If you are working in a classroom your tutor will have prepared the email messages for you to complete the tasks in this element and will have sent them to your email address.

Self-study home user

If you are using this book to study at home, then you will need to send two email messages, with attachments, to yourself so that you can complete the tasks. The text and attachments for the email messages can be found on the accompanying CD-ROM. (You may need to refer to the instructions in Tasks 3, 4 and 9 in order to send these emails.)

Email software matching guide

Assessment objective	Outlook	Yahoo! Mail
1.1a **Create new message**	Click on: 📧 New **New Message** button; key in recipient's email address; key in subject heading; key in message text.	Click on: the **Compose** link below **Yahoo! Options**; key in recipient's email address; key in subject heading; key in message text.

Assessment objective	Outlook	Yahoo! Mail
1.1b **Use Reply facility**	Open required e-mail message; click on: **Reply** button; key in new message above original message; click on: **Send** button.	Open required email message; click on: **Reply** button; key in new message above original message; click on: **Send** button.
1.1c **Use Forward facility**	Open required email message; click on: **Forward** button; key in new message above original message; click on: **Send** button.	Open required email message; click on: **Forward** button; key in new message above original message; click on: **Send** button.
1.1d **Send mail to more than one recipient with equal priority**	Click on: **New Message** button; click in **To** box; key in first recipient's email address; key in semi colon; key in second recipient's email address.	Click on: **Compose** link; click in **To** box; key in first recipient's email address; key in comma; key in second recipient's email address (no spaces after comma).
1.1e **Copy message to second recipient**	Click in **Cc** box; key in email address of person to receive copy: Cc...	Click in **Cc** box; key in email address of person to receive copy: **Cc:**
1.1f **Attach file to outgoing message**	Click on: **Insert File** button. *or* From the **Insert** menu, select **File**. Select location from **Look in:** box; select file to attach; click on: arrow to right of **Insert** button; select **Insert as Attachment**.	Click on: **Add/Delete Attachments** link at bottom of message box; click on: **Browse** to select location of file; click on attachment; click on: **Open**; click on: **Attach File** button. When attachment is shown in attachment box, click on: **Done**.
1.1h **Retrieve stored email address**	In **New Message** window, click on: **To...** button; select stored recipient's name; click on: **To** button; click on: **OK**.	Click on: **Address Book** link above **To** box; click to put a tick in **To** box next to recipient's email address.
1.1i **Store all outgoing messages**	Sent messages are saved automatically in Outlook.	Click on: **Options** link below **Yahoo! Mail**; click on: **Mail Preferences**; click to put a dot in circle next to **Yes Save Sent Messages**.

Assessment objective	Outlook	Yahoo! Mail
1.1j Send messages	Key in recipient's email address, subject heading and message text; click on: **Send** button. (If offline, click on: **Send/Receive** button to connect to Internet and send message.)	Key in recipient's email address, subject heading and message text; click on: **Send** button.
1.2a Access incoming message	Click on: **Inbox** in **Folder List**; double-click on message to open it.	Click on: **Check Mail** link below **Yahoo! Mail**; click on message to open it.
1.2b Access attachment	Click on: **Inbox** in **Folder List**; click on message with attachment; click on: **Paperclip** icon in top right-hand corner of preview pane. From the drop-down list select the document you wish to open.	Image attachments in Yahoo! Mail are shown at the bottom of the message. For other attachments: scroll down to bottom of message; click on: **Download File** link; click on: **Open this file from its current location**.
1.2c Store incoming message outside mailbox	Click on: **Inbox** in **Folder List**; click on message to store; from **File** menu, select: **Save As**; select location to save from **Save in:** box; click on: **Save**.	Click on: **Check Mail**; click on message to store; from **File** menu, select **Save As**; select location to save from **Save in:** box; click on: **Save**.
1.2d Store attachments outside mailbox	Open message from **Inbox**; from **File** menu, select: **Save Attachment**; select location to save from **Save in:** box; click on: **Save**. If there is more than one attachment: from **File** menu, select: **Save Attachments**; select location to save from **Save in:** box; click on: **Save**.	Open message. If image attachment, right-click on image; select **Save image as** (keep original filename). If other attachment, click on: **Download File**, when loaded into appropriate software, from **File** menu, select: **Save As** and keep original name.
1.2e Store email address in appropriate facility	Open incoming message; right-click on email address of sender in **From** field; click on: **Add to Contacts**; click on: **Save and Close** button.	Click on: **Add to Address Book** link to right of sender's email address; click to put a tick in box to left of email address to be added; click on: **Add Checked**.

Assessment objective	Outlook	Yahoo! Mail
1.2f **Delete message**	Click on: **Inbox** in **Folder List**; click once on message to delete; click on ✖ **Delete** button.	Click on: **Check Mail** folder; click to put a tick in box to left of message to be deleted; click on: Delete **Delete** button.
1.3d **Print sent messages**	Click on: **Sent** in **Folder List**; click on message to print; click on: 🖨 **Print** button. *or* From **File** menu, select: **Print**.	Click on: cross to left of **Folders** link below **Yahoo! Mail**; click on **Sent** folder; click to open message to print; click on: 🖨 Print **Print** button.

Objectives

What you will achieve in this element

Each task in this element has been designed to guide you through the OCR requirements for Element One. It is important that you complete the tasks in the order shown.

The syllabus matching chart on page 6 shows which tasks fulfil each of the OCR requirements.

Each task includes step-by-step instructions for completing it. It is important that you check each of your tasks carefully when you have finished. This is known as self-assessment and will help with your learning process. It is now also a requirement in many educational institutions. Check your completed tasks carefully and make any necessary amendments. The tasks are followed by build-up tasks and two full practice assignments to help consolidate your new skills.

Classroom situation

If you are using this book in a classroom, to further enhance your new skills, OCR has produced a series of practice assignment papers for each element of the award. Your tutor will tell you about this.

Self-study home user

If you are using this book to study at home, then completing the tasks will give you a good grounding in the skills involved, as well as providing the basis for completing Element One, should you decide to enrol at a college to work towards the award.

Assessment objectives	_	1	2	3	4	5	6	7	8	9	10	11	12	13	14	15	B1	B2	C1	C2
1.1 Transmit messages electronically																				
a create new message				●			●			●		●				●	●	●	●	●
b use reply facility as specified						●											●	●	●	●
c use forward facility as specified											●						●	●	●	●
d send message to more than one recipient with equal priority												●					●	●	●	●
e Copy message to a second recipient							●										●	●	●	●
f attach file to outgoing message				●			●			●		●					●	●	●	●
g address all outgoing messages				●						●							●	●	●	●
h retrieve stored email address				●						●							●	●	●	●
i store all outgoing messages				●			●			●		●					●	●	●	●
j send messages				●		●	●			●	●	●					●	●	●	●
1.2 Receive messages electronically																				
a access incoming message					●									●			●	●	●	●
b access attachment									●						●		●	●	●	●
c store incoming message outside mailbox structure														●			●	●	●	●
d store attachment outside mailbox structure													●	●			●	●	●	●
e store email address in appropriate facility		●			●								●				●	●	●	●
f delete message													●				●	●	●	●
1.3 Use appropriate software accurately and within regulations																				
a select and use appropriate software		●	●	●	●	●	●	●	●	●	●	●	●	●	●	●	●	●	●	●
b access mail server		●	●	●	●	●	●	●	●	●	●	●	●	●	●	●	●	●	●	●
c enter data as specified ensuring there are no more than 3 data entry errors in total		●	●	●	●	●	●	●	●	●	●	●	●	●	●	●	●	●	●	●
d print all messages and attachments as specified		●	●	●	●	●	●	●	●	●	●	●	●	●	●	●	●	●	●	●
e exit software following correct procedures		●	●	●	●	●	●	●	●	●	●	●	●	●	●	●	●	●	●	●
f use computer within basic health and safety regulations		●	●	●	●	●	●	●	●	●	●	●	●	●	●	●	●	●	●	●

Task number

Use electronic mail for business communications

Setting up an email account

Outlook

Check mail options

Objectives

- Load Microsoft Outlook
- Change view options
- Check mail options
- Exit Microsoft Outlook and shut down computer

Loading Microsoft Outlook

☐ Method

1   *Either:* click on: the 🕑 **Microsoft Outlook** shortcut icon on the desktop,
    or: click on the Start button in the bottom left-hand corner of the screen and,
    from the pop-up menu that appears, select **Programs**, then **Microsoft
    Outlook**.

The **Microsoft Outlook** window appears on screen (see Figure 1.1.1-1). There
are options available in the **Outlook** window that you will not need to complete
the following tasks. The grey bar on the left is the **Outlook Bar**. The options in
the **Outlook Bar** are also available in the **Folder List** so it is not necessary to
show the **Outlook Bar**.

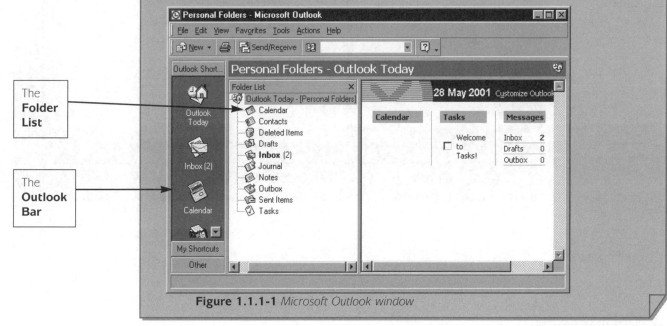

Figure 1.1.1-1 *Microsoft Outlook window*

The **Folder List**

The **Outlook Bar**

Changing view options

Removing Outlook Bar

It will be useful, while working through the tasks, if the window you are viewing is similar to the screen shots shown in this book. As you are unlikely to need the **Outlook Bar**, you can remove it from the window.

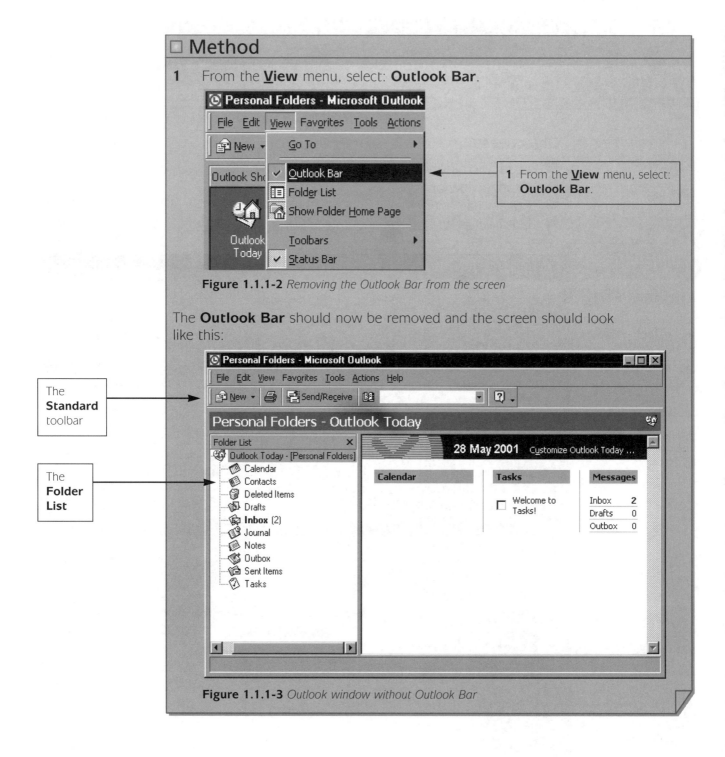

☐ Method

1   From the **View** menu, select: **Outlook Bar**.

> 1   From the **View** menu, select: **Outlook Bar**.

Figure 1.1.1-2 *Removing the Outlook Bar from the screen*

The **Outlook Bar** should now be removed and the screen should look like this:

The **Standard** toolbar

The **Folder List**

Figure 1.1.1-3 *Outlook window without Outlook Bar*

Displaying the standard toolbar

In Figure 1.1.1-3, the **Standard** toolbar is shown. If your toolbar is the same, then leave it. However, if your toolbar looks different, or no toolbar appears, you need to change the options so that it looks the same.

☐ Method

1   From the **View** menu, select: **Toolbars** and check that there is a tick only next to **Standard**. If there is no tick, then click on it to put a tick there; if there is a tick on any of the other options, then click on it to remove the tick.

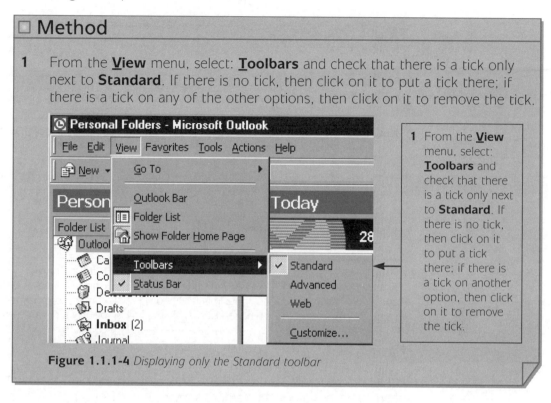

1 From the **View** menu, select: **Toolbars** and check that there is a tick only next to **Standard**. If there is no tick, then click on it to put a tick there; if there is a tick on another option, then click on it to remove the tick.

Figure 1.1.1-4 *Displaying only the Standard toolbar*

Displaying the Folder List

In Figure 1.1.1-3, the **Folder List** is on the left. If you do not see the folder list, then you will need to display it.

☐ Method

1   From the **View** menu, select **Folder List**.

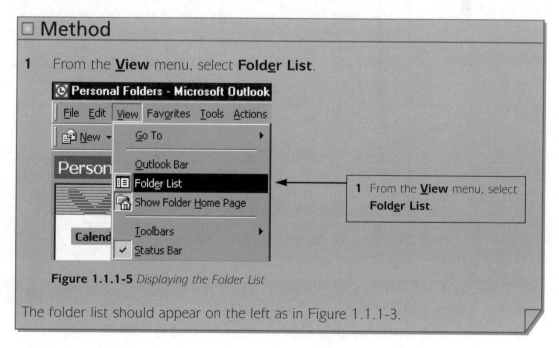

1 From the **View** menu, select **Folder List**.

Figure 1.1.1-5 *Displaying the Folder List*

The folder list should appear on the left as in Figure 1.1.1-3.

The Outlook window explained

Figure 1.1.1-6 shows the Outlook **menu bar**. When you click on an item on the menu bar, a drop-down menu appears (as you have already seen in Figures 1.1.1-2, 1.1.1-4 and 1.1.1-5).

When you click on an item, a drop-down menu appears.

Figure 1.1.1-6 *Outlook menu bar*

The **Standard** toolbar is shown in Figure 1.1.1-7. There are a number of shortcut buttons that you can click to access various functions.

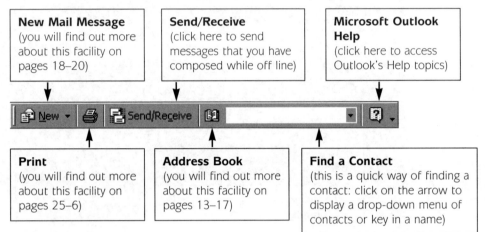

New Mail Message
(you will find out more about this facility on pages 18–20)

Send/Receive
(click here to send messages that you have composed while off line)

Microsoft Outlook Help
(click here to access Outlook's Help topics)

Print
(you will find out more about this facility on pages 25–6)

Address Book
(you will find out more about this facility on pages 13–17)

Find a Contact
(this is a quick way of finding a contact: click on the arrow to display a drop-down menu of contacts or key in a name)

Figure 1.1.1-7 *Standard toolbar*

Figure 1.1.1-8 shows the **Folder List**. For the tasks in this element, you will not need to access all of the folders shown. A brief description of the folders is given.

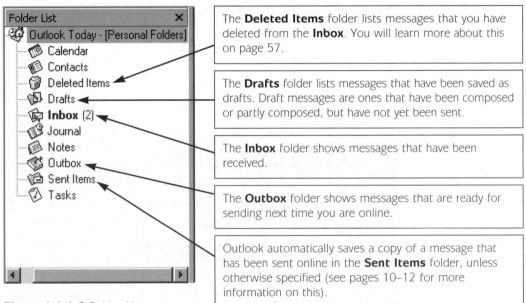

The **Deleted Items** folder lists messages that you have deleted from the **Inbox**. You will learn more about this on page 57.

The **Drafts** folder lists messages that have been saved as drafts. Draft messages are ones that have been composed or partly composed, but have not yet been sent.

The **Inbox** folder shows messages that have been received.

The **Outbox** folder shows messages that are ready for sending next time you are online.

Outlook automatically saves a copy of a message that has been sent online in the **Sent Items** folder, unless otherwise specified (see pages 10–12 for more information on this).

Figure 1.1.1-8 *Folder List*

Checking mail options

Ensuring Outlook will save sent messages

For the OCR Internet Technologies award you are required to save a copy of every email message you send. Microsoft Outlook should automatically save all sent messages in the **Sent Items** folder. However, it is important to check this.

☐ Method

1 From the **Tools** menu, select: **Options...**

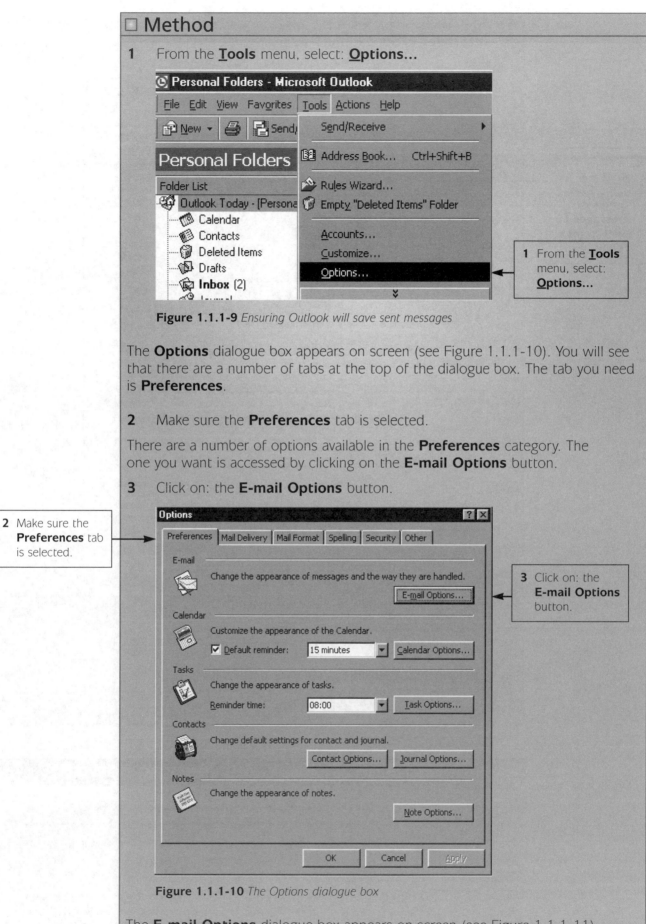

1 From the **Tools** menu, select: **Options...**

Figure 1.1.1-9 *Ensuring Outlook will save sent messages*

The **Options** dialogue box appears on screen (see Figure 1.1.1-10). You will see that there are a number of tabs at the top of the dialogue box. The tab you need is **Preferences**.

2 Make sure the **Preferences** tab is selected.

There are a number of options available in the **Preferences** category. The one you want is accessed by clicking on the **E-mail Options** button.

3 Click on: the **E-mail Options** button.

2 Make sure the **Preferences** tab is selected.

3 Click on: the **E-mail Options** button.

Figure 1.1.1-10 *The Options dialogue box*

The **E-mail Options** dialogue box appears on screen (see Figure 1.1.1-11). In the **Message handling** section, there are a number of small white boxes with further email options.

4 Make sure there is a tick in the second box (to the left of **Save copies of messages in Sent Items folder**). If not, then click in the box to put a tick in it.

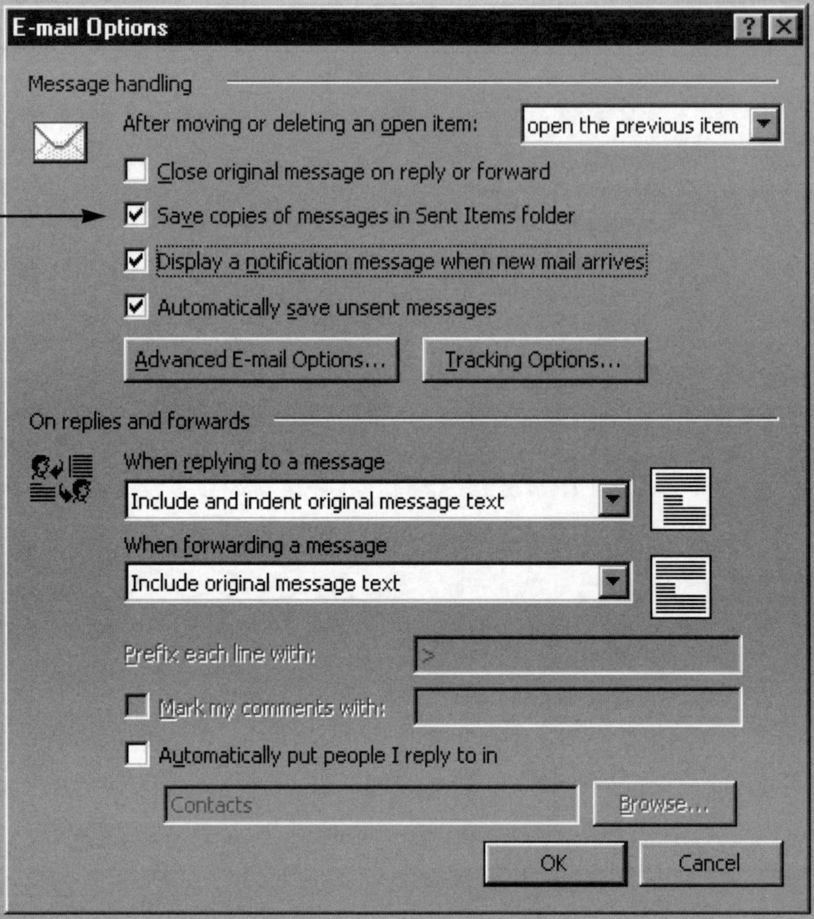

4 Make sure there is a tick in the **Save copies of messages in Sent Items folder** box.

E-mail Options

Message handling

After moving or deleting an open item: open the previous item

☐ Close original message on reply or forward

☑ Save copies of messages in Sent Items folder

☑ Display a notification message when new mail arrives

☑ Automatically save unsent messages

Advanced E-mail Options...   Tracking Options...

On replies and forwards

When replying to a message
Include and indent original message text

When forwarding a message
Include original message text

Prefix each line with: >

☐ Mark my comments with:

☐ Automatically put people I reply to in
Contacts   Browse...

OK   Cancel

Figure 1.1.1-11 *E-mail Options dialogue box*

When this option is selected, a copy of each email message you send will automatically be saved in the **Sent Items** folder. This allows you to access email messages that you have sent.

5 Click on: **OK**.

The **Options** dialogue box will still be on the screen.

6 Click on: **OK** again to exit the **Options** dialogue box.

Exiting Microsoft Outlook and shutting down

☐ Method

1 From the **File** menu, select: **Exit**.

2 Make sure that all other applications are closed.

3 Click on: the **Start** button and, from the pop-up menu, select **Shut Down** and then **Shut Down** from the options that appear.

4 Click on: **OK**.

Outlook

Add new contacts to Address Book

Objectives

- Access the **Address Book**
- Create a new contact
- Add a second contact
- Exit the **Address Book**

For the OCR Internet Technologies award you are required to access an email address book facility and enter email addresses.

There is an **Address Book** facility in most email applications. Making entries in the **Address Book** is very much like adding addresses to a personal address book.

One of the advantages of using this facility is that you are less likely to make a keying-in error in an email address. Another advantage is that it is less time-consuming than having to key in each email address every time you send a message as you can simply select the address you want from the address book.

Accessing the Address Book

☐ Method

1. If you do not already have Microsoft Outlook on screen, then load it (*either* click on: the **Microsoft Outlook** shortcut icon on the desktop, *or* click on the **Start** button and select: **Programs**, **Microsoft Outlook**).

2. Click on: the 📖 **Address Book** button.

The **Address Book** window appears on screen (see Figure 1.1.2-1). The **Address Book** window has its own menu bar and toolbar.

> If no-one else has used the **Address Book** before, you may see this **Welcome to Contacts** message, otherwise the Address Book will be empty (unless someone has already entered addresses in it).

Figure 1.1.2-1 *Address Book window*

Creating a new contact

☐ Method

1   Click on: the 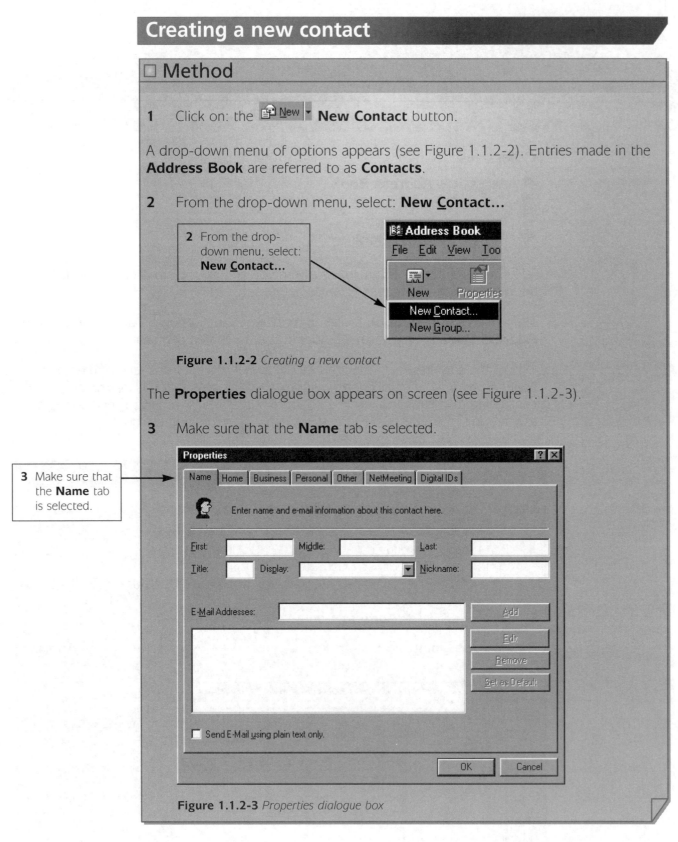 **New Contact** button.

A drop-down menu of options appears (see Figure 1.1.2-2). Entries made in the **Address Book** are referred to as **Contacts**.

2   From the drop-down menu, select: **New Contact...**

> **2** From the drop-down menu, select: **New Contact...**

Figure 1.1.2-2 *Creating a new contact*

The **Properties** dialogue box appears on screen (see Figure 1.1.2-3).

3   Make sure that the **Name** tab is selected.

> **3** Make sure that the **Name** tab is selected.

Figure 1.1.2-3 *Properties dialogue box*

You will be adding the email addresses of two of your fellow students (if you are using the book to study at home, then key in the email address of two friends or relatives instead).

For the purposes of this task, the only data you need to key in is the email address and a first name. Keying in a first name will help you to distinguish between different addresses. (If you were using this facility at home, for your personal use, you might want to complete the other address details as well.)

Entering the first name

☐ Method

1 Click inside the box next to **First** and key in the first name of your fellow student (or friend or relative).

When you have keyed in a name, it will appear in the title bar.

Key in the first name of your new contact.

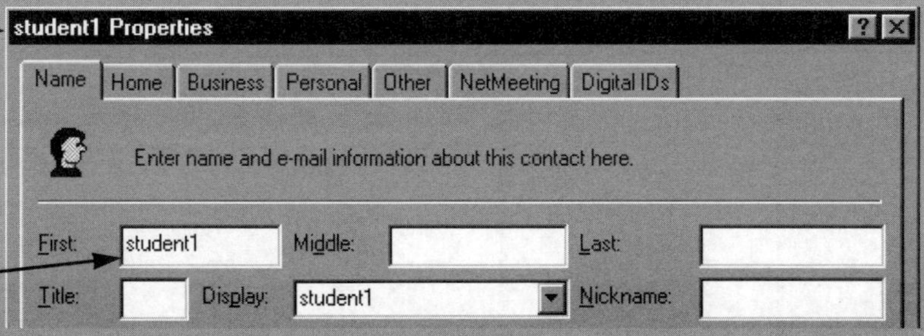

Figure 1.1.2-4 *Entering the first name*

Entering the email address

☐ Method

1 Click inside the **E-mail Addresses:** box and key in their complete email address.

E-Mail Addresses: student1@somewhere.co.uk | Add |

Figure 1.1.2-5 *Entering the email address*

☐ Hint

It is important to key in email addresses accurately as, if there were an error, the messages would not be delivered to the correct person (if at all).

2 Click on: the **Add** button.

The email address you have added will be shown in the white box at the bottom of the dialogue box (see Figure 1.1.2-6).

The email address will be shown here.

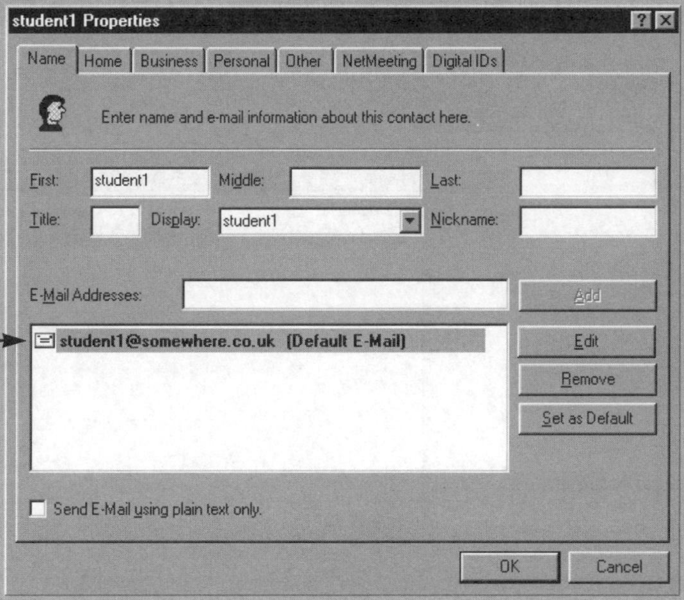

Figure 1.1.2-6 *Email address added*

3 Click on: **OK**.

The new contact will now be listed in the white box at the bottom of the **Address Book** window (see Figure 1.1.2-7).

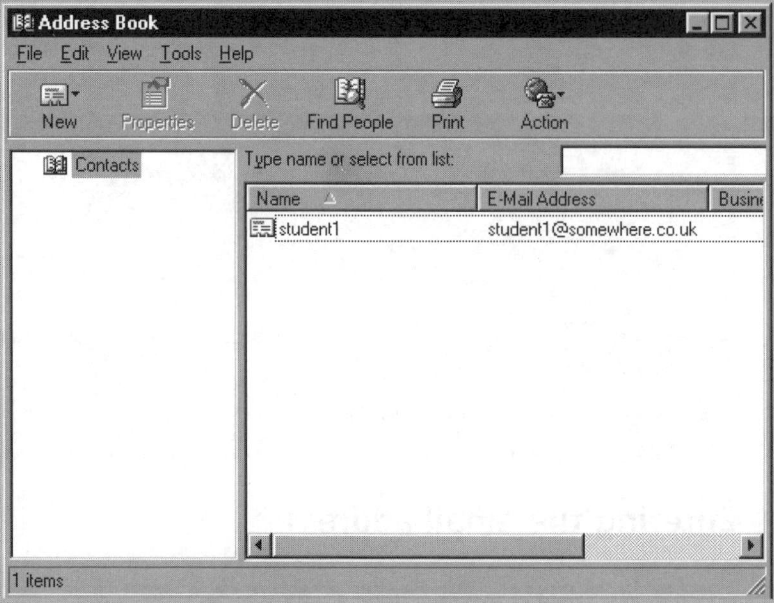

The new contact has now been added to the **Address Book**.

Figure 1.1.2-7 *New contact added*

Adding a second contact

You will now add the second contact to the **Address Book**.

☐ Method

1 Follow the same instructions as you did when adding the first contact (but use a different name and email address).

The **Address Book** should now have two new contacts (see Figure 1.1.2-8). At the bottom left of the dialogue box it should now show **2 items**.

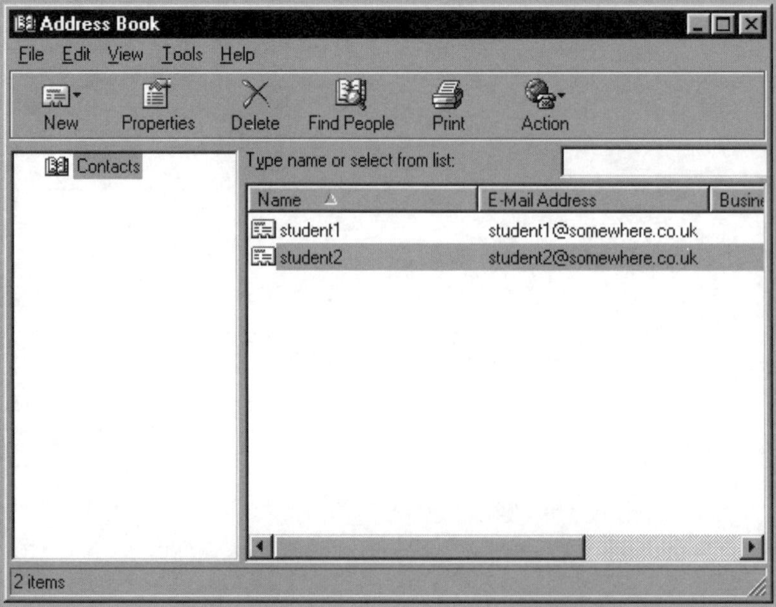

There should now be **2 items** shown here.

Figure 1.1.2-8 *Two contacts added*

Exiting the Address Book

☐ Method

1   From the **File** menu, select: **Exit** (see Figure 1.1.2-9).

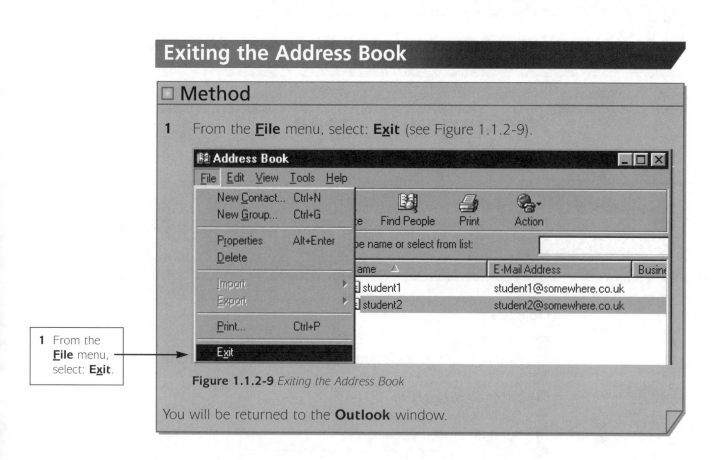

1 From the **File** menu, select: **Exit**.

Figure 1.1.2-9 *Exiting the Address Book*

You will be returned to the **Outlook** window.

Exiting Outlook and shutting down

If your session is finished, then exit Outlook (from the **File** menu, select **Exit** *or* click on: the ☒ cross in the top right-hand corner) and shut down your computer (exit all other applications; click on: the **Start** button; select **Shut Down**; select **Shut Down**; click on: **OK**). Otherwise, move straight on to the next task.

Use electronic mail for business communications

Working with email

Outlook

Create and send an email message

Objectives

- Create a new mail message
- Add a recipient email address from the **Address Book**
- Enter a subject heading
- Enter message text
- Spellcheck and proof-read a message
- Send an email message
- Print a message from the **Sent Items** folder

In this task, you will create and send an email message. Instead of keying in the email address of the recipient (the person to whom you are sending the email), you will insert an email address from one of the entries you made in the **Address Book** in Task 2.

Creating a new mail message

☐ Method

1   If you do not already have Microsoft Outlook on screen, then load it (*either* click on: the **Microsoft Outlook** shortcut icon on the desktop, *or* click on the **Start** button and select: **Programs**, **Microsoft Outlook**).

2   Click on: the 📧 <u>New</u> ▾ **New Message** button.

The **Untitled – Message** window appears on screen (see Figure 1.2.3-1). This dialogue box has its own menu bar and toolbar.

The Message window explained

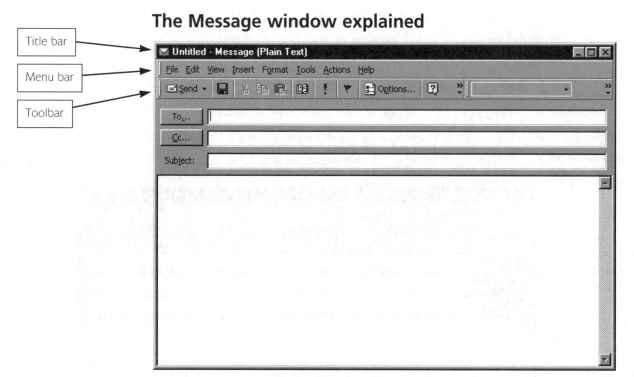

Figure 1.2.3-1 *Message window dialogue box*

The **title bar** shows the name of the message. So far, this message doesn't have a name, so it just says **Untitled**. The **menu bar** contains various options, including ones for formatting and editing an email message. You will be introduced to these different options as and when it becomes necessary. The **toolbar** contains buttons to access various functions (see Figure 1.2.3-2).

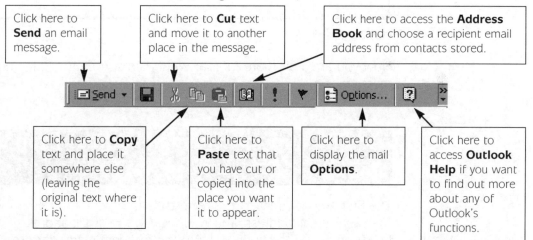

Figure 1.2.3-2 *Toolbar buttons*

Clicking the arrows at the far right of the toolbar will display a drop-down menu of more buttons (see Figure 1.2.3-3).

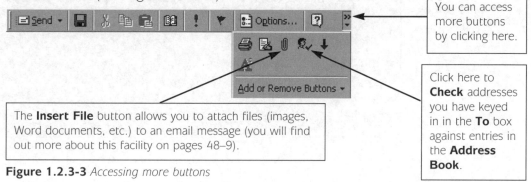

Figure 1.2.3-3 *Accessing more buttons*

There are four boxes in the **Message** window for keying text into (see Figure 1.2.3-4).

The details you enter in the three top boxes are known as the **Header details** of the email message. This shows whom you are sending the message to and the subject of the message.

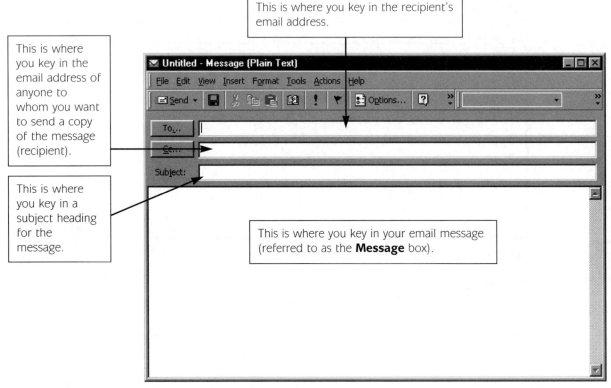

This is where you key in the recipient's email address.

This is where you key in the email address of anyone to whom you want to send a copy of the message (recipient).

This is where you key in a subject heading for the message.

This is where you key in your email message (referred to as the **Message** box).

Figure 1.2.3-4 *Where you key in text*

Now you are a bit more familiar with Microsoft Outlook, it's time to send an email message.

Adding a recipient email address from the Address Book

The first step is to insert the recipient's (the person to whom you are sending the message) email address. You could key in the email address in the **To...** box, however, in this task, you will add the recipient's email address from a contact entry you created in Task 2.

☐ Method

1   Click on: the ⬜ To: -> ⬜ **To...** button.

The **Select Names** dialogue box appears on screen (see Figure 1.2.3-5). The contacts you added in Task 2 should be listed here.

2   Click on: one of the contacts.

3 Click on: the To: -> **To->** button.

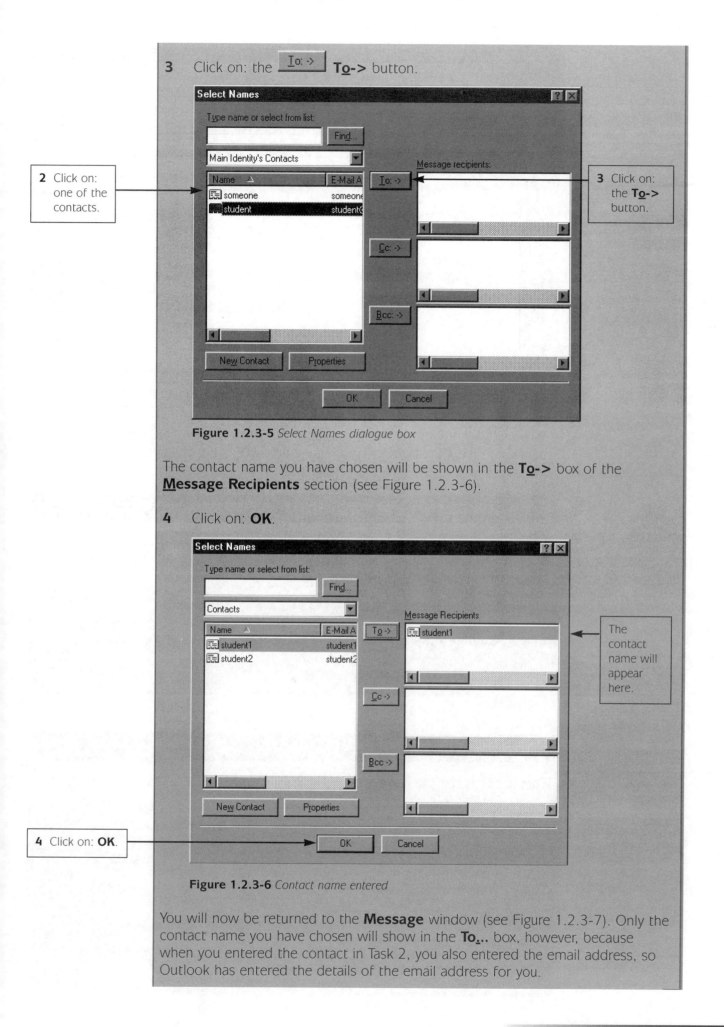

Figure 1.2.3-5 *Select Names dialogue box*

2 Click on: one of the contacts.

3 Click on: the **To->** button.

The contact name you have chosen will be shown in the **To->** box of the **Message Recipients** section (see Figure 1.2.3-6).

4 Click on: **OK**.

The contact name will appear here.

4 Click on: **OK**.

Figure 1.2.3-6 *Contact name entered*

You will now be returned to the **Message** window (see Figure 1.2.3-7). Only the contact name you have chosen will show in the **To...** box, however, because when you entered the contact in Task 2, you also entered the email address, so Outlook has entered the details of the email address for you.

The Contact name has now been entered in **To₁..** box.

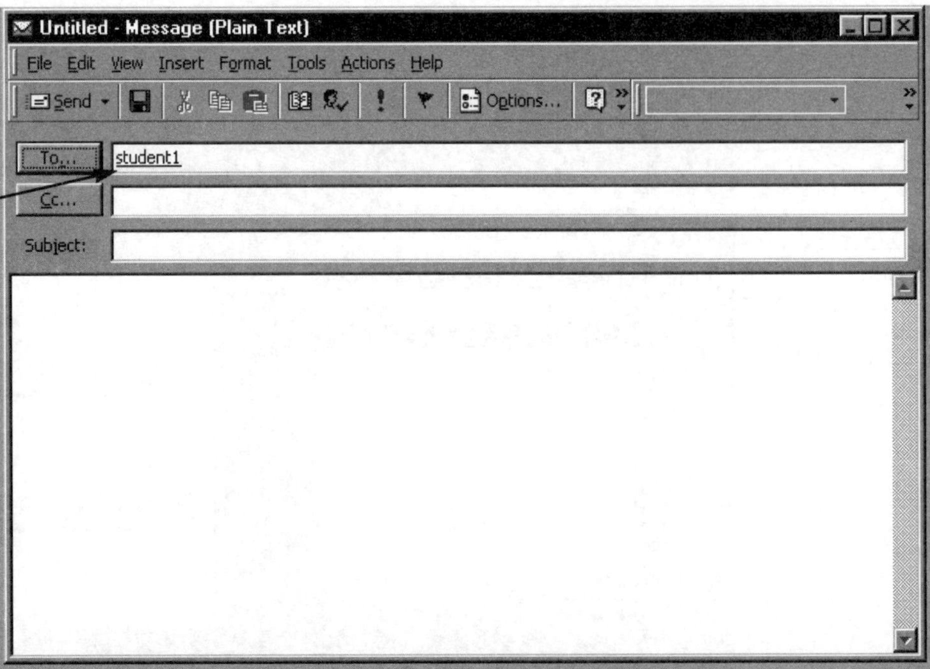

Figure 1.2.3-7 *Contact name entered in* **To₁..** *box*

As we only want to send this message to one person, there is no need to enter anything in the **Cc...** box (you will learn more about this on pages 35–6).

Entering a subject heading

The next step is to key in a subject heading for the message. This is important as it will give the recipient an idea of what the message is about. It will also help you find a particular message at a later date.

☐ Method

1   Click in the **Subject:** box and key in the following text exactly as shown:

    EMAIL USING ADDRESS BOOK

Entering message text

The message box (the large white box) is where you key in the actual message.

☐ Method

1   Click in the message box and key in the following message text exactly as shown:

    I am sending this message to test an entry made in the Address Book.

2   Key in your name, date, centre number (if you are working at college or school) and task number below the message text.

Hint

Make sure there is one clear line space after the message (by pressing: **Enter** twice) before you key in your personal details.

Spellchecking and proof-reading a message

For the OCR Internet Technologies award you are only allowed three data entry errors in the email assignment. Outlook has a **Spellcheck** facility and you should get into the habit of using this as well as proof-reading your messages for errors.

Method

1 From the **Tools** menu, select: **Spelling...**

Notice that the title bar now shows the subject heading.

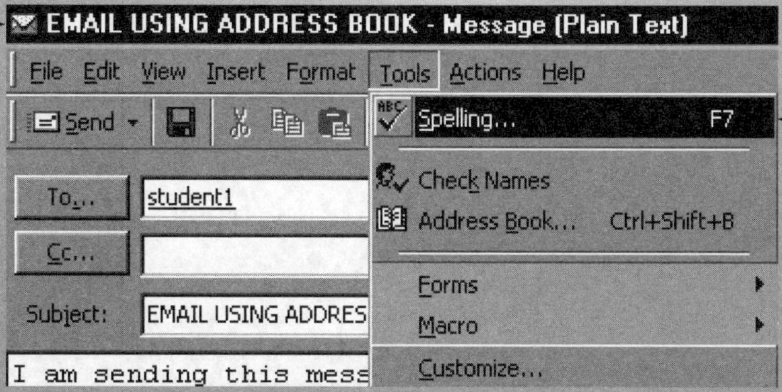
EMAIL USING ADDRESS BOOK - Message (Plain Text)
File Edit View Insert Format Tools Actions Help
Send
Spelling... F7
Check Names
Address Book... Ctrl+Shift+B
Forms
Macro
Customize...
To...
student1
Cc...
Subject:
EMAIL USING ADDRES
I am sending this mess

1 From the **Tools** menu, select: **Spelling...**

Figure 1.2.3-8 *Accessing the Spellcheck facility*

If the spelling in the message is correct you will see a prompt box telling you so (see Figure 1.2.3-9).

2 Click on: **OK**.

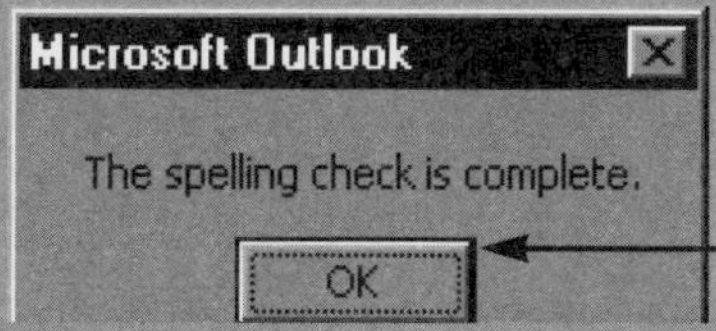
Microsoft Outlook
The spelling check is complete.
OK

2 Click on: **OK**.

Figure 1.2.3-9 *Spelling check complete prompt box*

Info

If you have spelt a word incorrectly, then the **Spelling** dialogue box will appear on screen (see Figure 1.2.3-10). As an example, the word **message** has been spelt wrongly on purpose to show you how to correct this using the **Spellcheck** facility.

The wrong spelling of the word **message** is shown in the **Not in Dictionary:** box.

A list of possible words is shown in the **Suggestions:** box. In this example, the correct spelling of the word **message** is listed. Click on: the correct spelling and then click on: **Change**. The **Spelling** dialogue box will then display the next spelling error, until there are none remaining.

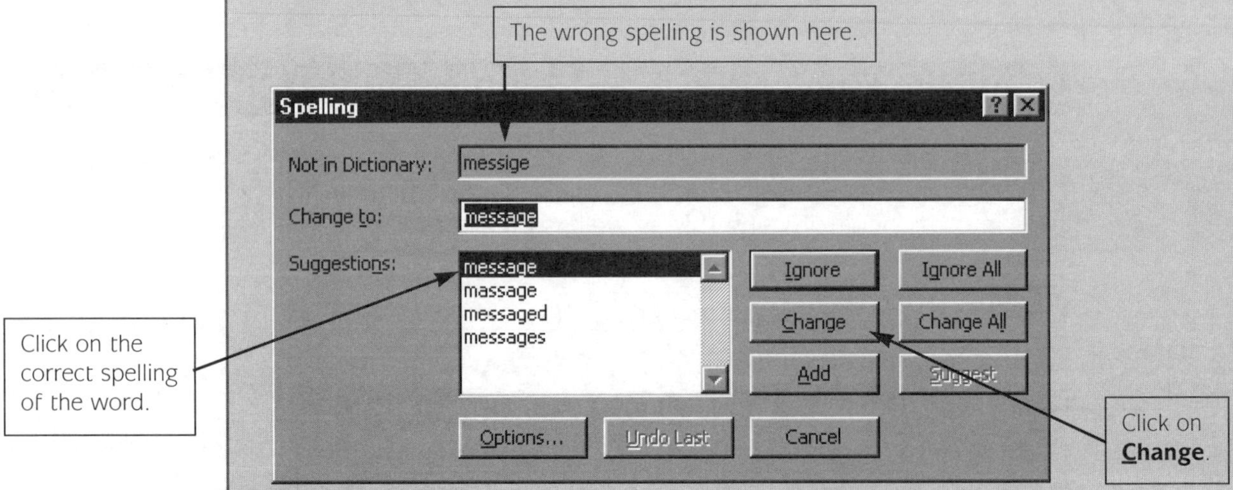

The wrong spelling is shown here.

Spelling   ? ✕

Not in Dictionary: messige

Change to: message

Suggestions: message   ▲   Ignore   Ignore All
               massage
               messaged   Change   Change All
               messages
                                 ▼   Add   Suggest

               Options...   Undo Last   Cancel

Click on the correct spelling of the word.

Click on **Change**.

Figure 1.2.3-10 *Spelling dialogue box*

When the **Spellcheck** is complete, the prompt box (see Figure 1.2.3-9) will appear on screen. Click on: **OK**.

4   Proof-read the text carefully for errors that the **Spellcheck** might have missed (by reading what's on screen against the original text in this book).

Your email message should now look like the one shown below (except with different recipient name and with your own personal details shown at the bottom of the message text).

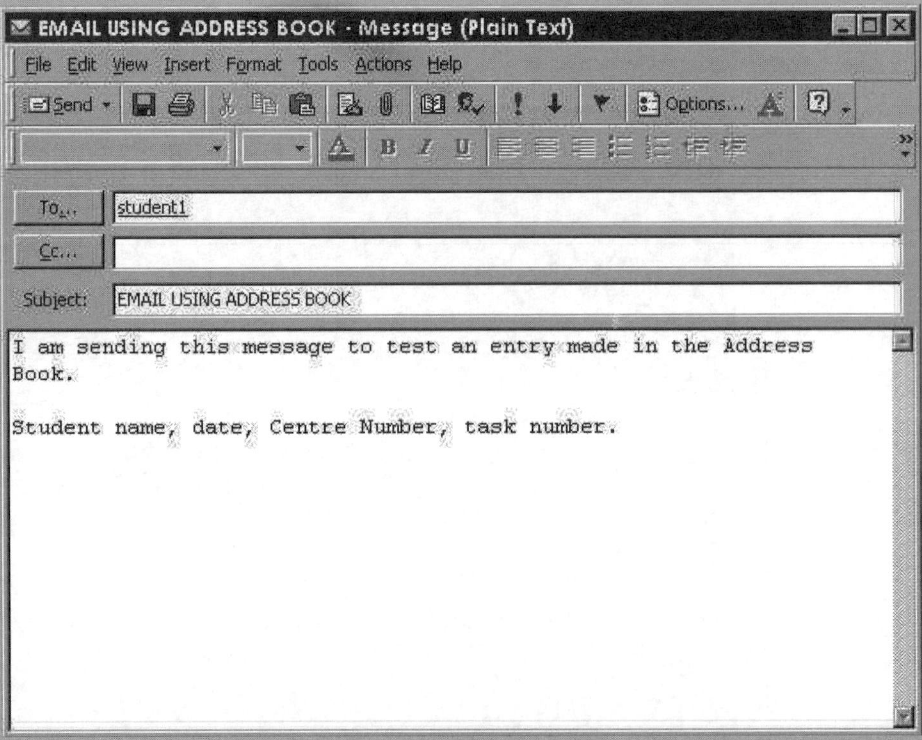

✉ **EMAIL USING ADDRESS BOOK - Message (Plain Text)**   _ ☐ ✕

File Edit View Insert Format Tools Actions Help

Send ▾   🖫 🖨 ✂ 📋 📋 📇 ℞ 📇 ℞ ! ↓ ▼ 📇 Options... A̲ ☑

───────── ▾ ─ A̲ B I U ▤ ▤ ▤ ⫶⫶ ⫶⫶ ⫶⫶ ⟫

To...   student1

Cc...

Subject: EMAIL USING ADDRESS BOOK

I am sending this message to test an entry made in the Address
Book.

Student name, date, Centre Number, task number.

Figure 1.2.3-11 *Completed email message*

Sending an email

You are now ready to send your email.

□ Method

1   Click on: the 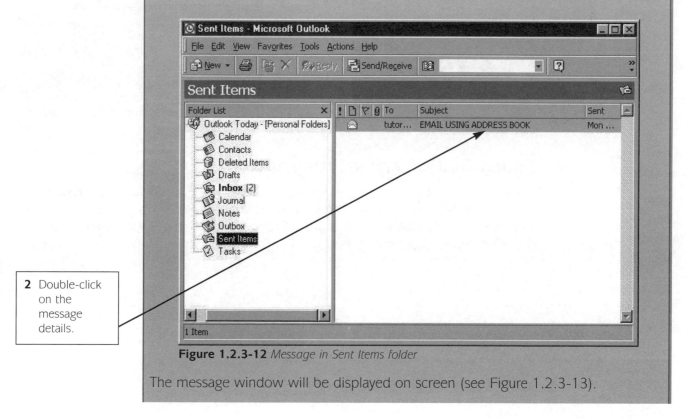 **Send** button.

You will be returned to the Outlook window. If you are working in a college, then the email will probably have been sent immediately and will now be in the **Sent Items** folder. However, if you are working offline at home, the email will be in the **Outbox** waiting for you to connect to the Internet. In this case, you need to click on: the **Send/Receive** button in order for the message to be delivered (when you have done that the message will be put in the **Sent Items** folder).

Printing a message from the Sent Items folder

For the OCR Internet Technologies award you are required to print messages that have been sent. To do this, you will need to access the **Sent Items** folder.

□ Method

1   Click on: **Sent Items** in the **Folder List**.

The details of the message you have just sent will be displayed on the right of the window (see Figure 1.2.3-12).

2   Double-click on the message details (click twice quickly with the left mouse button) to open the message.

> **2** Double-click on the message details.

Figure 1.2.3-12 *Message in Sent Items folder*

The message window will be displayed on screen (see Figure 1.2.3-13).

When viewing an email message from the **Sent Items** folder in Outlook, you will see that the sent message shows all four header details:

From: Who sent the message   **Sent:** The date the message was sent

To: The recipient's email address

Subject: Details of the content of the message

3   Click on: the 🖨 **Print** button to print the message.

3 Click on: the **Print** button.

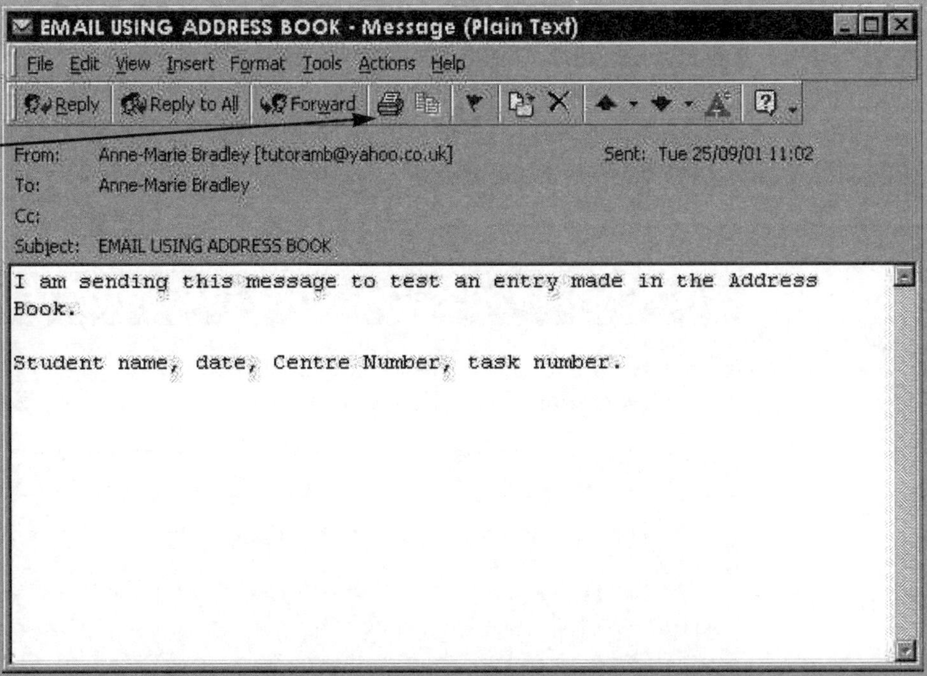

Figure 1.2.3-13 *Printing an email message*

This will print the message to the default printer. If you are working in a classroom, your tutor will tell you where this is. If you are working at home, the message will print to your printer.

4   From the **File** menu, select: **Close** to close the message. You will now be returned to the **Outlook** window.

Exiting Outlook and shutting down

If your session is finished, then exit Outlook (from the **File** menu, select **Exit** *or* click on: the ⊠ cross in the top right-hand corner) and shut down your computer (exit all other applications; click on: the **Start** button; select **Shut Down**; click on: **OK**). Otherwise, move straight on to the next task.

Outlook

Read, print and save an email message

Objectives

- Open the **Inbox**
- Open and read an email message
- Add a sender's address to the **Address Book**
- Save an email message
- Print an email message

Scenario: office safety

This scenario applies from this task up to Task 12.

You are the administrator in the Occupational Health department of a large organisation. You are in the process of producing an *Office Safety Awareness* booklet for staff, which deals with all aspects of health and safety in an office environment. A technician in the IT department is working with you and is trying to find suitable images to include in the booklet.

You have to attend an urgent meeting and only have time to read and print the message from the technician.

Remember: If you are working at home, you must send the two emails to yourself before starting on this task (see page 2 for instructions).

Opening the Inbox

☐ Method

1   If you do not already have Microsoft Outlook on screen, then load it (*either* click on: the **Microsoft Outlook** shortcut icon on the desktop, *or* click on the **Start** button and select: **Programs**, **Microsoft Outlook**).

If you look in the **Folder List** you will see that there are messages in your **Inbox** (see Figure 1.2.4-1).

2   Click on: **Inbox** in the **Folder List**.

2 Click on: **Inbox** in the **Folder List** to open the **Inbox**.

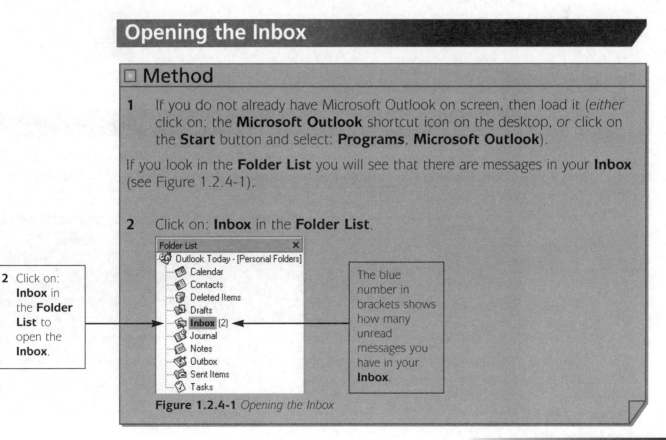

The blue number in brackets shows how many unread messages you have in your **Inbox**.

Figure 1.2.4-1 *Opening the Inbox*

The **Inbox** appears on the right side of the window (see Figure 1.2.4-2). The **Inbox** displays information about the email messages you have received. The **Header** section appears at the top and the **Preview Pane** appears underneath.

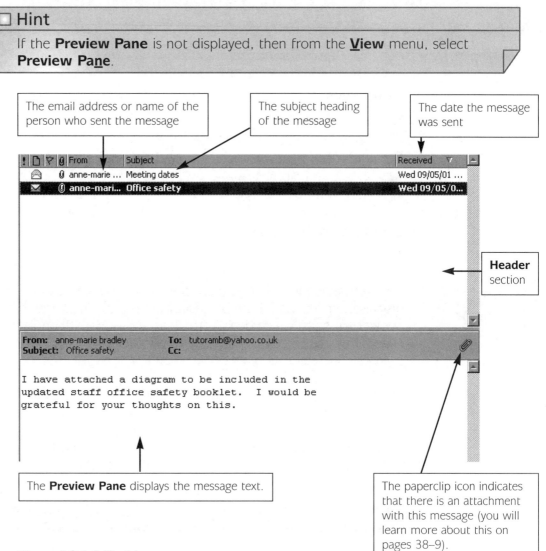

The email address or name of the person who sent the message

The subject heading of the message

The date the message was sent

Header section

From: anne-marie bradley   **To:** tutoramb@yahoo.co.uk
Subject: Office safety   **Cc:**

I have attached a diagram to be included in the updated staff office safety booklet. I would be grateful for your thoughts on this.

The **Preview Pane** displays the message text.

The paperclip icon indicates that there is an attachment with this message (you will learn more about this on pages 38–9).

Figure 1.2.4-2 *The Inbox*

Opening and reading an email message

You can read the message in the **Preview Pane**. However, if you actually open the message, then the message toolbar and menu bar will be displayed, allowing you to access more functions.

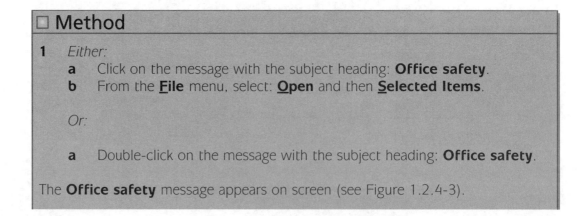

☐ **Method**

1   *Either:*
    a   Click on the message with the subject heading: **Office safety**.
    b   From the **File** menu, select: **Open** and then **Selected Items**.

    Or:

    a   Double-click on the message with the subject heading: **Office safety**.

The **Office safety** message appears on screen (see Figure 1.2.4-3).

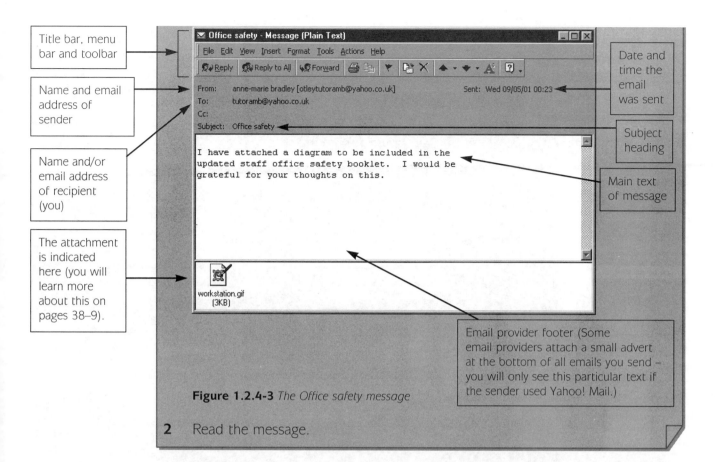

Figure 1.2.4-3 *The Office safety message*

Title bar, menu bar and toolbar

Name and email address of sender

Name and/or email address of recipient (you)

The attachment is indicated here (you will learn more about this on pages 38–9).

Date and time the email was sent

Subject heading

Main text of message

Email provider footer (Some email providers attach a small advert at the bottom of all emails you send – you will only see this particular text if the sender used Yahoo! Mail.)

2 Read the message.

Adding a sender's address to the Address Book

If the email is from someone new (i.e. someone whose details are not already stored in your **Address Book**), then you can easily add their email address to the **Address Book**.

☐ Method

1 Right-click on: the name of the sender to the right of **From:**. A drop-down menu appears (see Figure 1.2.4-4). Click on: **Add to Contacts**.

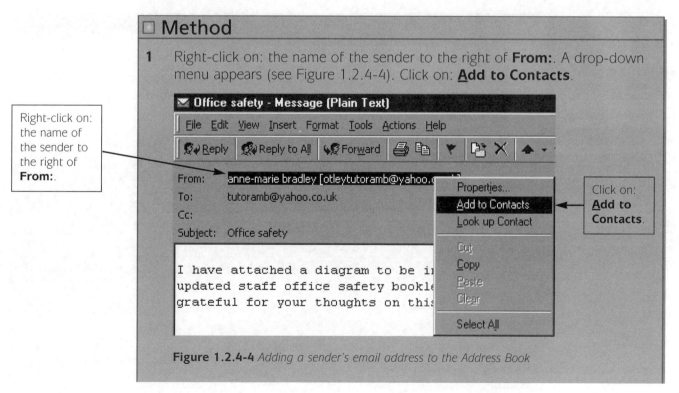

Right-click on: the name of the sender to the right of **From:**.

Click on: **Add to Contacts**.

Figure 1.2.4-4 *Adding a sender's email address to the Address Book*

The **Contact** dialogue box appears on screen (see Figure 1.2.4-5). Make sure the **General** tab is selected. Don't worry if this looks a bit daunting. The important details of the contact address have already been added for you – their name and email address. The important point is that you now need to save the new contact.

2   Click on: the **Save and Close** button.

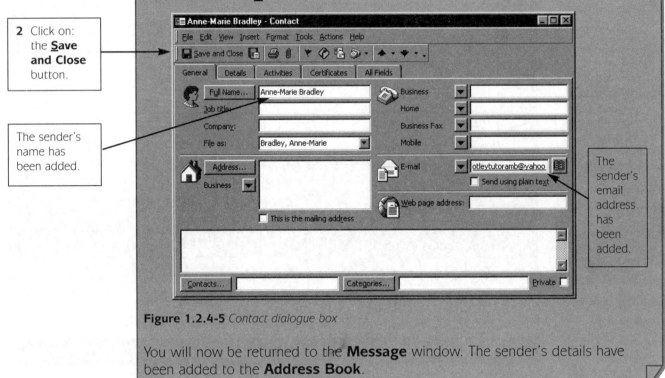

2 Click on: the **Save and Close** button.

The sender's name has been added.

The sender's email address has been added.

Figure 1.2.4-5 *Contact dialogue box*

You will now be returned to the **Message** window. The sender's details have been added to the **Address Book**.

Saving an email message

The email message is automatically saved in your **Inbox**. You can also save the message somewhere else if you wish. For example, you may want to store it in a folder with other related documents or you may want to save it onto a floppy disk so that it is portable.

☐ Method

1   From the **File** menu, select **Save As...**

The **Save As** dialogue box appears on screen (see Figure 1.2.4-6).

☐ Info

For the purposes of this task the message will be saved on a floppy disk. However, you can save the message wherever you prefer to save your files (e.g. in your network folder at college; in **My Documents** folder at home).

2   Click on: the small arrow to the right of the **Save in:** box and select the location to save the message.

3 In the **File name:** box, make sure that **Office safety** appears. If not, then key it in.

4 Click on: the **Save** button.

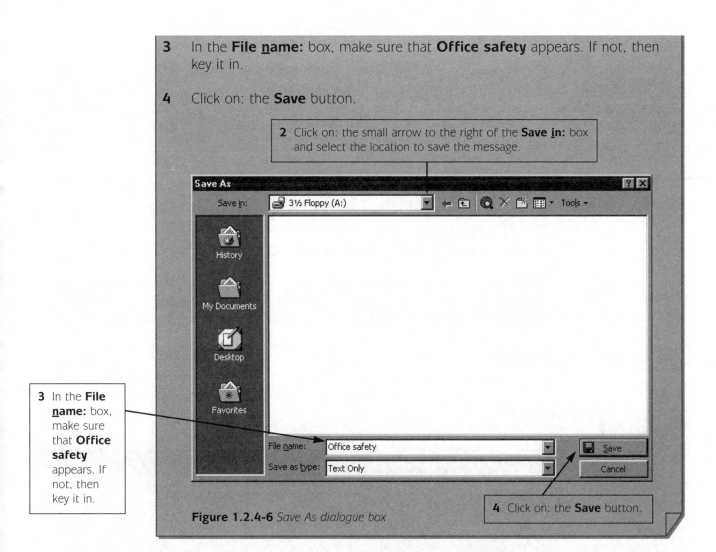

2 Click on: the small arrow to the right of the **Save in:** box and select the location to save the message.

3 In the **File name:** box, make sure that **Office safety** appears. If not, then key it in.

4 Click on: the **Save** button.

Figure 1.2.4-6 *Save As dialogue box*

Printing an email message

☐ Method

1 Click on: the 🖨 **Print** button.

2 Write your name, date, centre number and task number on the top of the printout.

3 From the **File** menu, select: **Close** to close the message.

You will now be returned to the **Outlook** window.

Exiting Outlook and shutting down

If your session is finished, then exit Outlook (from the **File** menu, select **Exit** *or* click on: the ☒ cross in the top right-hand corner) and shut down your computer (exit all other applications; click on: the **Start** button; select **Shut Down**; select **Shut Down**; click on: **OK**). Otherwise, move straight on to the next task.

Outlook

Reply to an email message

Objectives

- Reply to a message
- Send the reply
- Print a reply from the **Sent Items** folder

When you have been sent an email message, there is a facility that allows you to reply directly to the person who sent you the message, without re-entering the email address and subject heading as Outlook will automatically do this for you.

Scenario

The technician assisting you with the new *Office Safety Awareness* booklet has attached a diagram to the message. She would like to know what you think of the diagram.

Replying to a message

☐ Method

1 If you do not already have Microsoft Outlook on screen, then load it (*either* click on: the **Microsoft Outlook** shortcut icon on the desktop, *or* click on the **Start** button and select: **Programs**, **Microsoft Outlook**).

2 Click on: **Inbox** in the **Folders List**.

3 Open the **Office safety** message (from the **File** menu, select **Open** *or* double-click on the message).

4 Click on: the **Reply** button.

The **Reply** window appears on screen. The recipient address and the subject heading have been inserted automatically. The letters **RE:** before the subject heading indicate that this is a reply. The original message is shown.

In this task you will key in the text for your reply above the original message.

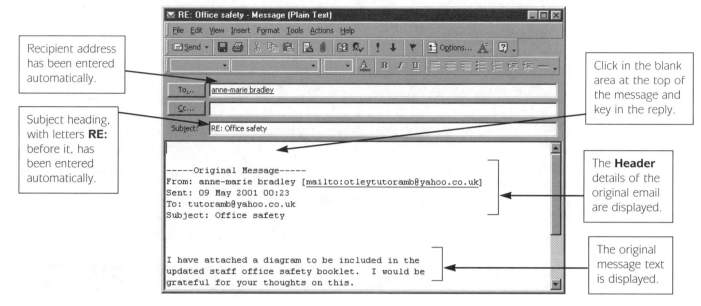

Recipient address has been entered automatically.

Subject heading, with letters **RE:** before it, has been entered automatically.

Click in the blank area at the top of the message and key in the reply.

The **Header** details of the original email are displayed.

The original message text is displayed.

Figure 1.2.5-1 *The Reply window*

Entering the reply text

□ Method

1   Click in the blank area at the top of the message screen, above the details of the person who sent the original message.

2   Key in the following reply text:

   The diagram you sent looks great, well done.

□ Hint

There should be one clear space after a comma.
There should be one clear line space between paragraphs.

3   Press: **Enter** twice and key in your personal details (name, date, centre number and task number).

4   To make the message look less cluttered, press: **Enter** twice to separate your new text from the original message.

5   Spellcheck the message, making any necessary amendments (from the **Tools** menu, select **Spelling**).

6   Proof-read the new text carefully, looking for any errors that the Spellcheck might have missed (e.g. if you had keyed in **bee** instead of **be** the Spellcheck would not have recognised it as an error), and make any necessary amendments.

Sending the reply

☐ Method

1   Click on: the 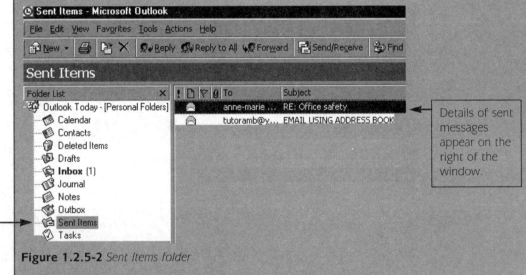**Send** button.

☐ Hint

If the original message is open, close it down.

You will be returned to the **Outlook** window (if you are working offline, you will need to click on: the **Send/Receive** button to send the message across the Internet).

Printing a reply from the Sent Items folder

☐ Method

1   Click on: **Sent Items** in the **Folder List**.

Details of the messages that have been sent appear on the right of the window (see Figure 1.2.5-2).

Clicking on **Sent Items** in the **Folder List** will display details of messages that have been sent.

Details of sent messages appear on the right of the window.

Figure 1.2.5-2 *Sent Items folder*

In Outlook, you can print messages directly from folders without opening the message.

2   Right-click on the message you have just sent. A drop-down menu appears.

3   Click on: **Print**.

To help you keep track of the tasks you are printing, highlight the fact that this is a reply on the printout. (Using a highlighter pen or pencil, mark the **RE:** part in the subject heading.)

Exiting Outlook and shutting down

If your session is finished, then exit Outlook (from the **File** menu, select **Exit** *or* click on: the ⊠ cross in the top right-hand corner) and shut down your computer (exit all other applications; click on: the **Start** button; select **Shut Down**; select **Shut Down**; click on: **OK**). Otherwise, move straight on to the next task.

Task 6 Outlook

Send a copy of an email message

Objective

- Send a copy of a new message to second recipient

For the OCR Internet Technologies award you are required to send an email message and send a copy of the message to a second recipient. This is often the case when you want to inform a third party about something that may concern them.

In this task you will compose a new email message and, as well as sending the message to a recipient, you will use the **Cc** facility to send a copy of the message to a second recipient (someone else). **Cc** stands for 'Courtesy copy'. When you send a copy of a message, the first recipient will know (from the **Header** details) that it has been copied to the second recipient and the second recipient will know that their message is a copy.

Sending a copy of a new message to second recipient

☐ Method

1 If you do not already have Microsoft Outlook on screen, then load it (*either* click on: the **Microsoft Outlook** shortcut icon on the desktop, *or* click on the **Start** button and select: **Programs**, **Microsoft Outlook**).

2 Create a new message (click on: the ⊞ New ▾ **New Message** button *or*, from the **File** menu, select **Mail message**).

The **Message** window appears on screen (see Figure 1.2.6-1).
In this task you will key in the recipient email addresses, rather than entering them from the **Address Book**.

3 Click in the **To...** box and key in the email address of a fellow student (or friend).

☐ Hint

It is important that the email address is keyed in accurately or it will not arrive.

To send a copy of a message to another recipient you enter their email address in the **Cc** box.

4 Click in the **Cc...** box and key in the email address of another student (or friend).

4 Click in the **Cc...** box and key in the email address of another student (or friend).

3 Click in the **To...** box and key in the email address of a fellow student (or friend).

Figure 1.2.6-1 *Message window*

If you keyed in email addresses that are not in the **Address Book**, then the addresses will stay the same (as in Figure 1.2.6-1). However, if you keyed in email addresses that are stored in the **Address Book**, then Outlook will automatically have inserted their names as you entered them (see Figure 1.2.6-2).

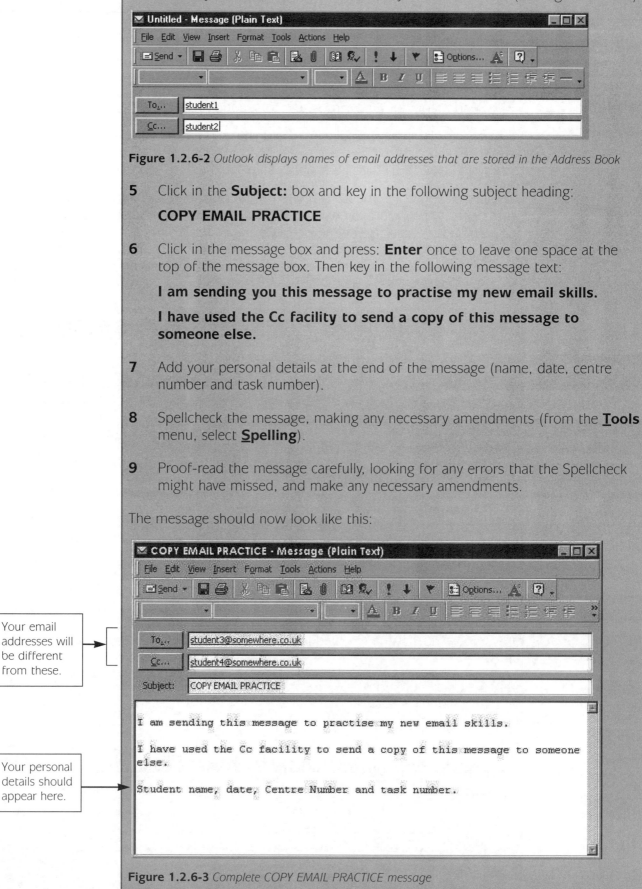

Figure 1.2.6-2 *Outlook displays names of email addresses that are stored in the Address Book*

5 Click in the **Subject:** box and key in the following subject heading:

COPY EMAIL PRACTICE

6 Click in the message box and press: **Enter** once to leave one space at the top of the message box. Then key in the following message text:

I am sending you this message to practise my new email skills.

I have used the Cc facility to send a copy of this message to someone else.

7 Add your personal details at the end of the message (name, date, centre number and task number).

8 Spellcheck the message, making any necessary amendments (from the **Tools** menu, select **Spelling**).

9 Proof-read the message carefully, looking for any errors that the Spellcheck might have missed, and make any necessary amendments.

The message should now look like this:

Your email addresses will be different from these.

Your personal details should appear here.

Figure 1.2.6-3 *Complete COPY EMAIL PRACTICE message*

10 Click on: the ⌨ **S̲end** ▾ **Send** button. (If you are working offline, *remember* to click on the **Send/Receive** button so the message is sent over the Internet.)

A copy of the message you have just sent will automatically be placed in the **Sent Items** folder.

11 Print the message from the **Sent Items** folder (click on: **Sent Items** in the **Folder List**; right-click on the message you have just sent; click on: **P̲rint**).

12 Circle or highlight the **Cc** details on the printout to remind you that you used the **Cc** facility in this task.

Exiting Outlook and shutting down

If your session is finished, then exit Outlook (from the **F̲ile** menu, select **E̲xit** *or* click on: the ☒ cross in the top right-hand corner) and shut down your computer (exit all other applications; click on: the **Start** button; select **Sh̲ut Down**; select **S̲hut Down**; click on: **OK**). Otherwise, move straight on to the next task.

Outlook

Task 7

Save an email attachment

Objectives

▪ View an attachment
▪ Open an attachment
▪ Save an attachment

If you receive an attachment you may want to save it for future use. Once it has been saved on your computer, you can use it or edit it just as you would any other file you have created yourself. For the OCR Internet Technologies award you are required to save an email attachment. In this task, the attachment is a graphic image. The examples here show the attachment being saved to a floppy disk for use in another task. However, you can save the attachment in your usual place – for example, in your network folder at college or in **My Documents** folder at home.

Scenario

A colleague sent you an email message and attached a graphic image to be included in the new staff office safety booklet. Due to your busy schedule, when you read the message, you forgot to save the image for future reference.

Viewing and opening an attachment

☐ Method

1 If you do not already have Microsoft Outlook on screen, then load it (*either* click on: the **Microsoft Outlook** shortcut icon on the desktop, *or* click on the **Start** button and select: **Programs**, **Microsoft Outlook**).

2 Click on: **Inbox** in the **Folder List** to display your email messages.

A preview of the message will be shown in the **Preview Pane** (if you can't see the **Preview Pane**, then from the **View** menu, select **Preview Pane**). If you look in the grey shaded area above the message text you will see a small paperclip icon on the right. This indicates that there is an attachment to this email message (see Figure 1.2.7-1).

> The paperclip icon indicates there is an attachment.

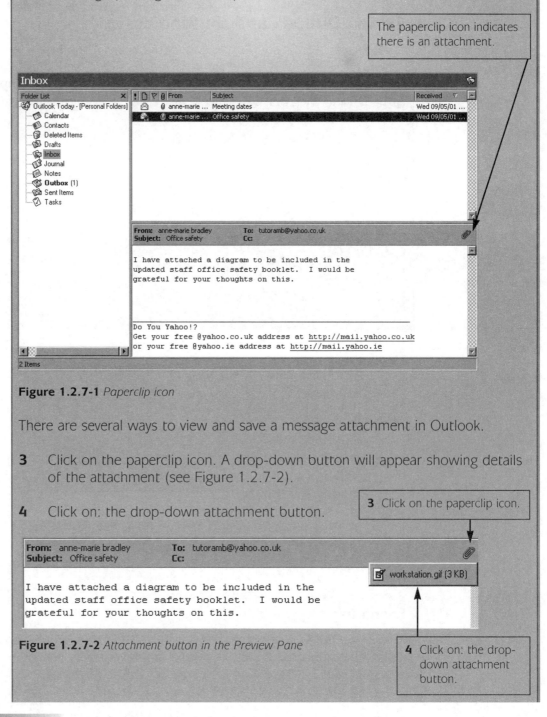

Figure 1.2.7-1 *Paperclip icon*

There are several ways to view and save a message attachment in Outlook.

3 Click on the paperclip icon. A drop-down button will appear showing details of the attachment (see Figure 1.2.7-2).

4 Click on: the drop-down attachment button.

> **3** Click on the paperclip icon.

From: anne-marie bradley   **To:** tutoramb@yahoo.co.uk
Subject: Office safety   **Cc:**

✉ workstation.gif (3 KB)

I have attached a diagram to be included in the
updated staff office safety booklet.   I would be
grateful for your thoughts on this.

Figure 1.2.7-2 *Attachment button in the Preview Pane*

> **4** Click on: the drop-down attachment button.

The **Opening Mail Attachment** prompt box appears on screen (see Figure 1.2.7-3). Your school or college will most likely have software installed on the computer that will check for viruses. A virus is a program that can damage the programs installed on your computer. As you know where this attachment has come from, it is safe to open it.

You will see that there are two options – **Open it** or **Save it to disk**. Because you need to view the attachment in this task you will choose the **Open it** option.

5 Click to put a dot in the circle to the left of **Open it** and then click on: **OK**.

Click to put a dot in the circle to the left of **Open it**.

Click on: **OK**.

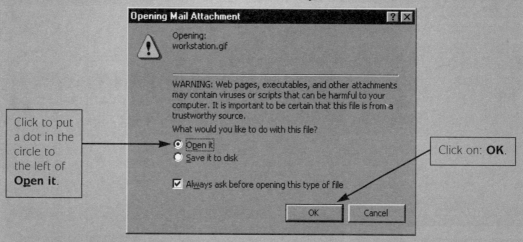

Figure 1.2.7-3 *Opening Mail Attachment prompt box*

In this example, the attachment is loaded into the web browser (see Figure 1.2.7-4) because it is a **.gif** file – **.gif** and **.jpg** files are usually opened in your web browser. Other attachments are usually loaded into the application in which they were produced – for example, if it is a text attachment it will be loaded into Windows Notepad; if it is a Word document it will be loaded into Microsoft Word, etc.

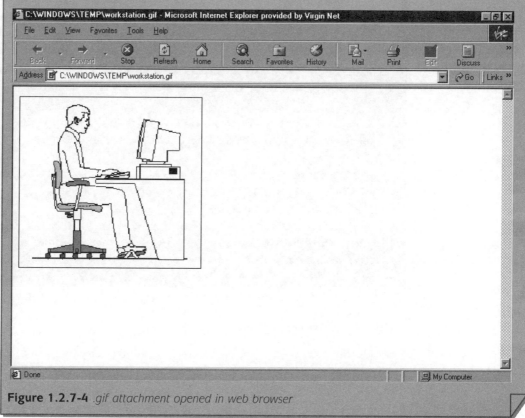

Figure 1.2.7-4 *.gif attachment opened in web browser*

Saving an attachment

Saving an opened attachment

☐ **Method**

1 From the **File** menu, select **Save As...**

> **1** From the **File** menu, select **Save As....**

Microsoft Photo Editor - workstation.gif

File Edit View Image Effects Window Help

New...	Ctrl+N
Open...	Ctrl+O
Close	
Save	Ctrl+S
Save As...	
Revert	Ctrl+R
Scan Image...	
Select Scanner Source...	
Print...	Ctrl+P
Send...	
Properties	Alt+Enter
1 C:\DOCUME~1\gb20723\LOCALS~1\Temp\workstation.gif	
2 L:\Gillian\Internet Technologies\Second proof additional stuff\2.2.10-8 favorite.tif	
3 L:\Gillian\Internet Technologies\Fig 2.2.11-1.tif	
4 L:\Gillian\top_02.gif	
Exit	

Figure 1.2.7-5 *Saving the image attachment from within the web browser*

The **Save As** dialogue box appears on screen (see Figure 1.2.7-6). In the example shown, the attachment is being saved on floppy disk. However, you should save the attachment wherever you usually save your files – for example, in your network folder or in **My Documents**.

2 Click on: the small arrow to the right of the **Save in:** box and, from the drop-down menu, select the location to save the file.

For the OCR Internet Technologies award you are required to save attachments using their original name. This is important, as you will be attaching this file to an email message in a later task.

3 In the **File name:** box, make sure the name is **workstation**. If not, key in **workstation** (this must be keyed in in lower case, exactly as it appears).

4 Click on: the **Save** button.

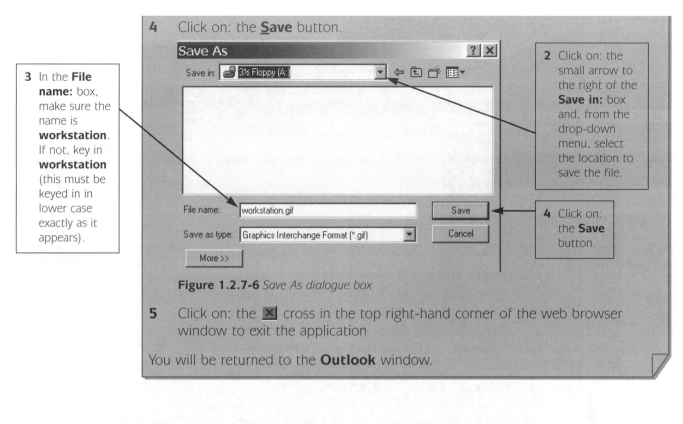

3 In the **File name:** box, make sure the name is **workstation**. If not, key in **workstation** (this must be keyed in in lower case exactly as it appears).

2 Click on: the small arrow to the right of the **Save in:** box and, from the drop-down menu, select the location to save the file.

4 Click on: the **Save** button.

Figure 1.2.7-6 *Save As dialogue box*

5 Click on: the ☒ cross in the top right-hand corner of the web browser window to exit the application

You will be returned to the **Outlook** window.

Saving an attachment using the File menu

You can also save an attachment without opening it, using the **File** menu.

☐ Method

1 Click on: **Inbox** in the **Folder List** and then click on: the **Office safety** message.

2 From the **File** menu, select **Save Attachments**. The attachment name appears to the right (see Figure 1.2.7-7).

3 Click on: the attachment name.

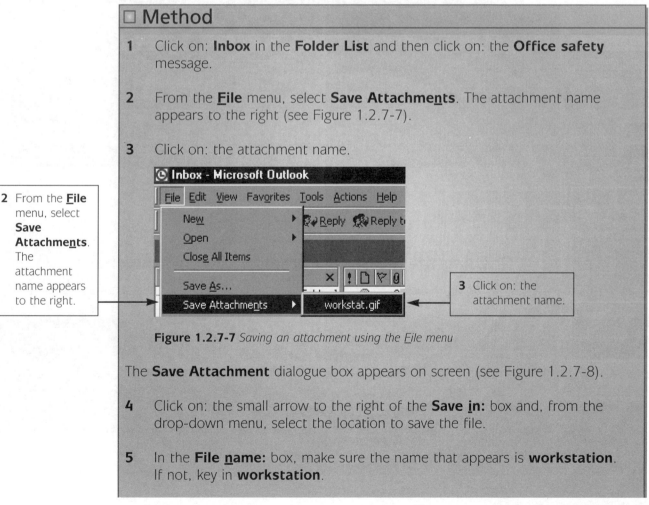

2 From the **File** menu, select **Save Attachments**. The attachment name appears to the right.

3 Click on: the attachment name.

Figure 1.2.7-7 *Saving an attachment using the File menu*

The **Save Attachment** dialogue box appears on screen (see Figure 1.2.7-8).

4 Click on: the small arrow to the right of the **Save in:** box and, from the drop-down menu, select the location to save the file.

5 In the **File name:** box, make sure the name that appears is **workstation**. If not, key in **workstation**.

6 Click on: the **Save** button.

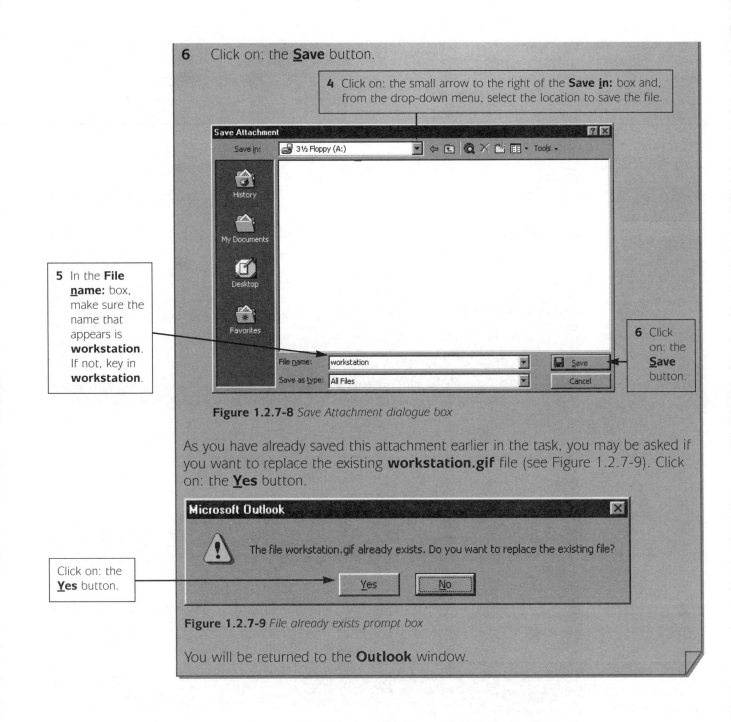

4 Click on: the small arrow to the right of the **Save in:** box and, from the drop-down menu, select the location to save the file.

5 In the **File name:** box, make sure the name that appears is **workstation**. If not, key in **workstation**.

6 Click on: the **Save** button.

Figure 1.2.7-8 *Save Attachment dialogue box*

As you have already saved this attachment earlier in the task, you may be asked if you want to replace the existing **workstation.gif** file (see Figure 1.2.7-9). Click on: the **Yes** button.

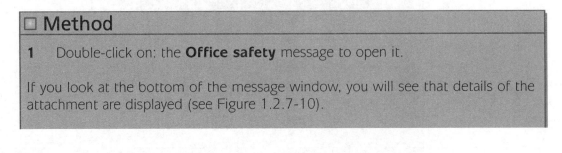

Click on: the **Yes** button.

Figure 1.2.7-9 *File already exists prompt box*

You will be returned to the **Outlook** window.

Opening the message and saving the attachment

You can also save an attachment from an opened email message.

☐ Method

1 Double-click on: the **Office safety** message to open it.

If you look at the bottom of the message window, you will see that details of the attachment are displayed (see Figure 1.2.7-10).

2 Double-click on: the attachment.

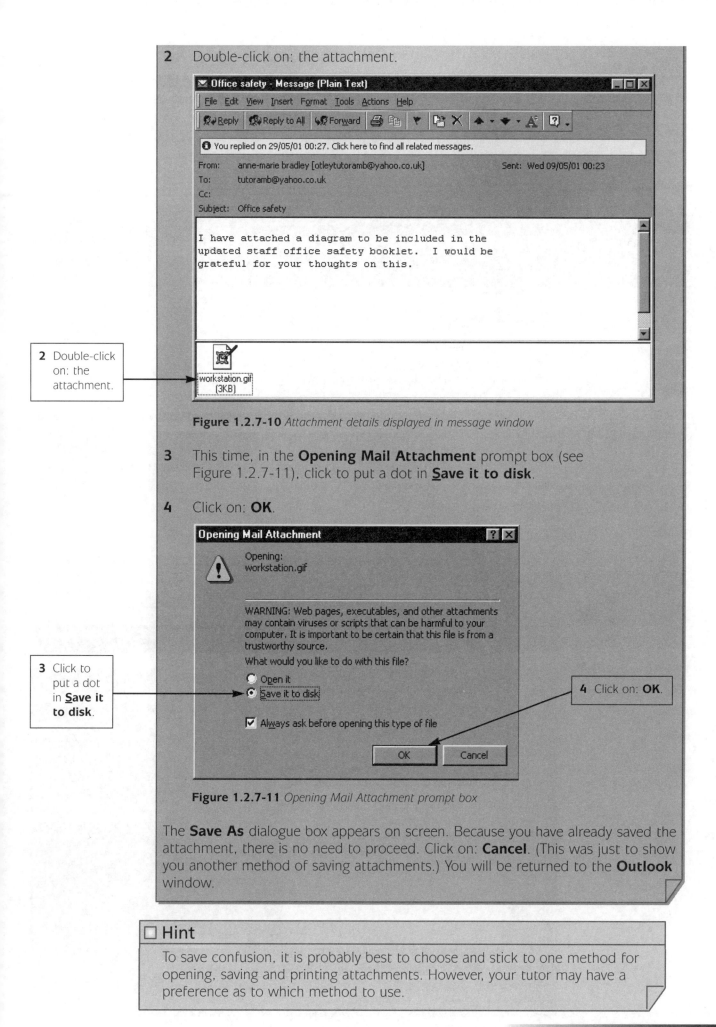

2 Double-click on: the attachment.

Figure 1.2.7-10 *Attachment details displayed in message window*

3 This time, in the **Opening Mail Attachment** prompt box (see Figure 1.2.7-11), click to put a dot in **Save it to disk**.

4 Click on: **OK**.

3 Click to put a dot in **Save it to disk**.

4 Click on: **OK**.

Figure 1.2.7-11 *Opening Mail Attachment prompt box*

The **Save As** dialogue box appears on screen. Because you have already saved the attachment, there is no need to proceed. Click on: **Cancel**. (This was just to show you another method of saving attachments.) You will be returned to the **Outlook** window.

☐ **Hint**

To save confusion, it is probably best to choose and stick to one method for opening, saving and printing attachments. However, your tutor may have a preference as to which method to use.

Exiting Outlook and shutting down

If your session is finished, then exit Outlook (from the **File** menu, select **Exit** *or* click on: the ⊠ cross in the top right-hand corner) and shut down your computer (exit all other applications; click on: the **Start** button; select **Shut Down**; select **Shut Down**; click on: **OK**). Otherwise, move straight on to the next task.

Outlook

Open and print saved attachment

Objectives

- Load Windows Paint
- Open a saved attachment from an external application
- Print a saved attachment from an external application

If you receive and save an attachment, it is likely that you may want to print it at a later date. For the OCR Internet Technologies award you are required to open a saved attachment from an external application. As this attachment is a graphic image, in this task you will view and print the attachment using the Windows **Paint** program. The **Paint** program will open images in several different formats – **.bmp**, **.jpg** and **.gif** (which is the format of the image in this task).

Scenario

The IT technician working on the *Office Safety Awareness* booklet is on annual leave, so the Design department has asked if you have a copy of the graphic image for the booklet. First, you want to check that the attachment you saved is OK.

Loading Windows Paint

☐ Method

1   Click on: the **Start** button and, from the pop-up menu, select: **Programs**, **Accessories**, **Paint**.

The **Paint** window appears on screen (see Figure 1.2.8-1).

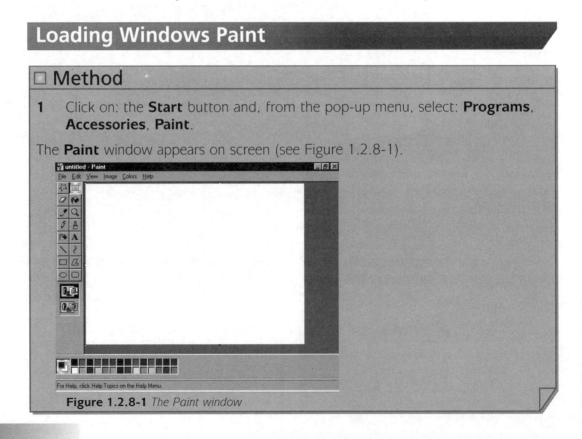

Figure 1.2.8-1 *The Paint window*

Opening a saved attachment from an external application

☐ Method

1 From the **File** menu, select: **Open**.

The **Open** dialogue box appears on screen (see Figure 1.2.8-2).

2 Click on: the small arrow to the right of the **Look in:** box and, from the drop-down menu, select the location where you saved the file in Task 7.

In the example shown, the image attachment is being opened from the floppy disk where it was saved earlier. You will need to open it from wherever you saved it before.

Don't worry if there are no files showing. This is because, in the **Files of type:** box, it says **Bitmap Files** and the image you want to view is in **.gif** format. Therefore, you need to change this so that you can view your saved attachment.

3 Click on: the small arrow to the right of the **Files of type:** box and, from the drop-down menu, select: **All Picture Files**.

<table>
<tr><td>

2 Click on: the small arrow to the right of the **Look in:** box and, from the drop-down menu, select the location where you saved the file in Task 7.

</td><td>

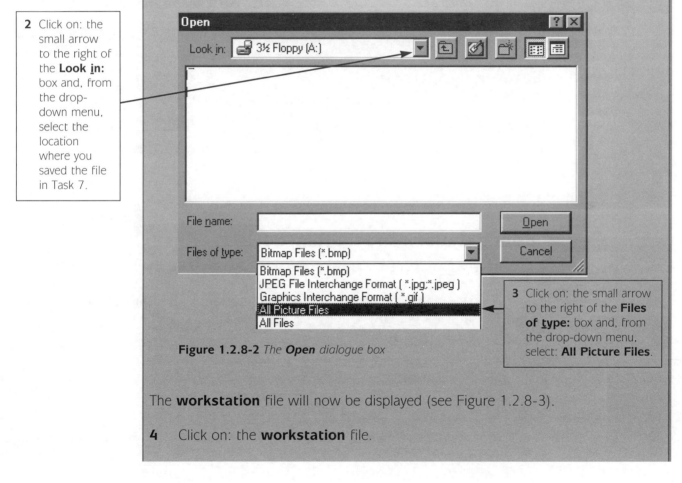

</td></tr>
</table>

Figure 1.2.8-2 *The Open dialogue box*

3 Click on: the small arrow to the right of the **Files of type:** box and, from the drop-down menu, select: **All Picture Files**.

The **workstation** file will now be displayed (see Figure 1.2.8-3).

4 Click on: the **workstation** file.

5 Click on: **Open**.

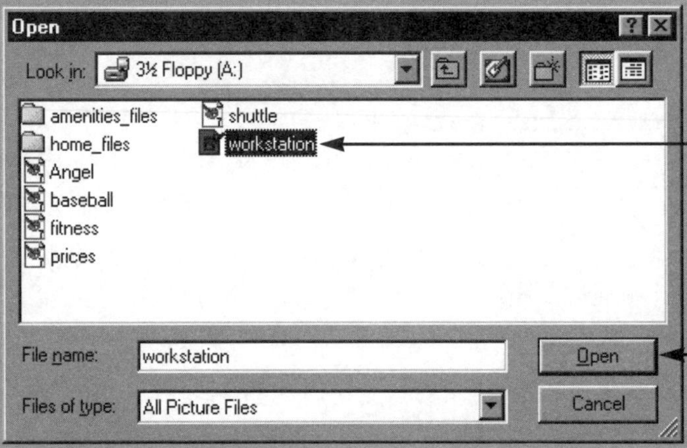

4 Click on: the **workstation** file.

5 Click on: **Open**.

Figure 1.2.8-3 *The workstation file is now displayed*

The **workstation** image appears in the **Paint** window.

Printing a saved attachment from an external application

Method

1 From the **File** menu, select **Print**.

2 Write your name, date, centre number and task number on the printout.

3 From the **File** menu, select **Exit** to exit **Paint**.

Exiting Outlook and shutting down

If your session is finished, then exit Outlook (from the **File** menu, select **Exit** *or* click on: the ☒ cross in the top right-hand corner) and shut down your computer (exit all other applications; click on: the **Start** button; select **Shut Down**; select **Shut Down**; click on: **OK**). Otherwise, move straight on to the next task.

Outlook

Attach a saved file to an email message

Objectives

- Create a new message
- Attach a saved file
- Save the message
- Send the message
- Print a message from the **Sent Items** folder

When sending an email message, you are likely to want to send an attachment. As you have seen, attachments can be any type of file. In this task, you will compose a new email message and attach to it the image that you saved in Task 7.

Scenario

The Design department has requested a copy of the image to be used in the new *Office Safety Awareness* booklet.

Creating a new message

☐ Method

1   If you do not already have Microsoft Outlook on screen, then load it (*either* click on: the **Microsoft Outlook** shortcut icon on the desktop, *or* click on the **Start** button and select: **Programs**, **Microsoft Outlook**).

2   Open a new mail message (click on: the ⊞ New ▾ **New Message** button).

☐ Info

If you are working in a college, you will send this email to your tutor. If you are working at home, then send it to a friend or relative.

3   Insert the recipient's email address from the **Address Book** (click on: the **To:..** button and select your tutor, friend or relative's name; click on the **To->** button to move it across into the **Message Recipients** box; click on: **OK**).

You will be returned to the message window and the recipient's name will be shown in the **To:..** box.

4   Enter the following in the **Subject:** box:

   Office safety image

5   Enter the following text in the message box:

   I have attached the office safety graphic image that you requested.

6 Press: **Enter** twice and then key in your personal details (name, date, centre number and task number).

7 Spellcheck the message, making any necessary amendments (from the **Tools** menu, select **Spelling**). Then proof-read the message carefully, looking for any errors that the Spellcheck might have missed, and make any necessary amendments.

Attaching a saved file

You will now attach the graphic image that you saved in Task 7.

□ Method

1 Click on: the 📎 **Insert File** button.

The **Insert File** dialogue box appears on screen (see Figure 1.2.9-1).

2 Click on: the small arrow to the right of the **Look in:** box and select the location where you saved the **workstation** image.

3 Click on: the **workstation** image.

> **2** Click on: the small arrow to the right of the **Look in:** box and select the location where you saved the **workstation** image.

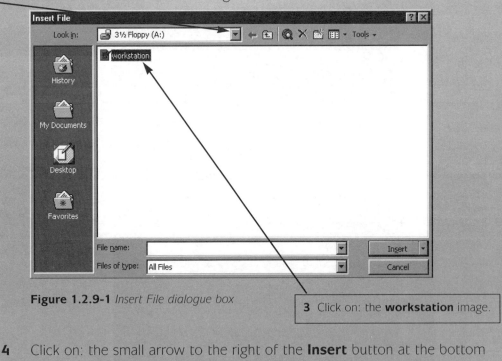

Figure 1.2.9-1 *Insert File dialogue box*

> **3** Click on: the **workstation** image.

4 Click on: the small arrow to the right of the **Insert** button at the bottom right of the dialogue box (see Figure 1.2.9-2).

5   Select **Insert as Attachment** from the drop-down menu.

4   Click on: the small arrow to the right of the **Insert** button at the bottom right of the dialogue box.

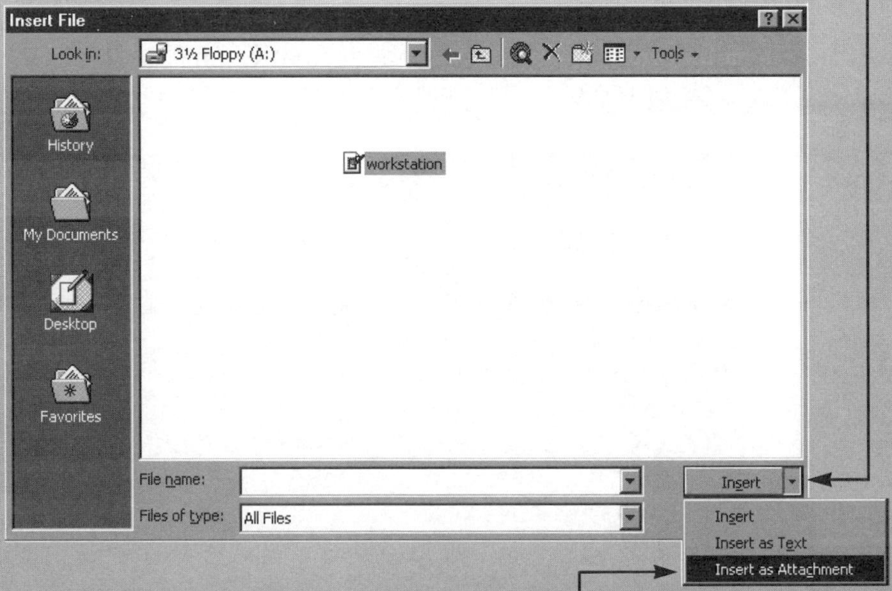

5   Select **Insert as Attachment** from the drop-down menu.

Figure 1.2.9-2 *Inserting an attachment*

Details of the file you have attached will be shown at the bottom of the message window (see Figure 1.2.9-3).

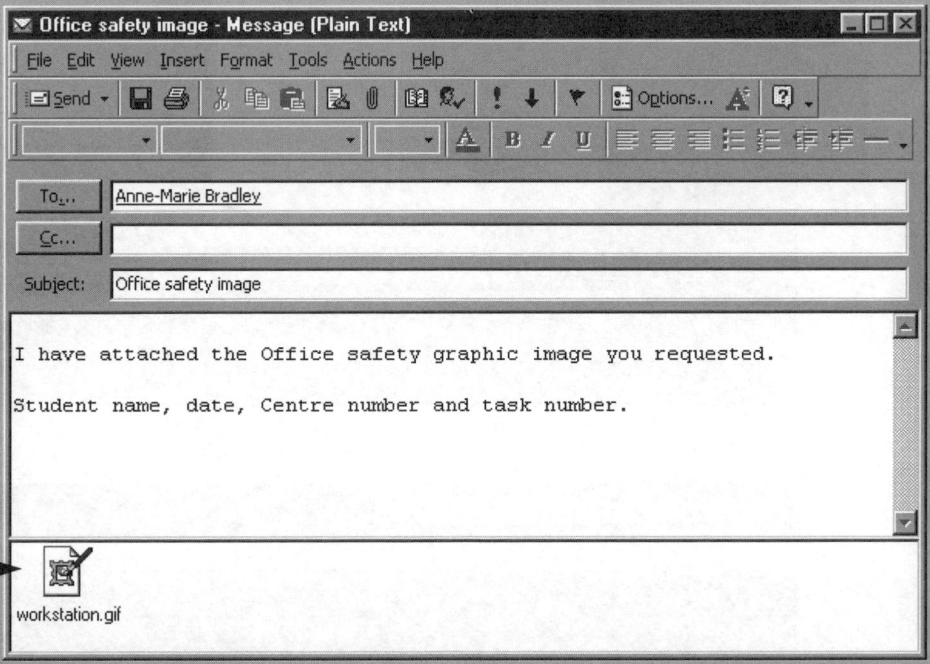

Details of the file you have attached will be shown at the bottom of the message window.

Figure 1.2.9-3 *Attached file inserted*

Saving the message

A copy of the message will automatically be saved in the **Sent Items** folder when you send the message. Sometimes however, you may want to store the message elsewhere with other related files. For the OCR Internet Technologies award, you are required to save an email message outside of the mailbox structure. An important point to remember is that when you do this in Outlook it only saves the text of the message, and not the attachment(s).

☐ Method

1   From the **File** menu, select **Save As**.

The **Save As** dialogue box appears on screen (see Figure 1.2.9-4).

2   From the **Save in:** box, select the location where you save your tasks.

3   In the **File name:** box, delete the suggested name for the file (double-click to select the text; press: **Delete**). Key in: **send saved attachment** followed by your initials.

4   Click on: the **Save** button.

2 From the **Save in:** box, select the location where you save your tasks.

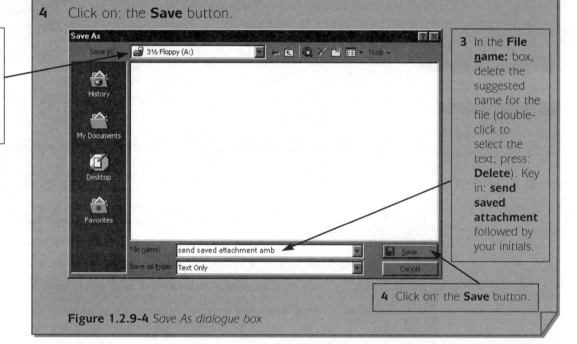

3 In the **File name:** box, delete the suggested name for the file (double-click to select the text; press: **Delete**). Key in: **send saved attachment** followed by your initials.

4 Click on: the **Save** button.

Figure 1.2.9-4 *Save As dialogue box*

Sending the message

☐ Method

1   Click on: the [Send] **Send** button. (If you are working offline, *remember* to click on: the **Send/Receive** button so that the message is sent over the Internet.)

Printing a message from the Sent Items folder

☐ Method

1   Click on: **Sent Items** in the **Folder List**.

2   Right-click on the message you have just sent and, from the drop-down menu, select: **Print**.

Exiting Outlook and shutting down

If your session is finished, then exit Outlook (from the **File** menu, select **Exit** *or* click on: the ⊠ cross in the top right-hand corner) and shut down your computer (exit all other applications; click on: the **Start** button; select **Shut Down**; select **Shut Down**; click on: **OK**). Otherwise, move straight on to the next task.

Outlook

Forward an email message

Objectives

- Open an email message
- Forward an email message
- Send the forwarded message
- Print the forwarded message

There is a facility in email packages that allows you to forward a message you have received to one or more recipients. In this task, you will open a message and use the **Forward** facility to pass the message on to another recipient.

Scenario

The personnel manager has requested to be kept informed of the progress of the *Office Safety Awareness* booklet. Forward a copy of the message and image attachment to keep him up to date.

Opening an email message

☐ Method

1   If you do not already have Microsoft Outlook on screen, then load it (*either* click on: the **Microsoft Outlook** shortcut icon on the desktop, *or* click on the **Start** button and select: **Programs**, **Microsoft Outlook**).

2   Open the **Office safety** message from the **Inbox** (click on **Inbox** in the **Folder List**; double-click on the **Office safety** message on the right of the window).

☐ Method

1 Click on: the 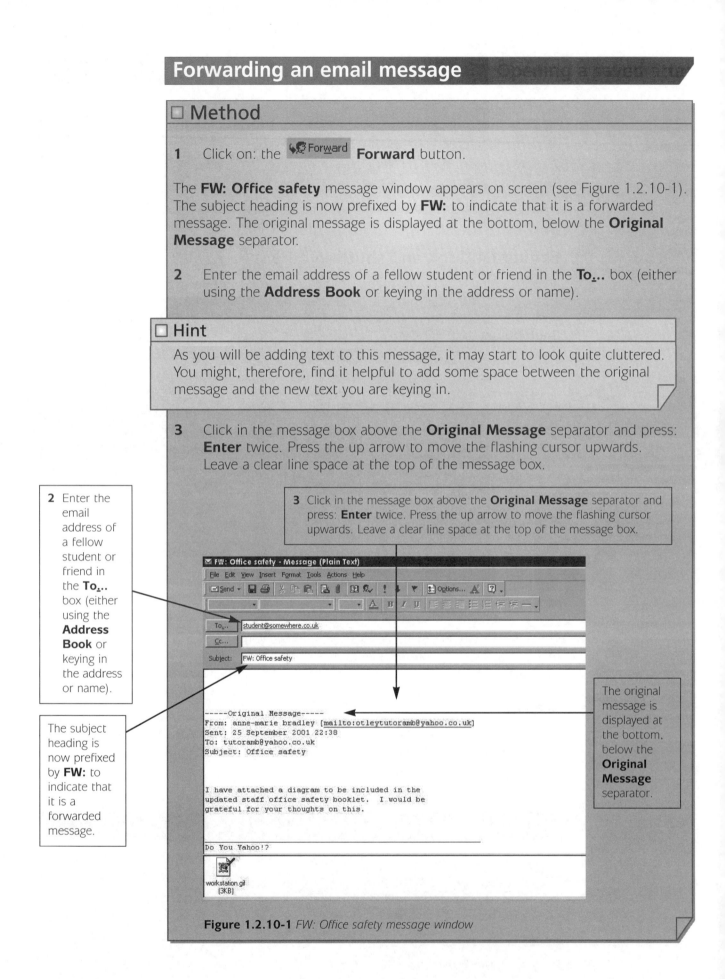**Forward** button.

The **FW: Office safety** message window appears on screen (see Figure 1.2.10-1). The subject heading is now prefixed by **FW:** to indicate that it is a forwarded message. The original message is displayed at the bottom, below the **Original Message** separator.

2 Enter the email address of a fellow student or friend in the **To:...** box (either using the **Address Book** or keying in the address or name).

☐ Hint

As you will be adding text to this message, it may start to look quite cluttered. You might, therefore, find it helpful to add some space between the original message and the new text you are keying in.

3 Click in the message box above the **Original Message** separator and press: **Enter** twice. Press the up arrow to move the flashing cursor upwards. Leave a clear line space at the top of the message box.

2 Enter the email address of a fellow student or friend in the **To:...** box (either using the **Address Book** or keying in the address or name).

The subject heading is now prefixed by **FW:** to indicate that it is a forwarded message.

3 Click in the message box above the **Original Message** separator and press: **Enter** twice. Press the up arrow to move the flashing cursor upwards. Leave a clear line space at the top of the message box.

The original message is displayed at the bottom, below the **Original Message** separator.

Figure 1.2.10-1 *FW: Office safety message window*

Adding text to a message

It is good practice to add a short message before you forward an email message, making a comment about the message you are forwarding.

☐ Method

1   Key in the following text in the message box, above the original message (leaving one clear line space at the top of the message box):

Message forwarded by (key in your name)

2   Add your personal details at the end of the message (name, date, centre number and task number).

The message should now look like the one shown below (Figure 1.2.10-2).

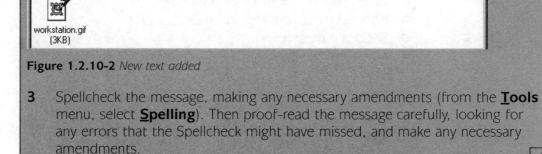

Figure 1.2.10-2 *New text added*

3   Spellcheck the message, making any necessary amendments (from the **Tools** menu, select **Spelling**). Then proof-read the message carefully, looking for any errors that the Spellcheck might have missed, and make any necessary amendments.

Sending the forwarded message

☐ Method

1   Click on: the ▣ Send ▾ **Send** button. (If you are working offline, *remember* to click on: the **Send/Receive** button so that the message is sent over the Internet.)

☐ Hint

If the original message is still open, close it down.

Printing the forwarded message

☐ Method

1 Print the message you have just sent (click on: **Sent Items** in the **Folder List**; right-click on the message you have just sent; select: **Print**).

2 On the printout, highlight the letters **FW:** in the subject heading.

Exiting Outlook and shutting down

If your session is finished, then exit Outlook (from the **File** menu, select **Exit** or click on: the ☒ cross in the top right-hand corner) and shut down your computer (exit all other applications; click on: the **Start** button; select **Shut Down**; select **Shut Down**; click on: **OK**). Otherwise, move straight on to the next task.

Outlook

Task 11

Send an email message to more than one recipient

Objectives

- Open a new mail message
- Enter two recipient email addresses
- Enter subject heading and message text
- Send the message
- Print the message

For the OCR Internet Technologies award you are required to send an email message to more than one recipient at the same time – this is referred to as 'equal priority'. This means you send the same message to two (or more) people at the same time.

Opening a new mail message

☐ Method

1 If you do not already have Microsoft Outlook on screen, then load it (*either* click on: the **Microsoft Outlook** shortcut icon on the desktop, *or* click on the **Start** button and select: **Programs**, **Microsoft Outlook**).

2 Click on: the 📧 New ▾ **New Message** button. The message window appears on screen.

Entering two recipient email addresses

There are two methods that can be used to enter recipient email addresses – by keying in the addresses or by adding addresses from the **Address Book**. In this task, for further practice, you will be keying in the required email addresses of both recipients.

☐ Method

1   Click in the **To...** box and key in your tutor's (or friend's) email address.

You now need to key in the second recipient's email address in the **To...** box. When sending a message to two recipients with equal priority, the email addresses must be separated in some way. To do this in Outlook, you use a semi-colon (;). You could also key in a comma (,) to separate the two addresses and Outlook would automatically replace this with a semi-colon (;).

2   Key in a semi-colon (;) – next to the letter **L** on the keyboard.

3   Key in a fellow student's (or another friend's) email address next to the semi-colon (;).

☐ Info

If you keyed in email addresses that are stored in the **Address Book** Outlook will automatically have changed them to the names as stored in the **Address Book**. Don't worry, the message will be sent to the correct address.

The addresses in the **To...** box should now look similar to those shown below (Figure 1.2.11-1).

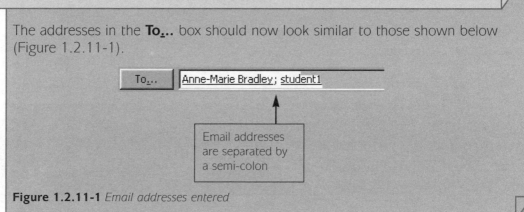

Figure 1.2.11-1 *Email addresses entered*

Entering subject heading and message text; sending and printing the message

☐ Method

1   Click in the **Subject:** box and key in the following subject heading:

Send a message to two recipients

2   Click in the message box, press: **Enter** once and key in the following message (it doesn't matter if the line endings are not the same as those shown):

This email message is an example of how you can send the same message to more than one recipient at the same time, with equal priority.

3 Press: **Enter** twice and key in your personal details at the end of the email message (name, date, centre number and task number).

4 Spellcheck the message, making any necessary amendments (from the **Tools** menu, select **Spelling**). Then proof-read the message carefully, looking for any errors that the Spellcheck might have missed, and make any necessary amendments.

5 Save the message where you normally save your tasks using the filename: **two recipients**.

6 Send the message. (If you are working offline, *remember* to click on: the **Send/Receive** button so that the message is sent over the Internet.)

7 Print the message you have just sent (click on: **Sent Items** in the **Folders List**; right-click on the message you have just sent; select **Print**).

Exiting Outlook and shutting down

If your session is finished, then exit Outlook (from the **File** menu, select **Exit** *or* click on: the ⊠ cross in the top right-hand corner) and shut down your computer (exit all other applications; click on: the **Start** button; select **Shut Down**; select **Shut Down**; click on: **OK**). Otherwise, move straight on to the next task.

Outlook

Task 12

Make a backup copy and delete an email message

Objectives

- Open a message
- Make a backup copy of a message
- Delete a message from the **Inbox**
- Restore a deleted message

A backup copy of a message (or any other file) ensures that you have an extra copy saved safely elsewhere. For the OCR Internet Technologies award you are required to make a backup copy of a message to be saved outside the mailbox structure and then delete the message from the **Inbox**. You should delete unwanted messages from time to time to 'tidy up' your **Inbox**. In this task, you will create a backup copy of the **Office safety** message and then delete it from your **Inbox**.

Scenario

Your organisation is setting up a new computer network system. You have been asked to save important messages outside the mailbox structure, in your relevant departmental user area, and then delete the messages from the **Inbox**.

Opening a message

☐ Method

1   If you do not already have Microsoft Outlook on screen, then load it (*either* click on: the **Microsoft Outlook** shortcut icon on the desktop, *or* click on the **Start** button and select: **Programs**, **Microsoft Outlook**).

2   Open the **Office safety** message (click on: **Inbox** in the **Folder List**; double-click on the message on the right of the window).

Making a backup copy of a message

Although you saved the **Office safety** message in Task 4, you will save it again here using a different filename.

☐ Method

1   From the **File** menu, select **Save As** and save the message where you usually save your files, using the filename: **Office safety backup** (followed by your initials).

This will only save the text in the message, but you already saved the attachment in Task 7, so you do not need to worry about that.

2   Close the message (from the **File** menu, select: **Close**).

You will be returned to the **Outlook** window.

Deleting a message from the Inbox

☐ Method

1   Click on: **Inbox** in the **Folder List**

2   Click once on the **Office safety** message.

3   Click on: the ✖ **Delete** button.

The **Office safety** message has been deleted from the **Inbox**. The deleted message is now stored in the **Deleted Items** folder (see Figure 1.2.12-1).

Restoring a deleted message

If you delete a message by mistake you can restore it and place it back in the **Inbox**. Deleted messages are put into the **Deleted Items** folder, which is like a waste-paper bin, except that you can still retrieve items from it.

☐ Method

1   Click on: **Deleted Items** in the **Folder List**. The deleted message is displayed on the right of the window (see Figure 2.12-1).

2 Click on the deleted message and, holding down the mouse button, drag the message to the **Inbox** folder in the **Folder List**. (You will briefly see a circle with a line through it, but do not worry about this.)

3 Release the mouse button when **Inbox** is highlighted.

1 Click on: **Deleted Items** in the **Folder List**. The deleted message is displayed on the right of the window.

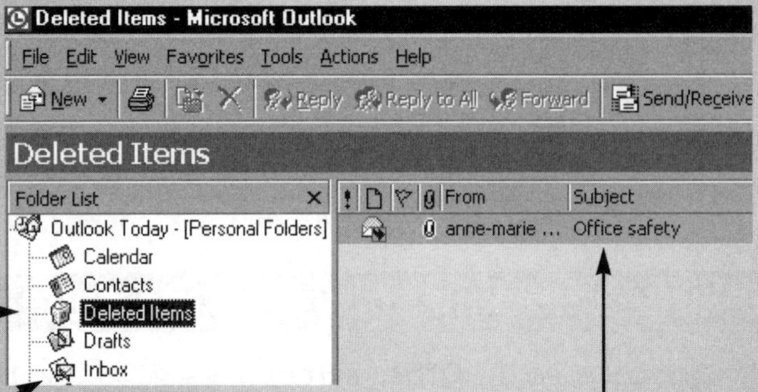

3 Release the mouse button when **Inbox** is highlighted.

2 Click on the deleted message and, holding down the mouse button, drag the message to the **Inbox** folder in the **Folder List**. (You will briefly seé a circle with a line through it, but do not worry about this.)

Figure 1.2.12-1 *Deleted Items folder*

The **Deleted Items** folder is now empty (see Figure 1.2.12-2). The deleted message has been restored to the **Inbox**.

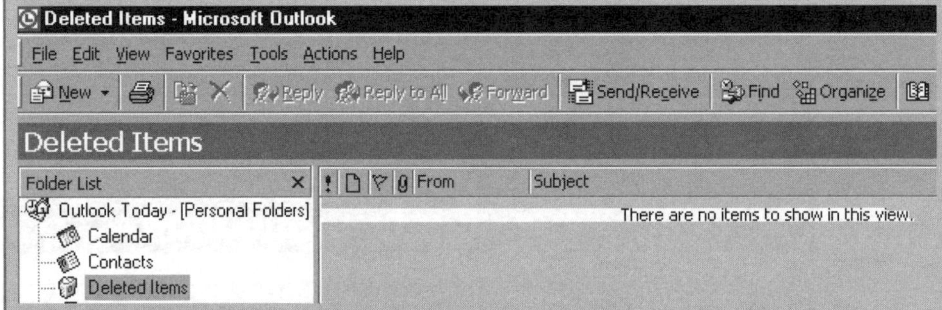

Figure 1.2.12-2 *Empty Deleted Items folder*

4 Click on: **Inbox** in the **Folder List**.

The **Office safety** message should be visible in the **Inbox** again (see Figure 1.2.12-3).

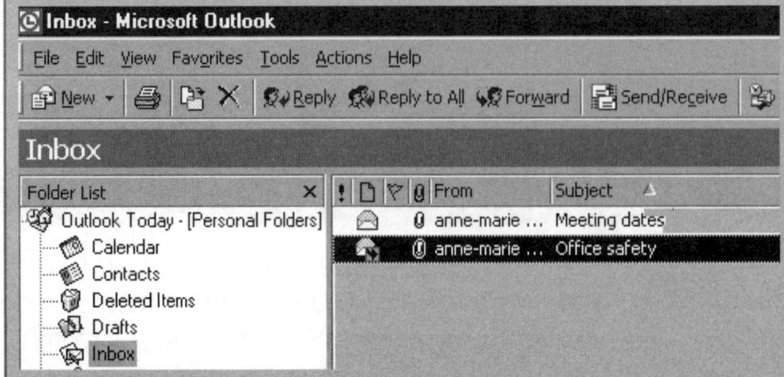

Figure 1.2.12-3 *Office safety message restored to Inbox*

Restoring the message was for practice only. Follow the instructions given for deleting the **Office safety** message from the **Inbox** – this time it is not necessary to restore it.

You can only restore deleted items while they are in the **Deleted Items** folder. When you exit Outlook and have messages in the **Deleted Items** folder a prompt box will appear asking if you want to delete the items in the **Deleted Items** folder.

If you are sure you do not want the items you have deleted, then click on: the **Yes** button, otherwise, click on the **No** button and the deleted messages will remain in the **Deleted Items** folder to be restored if necessary.

Exiting Outlook and shutting down

If your session is finished, then exit Outlook (from the **File** menu, select **Exit** *or* click on: the ☒ cross in the top right-hand corner) and shut down your computer (exit all other applications; click on: the **Start** button; select **Shut Down**; select **Shut Down**; click on: **OK**). Otherwise, move straight on to the next task.

Use electronic mail for business communication

Working with attachments

13 Outlook

Save text and Word attachments

Objectives

- Open and read a message
- Save attachments
- Print a message

Not all email attachments are images. Many file types can be attached to an email message. It is important to know how to view and save other types of attachment.

The email message in this task has two attached files. One has a **.doc** extension, which means it is a Microsoft Word document. For the OCR Internet Technologies award you will only work with image and text attachments. The word attachment in this task has only been supplied to give you extra practice in working with attachments. The other has a **.txt** extension, which means it is a text only document. It was created using Windows Notepad, which is a very simple package in which you can produce text files.

In this task, you will save both these types of attachment.

Scenario

You are an executive secretary in an engineering firm. You have been asked to arrange an urgent meeting of the heads of departments. To help save time you have decided to email the appropriate members of staff with several suggested meeting dates. You have been sent a message by another secretary with details of possible dates.

Opening and reading a message

☐ Method

1   If you do not already have Microsoft Outlook on screen, then load it (*either* click on: the **Microsoft Outlook** shortcut icon on the desktop, *or* click on the **Start** button and select: **Programs**, **Microsoft Outlook**).

2   Open the **Meeting** message.

3   Read the message.

If you look at the bottom of the message window you will see that there are two attachments to this email message (see Figure 1.3.13-1).

This is a Word attachment.

This is a text attachment.

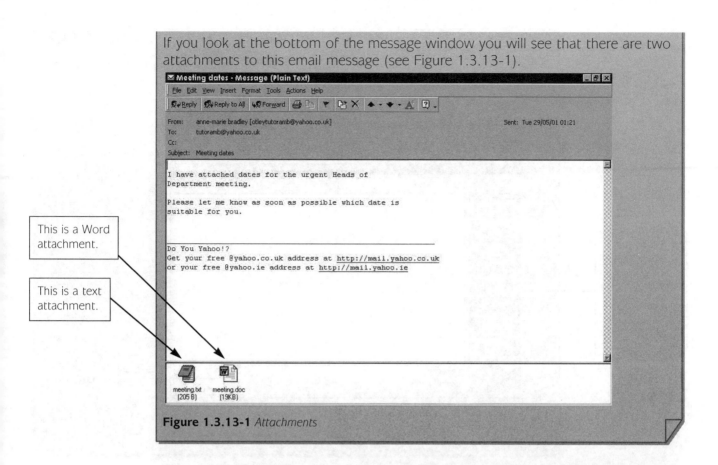

Figure 1.3.13-1 *Attachments*

Saving attachments

As you will be using these attachments in a later task, it is important to save them. It is possible to save the attachments separately, however, there is an excellent facility in Outlook that makes this process much easier.

☐ Method

1 From the **File** menu, select **Save Attachments…**

The **Save All Attachments** dialogue box appears on screen (see Figure 1.3.13-2).

2 Click on: **OK**.

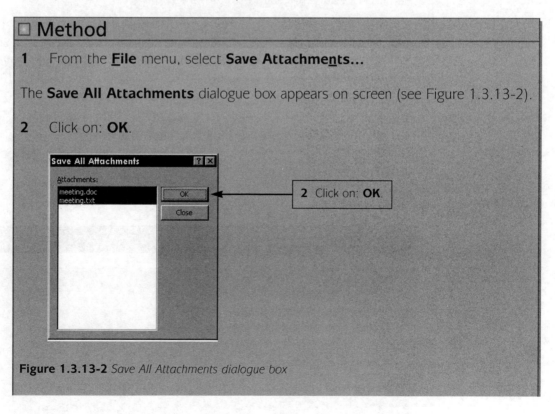

2 Click on: **OK**.

Figure 1.3.13-2 *Save All Attachments dialogue box*

A new **Save All Attachments** dialogue box appears on screen (see Figure 1.3.13-3).

In the example shown, the attachments are being saved on floppy disk. However, you should save them in the same place you have been saving other tasks in this book.

3   From the **Look in:** drop-down menu, select the location to save.

4   Click on: **OK**.

3 From the **Look in:** drop-down menu, select the location to save.

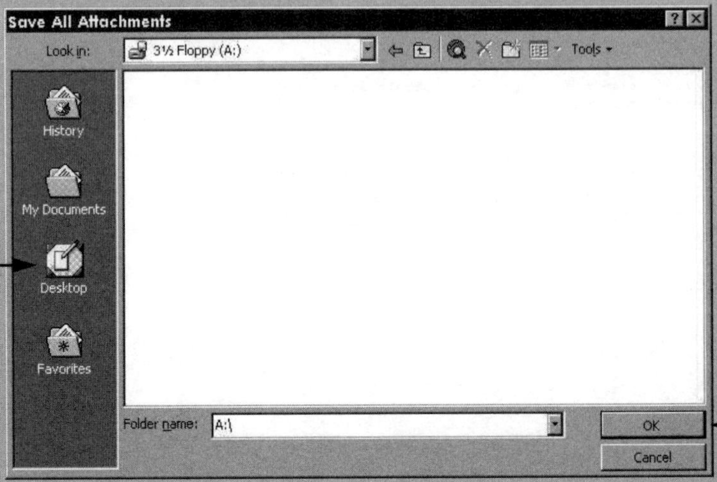

4 Click on: **OK**.

Figure 1.3.13-3 *Save All Attachments dialogue box*

You will be returned to the message window.

☐ Info

You could also save the attachments individually by right-clicking on each of them, selecting **Save As** and then using the **Save As** dialogue box to select the location to save them and clicking on: **Save**. You would need to follow the same procedure for each attachment.

You can also save attachments from the **Inbox** without actually opening the message. Click once on the message, then from the **File** menu, select **Attachments**, then **All Attachments**. This will bring up the **Save All Attachments** dialogue box and you would then follow steps **2** through **4** as above.

The method you used in this task is quick and simple. The extra information here is purely to give you more background knowledge of the software. As you use Outlook more and more, you will develop your own preferred methods of undertaking different tasks.

Printing a message

☐ Method

1   Click on: the 🖨 **Print** button.

When you print the message, the attachments will show above the message.

2   Write your name, date, centre number and task number on the printout.

3   Close the message (from the **File** menu, select: **Close**).

Exiting Outlook and shutting down

If your session is finished, then exit Outlook (from the **File** menu, select **Exit** *or* click on: the ☒ cross in the top right-hand corner) and shut down your computer (exit all other applications; click on: the **Start** button; select **Shut Down**; select **Shut Down**; click on: **OK**). Otherwise, move straight on to the next task.

Outlook

Open and print saved Word and text attachments

Objectives

- Open and print saved Word attachment
- Open and print saved text attachment

For the OCR Internet Technologies award you are required to open and print saved attachments. You could of course open and print the attachments from the email message. However, you need to show that you have saved the attachments and that you can find and print them from the location where they were saved.

In this task, you will open and print the text and Word attachments saved in Task 13. For the OCR Internet Technologies award you will not be required to open a word document. This task has been included to provide you with additional practice in working with attachments.

☐ Method

1 Double click on: [My Computer] **My Computer** icon on the desktop.

The **My Computer** window appears on screen (see Figure 1.3.14-1).

☐ Info

In the example shown, the attachments were saved on floppy disk. You will need to select the location where you saved the attachments.

2 Double-click on the drive where you saved your files, keep double-clicking on relevant folders until you reach the location where you saved your files.

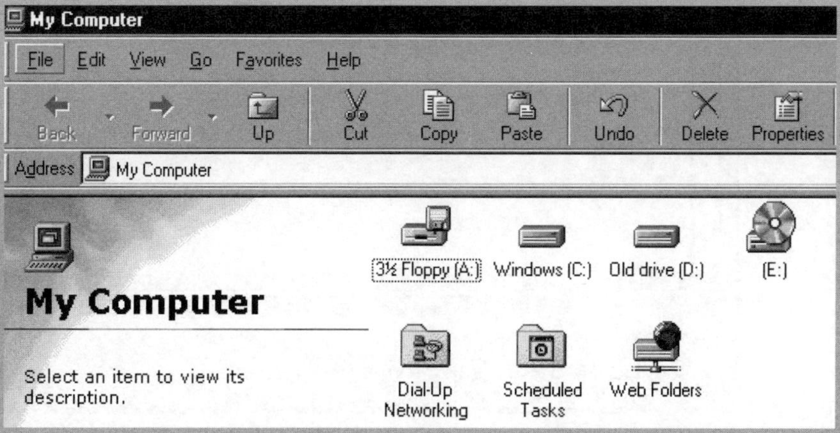

Figure 1.3.14-1 *My Computer window*

When you have reached the location where you have been saving your files, you should see the two attachments (see Figure 1.3.14-2).

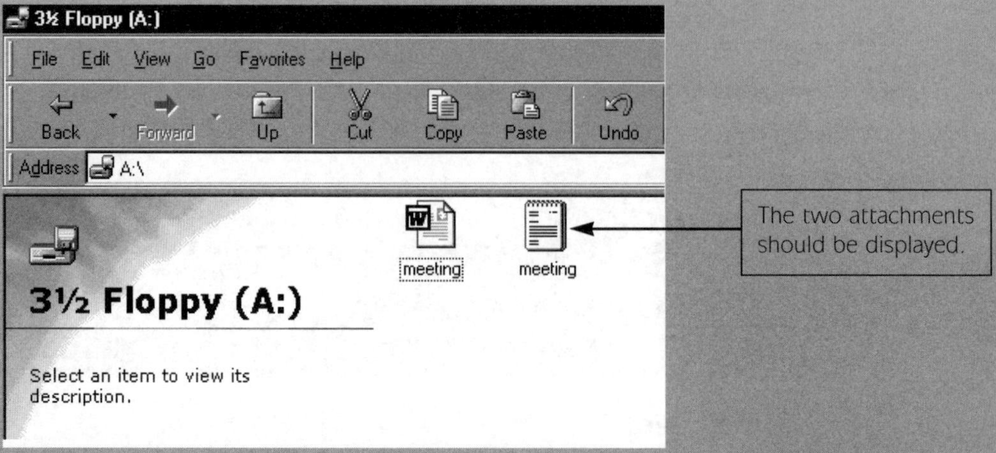

The two attachments should be displayed.

Figure 1.3.14-2 *Attachments*

Opening Word attachment

☐ Method

1   *Either* double-click on the Microsoft Word **meeting** document, *or* from the **File** menu, select: **Open**.

This will load the attachment into Microsoft Word (where it was originally produced) (see Figure 1.3.14-3).

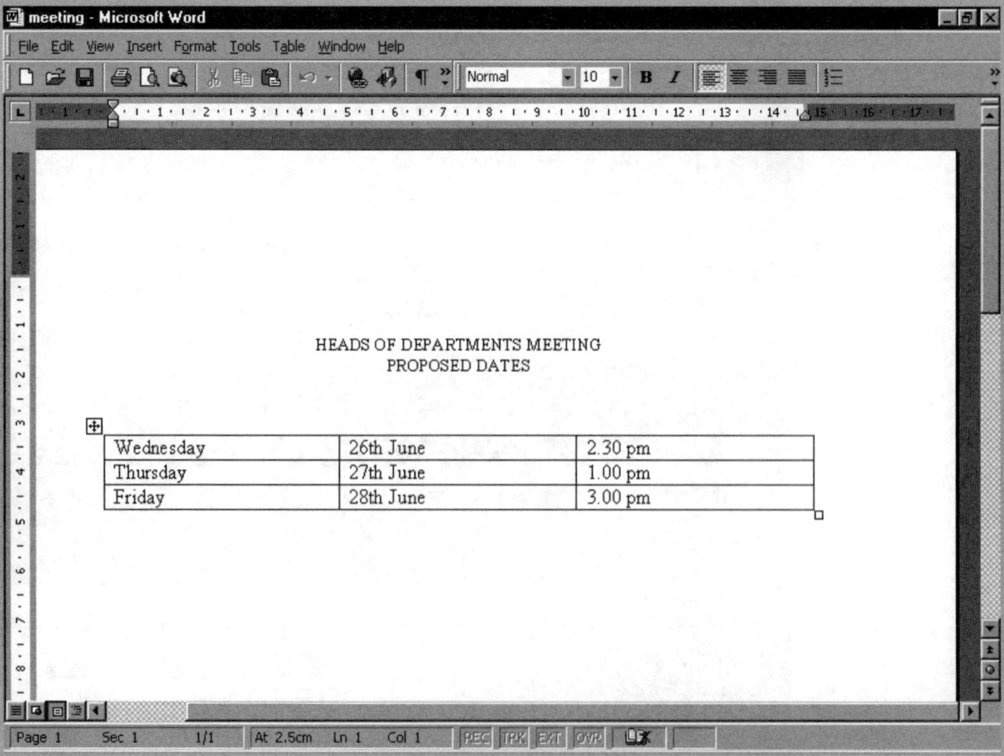

HEADS OF DEPARTMENTS MEETING
PROPOSED DATES

Wednesday	26th June	2.30 pm
Thursday	27th June	1.00 pm
Friday	28th June	3.00 pm

Figure 1.3.14-3 *Attachment loaded in Microsoft Word*

Printing Microsoft Word attachment

☐ Method

1 Click on: the 🖨 **Print** button.

2 Write your name, date, centre number and task number on the printout.

3 Close the document (from the **File** menu, select **Close**).

4 Exit Word (from the **File** menu, select **Exit**).

You will be returned to the Outlook window.

Opening and printing saved text attachment

☐ Method

1 *Either:* double-click on the **meeting** text attachment (see Figure 1.3.14-4), *or* click on the **meeting** text attachment and, from the **File** menu, select: **Open**.

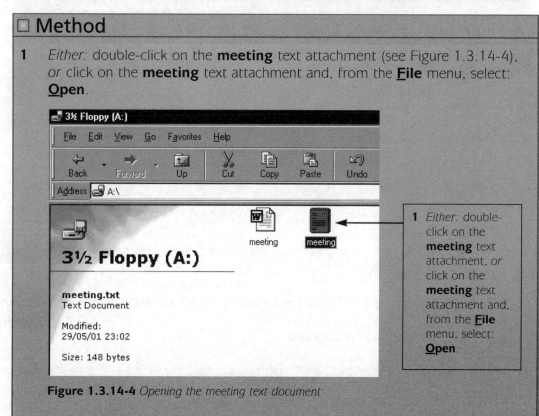

1 *Either:* double-click on the **meeting** text attachment, *or* click on the **meeting** text attachment and, from the **File** menu, select: **Open**.

Figure 1.3.14-4 *Opening the meeting text document*

This will load the text attachment into Windows Notepad (where it was originally produced) (see Figure 1.3.14-5).

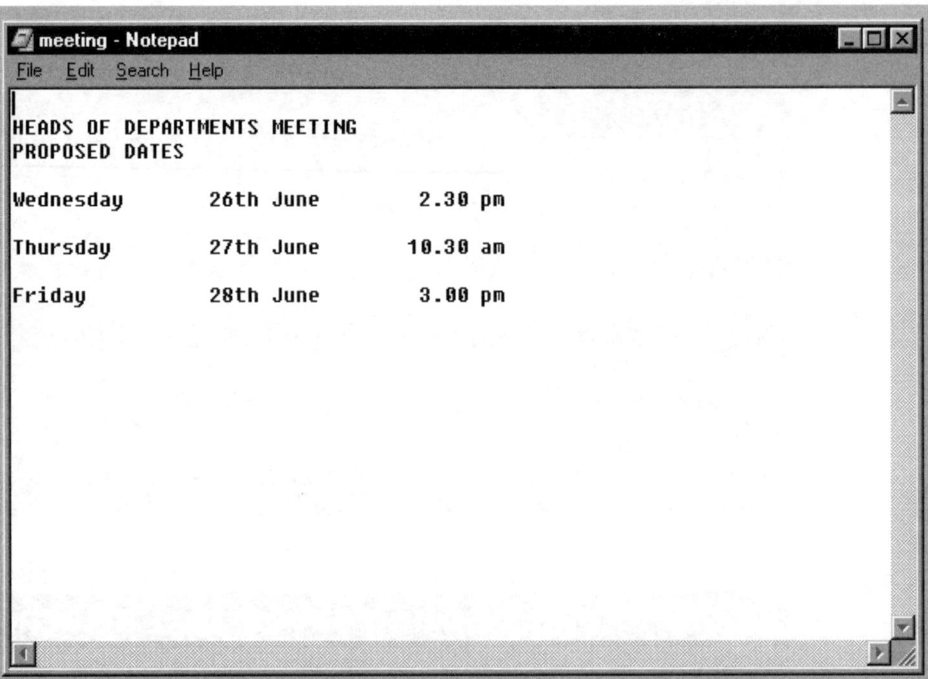

```
┌─────────────────────────────────────────────────────────┐
│ ▤ meeting - Notepad                          _ □ ✕ │
├─────────────────────────────────────────────────────────┤
│ File  Edit  Search  Help                                │
├─────────────────────────────────────────────────────────┤
│ |                                                   ▲    │
│ HEADS OF DEPARTMENTS MEETING                             │
│ PROPOSED DATES                                           │
│                                                          │
│ Wednesday         26th June         2.30 pm              │
│                                                          │
│ Thursday          27th June        10.30 am              │
│                                                          │
│ Friday            28th June         3.00 pm              │
│                                                          │
│                                                          │
│                                                     ▼    │
│ ◄                                               ►        │
└─────────────────────────────────────────────────────────┘
```

Figure 1.3.14-5 *Attachment loaded in Windows Notepad*

2   From the **File** menu, select: **Print**.

3   Write your name, date, centre number and task number on the printout.

4   Exit Notepad (from the **File** menu, select **Exit**).

You will be returned to the **My Computer** window.

5   Close **My Computer** (from the **File** menu, select **Close**).

□ Info

If you do not have access to **My Computer**, then you can also access files using **Windows Explorer**. You can usually access **Windows Explorer** by clicking on the **Start** button, then selecting **Programs**, **Accessories**, **Windows Explorer**.

In the **Windows Explorer** window (see Figure 1.3.14-6), you select the drive and then folders where your files are located by double-clicking on them in the **Folders** list on the left of the window.

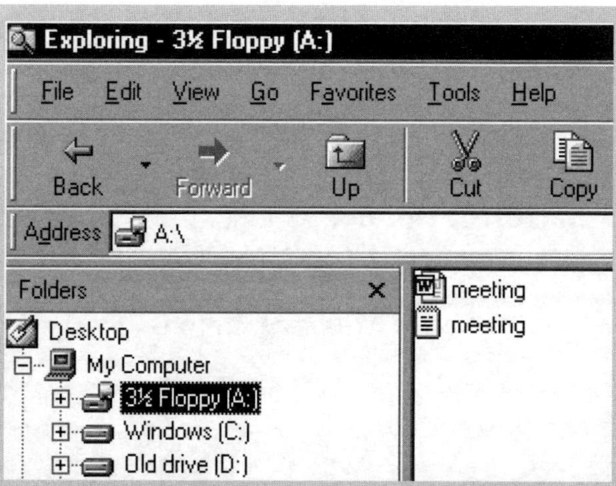

Figure 1.3.14-6 *Windows Explorer window*

The files are then displayed on the right-hand side of the window. You can then follow the same steps for opening and printing Word and text attachments, above.

Exiting Outlook and shutting down

If your session is finished, then exit Outlook (from the **File** menu, select **Exit** *or* click on: the ✕ cross in the top right-hand corner) and shut down your computer (exit all other applications; click on: the **Start** button; select **Shut Down**; select **Shut Down**; click on: **OK**). Otherwise, move straight on to the next task.

Task 15 Outlook

Attach saved text and Word files to new email message

Objectives

- Compose a new message
- Attach saved text and Word files

In Task 9 you attached a saved graphic image to an email message. As explained earlier, not all email attachments are images. In this task, you will attach the text file and the Word document that you saved in Task 13. Most email packages allow you to attach more than one file to an email message.

Scenario

You are the head of department for the Payroll section. You have received an email message regarding meeting dates for the heads of departments meeting. A colleague has not received a copy of the message and the secretary dealing with this is at lunch. You have agreed to let her have details of the message.

Compose a new message

☐ Method

1 If you do not already have Microsoft Outlook on screen, then load it (*either* click on: the **Microsoft Outlook** shortcut icon on the desktop, *or* click on the **Start** button and select: **Programs**, **Microsoft Outlook**).

2 Click on: the ⧉ New ▾ **New Message** button.

This message is to be sent to your tutor or, if you are working at home, to a friend or relative.

3 Enter the recipient's email address.

4 Key in the following subject heading:

Details of meeting

5 Key in the following message text:

Please find attached the meeting dates as promised.

6 Key in your personal details after the message text.

Attaching saved text and Word files

☐ Method

1 Click on: the 📎 **Insert File** button.

The **Insert Attachment** dialogue box appears on screen (see Figure 1.3.15-1).

2 From the **Look in:** box, select the location where you saved the attachments.

3 Click on the Word **meeting** attachment.

4 Click on: the arrow to the right of the **Insert** button at the bottom right of the dialogue box.

5 From the drop-down menu, select: **Insert as Attachment**.

2 From the **Look in:** box, select the location where you saved the attachments.

3 Click on the Word **meeting** attachment.

4 Click on: the arrow to the right of the **Insert** button at the bottom right of the dialogue box

5 From the drop-down menu, select: **Insert as Attachment**.

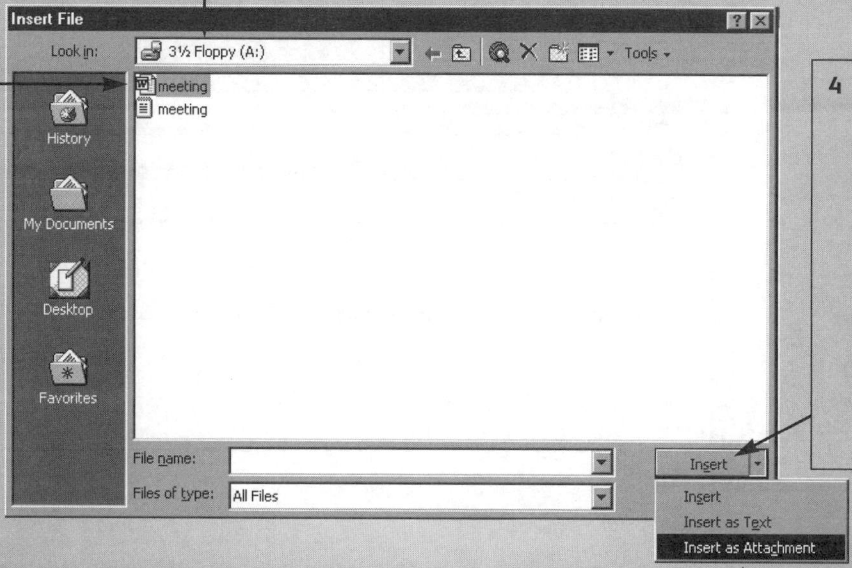

Figure 1.3.15-1 *Insert File dialogue box*

This will return you to the message window, where the Word attachment is shown at the bottom of the message (see Figure 1.3.15-2).

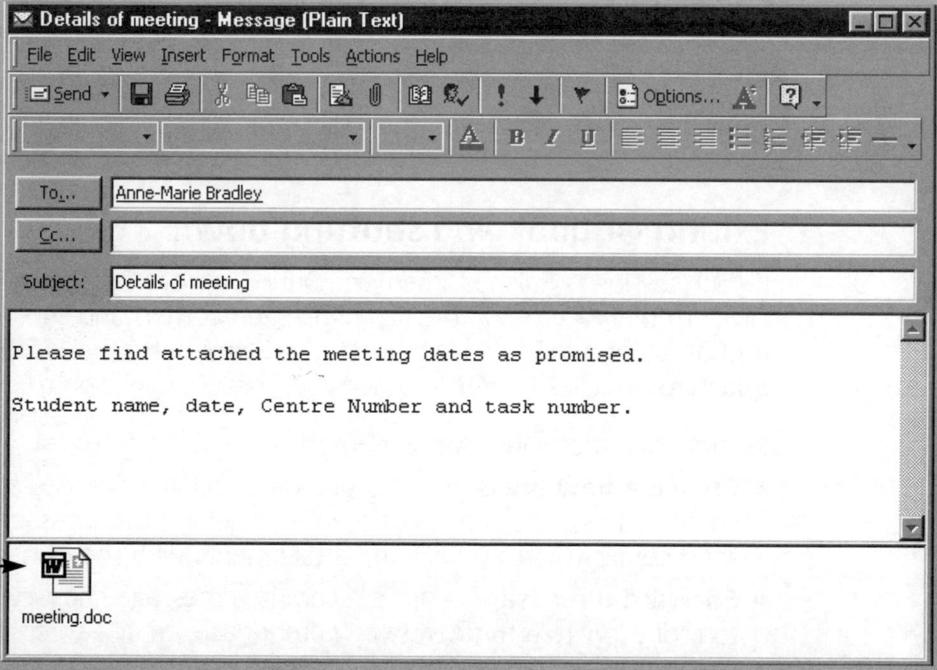

The Word attachment is now shown at the bottom of the message.

Figure 1.3.15-2 *Message window with Word attachment shown*

You now need to attach the text file to the email message.

6 Follow steps **1** through **5**, but this time, at step **3**, click on: the **meeting** text file.

Both attachments should now be shown at the bottom of the message (see Figure 1.3.15-3).

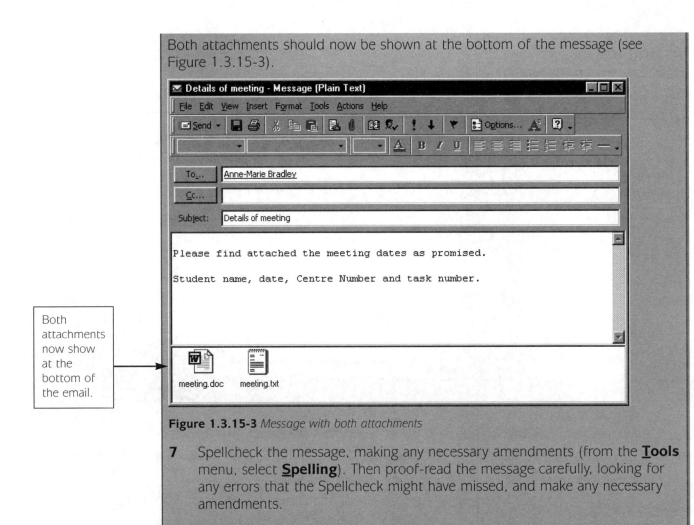

Both attachments now show at the bottom of the email.

Figure 1.3.15-3 *Message with both attachments*

7   Spellcheck the message, making any necessary amendments (from the **Tools** menu, select **Spelling**). Then proof-read the message carefully, looking for any errors that the Spellcheck might have missed, and make any necessary amendments.

8   Send the message. (If you are working offline, *remember* to click on: the **Send/Receive** button so that the message is sent over the Internet.)

9   Print the message you have just sent (click on: **Sent Items** in the **Folders List**; right-click on the message you have just sent; select **Print**).

Exiting Outlook and shutting down

If your session is finished, then exit Outlook (from the **File** menu, select **Exit** *or* click on: the ▄ cross in the top right-hand corner) and shut down your computer (exit all other applications; click on: the **Start** button; select **Shut Down**; select **Shut Down**; click on: **OK**). Otherwise, move straight on to the next task.

In summary, there are several methods of sending an email:

- **Create a new message** – requires you to initiate a message by entering the email address, the subject of the message and the message text itself. You can send copies (Cc) to others and attachments with the message.

- **Forward a message** – upon receiving a message choose the **Forward** option to redirect it to a third party by entering the email address and adding your own message to the original. FW: will appear automatically in front of the original subject heading to show it is a forwarded message. You can send copies (Cc) to others and attachments with the message.

- **Reply to a message** – upon receiving a message use the **Reply** option to respond. The message is automatically addressed back to the sender, allowing you to add your reply to the original message. RE: will appear in front of the original subject heading to show it is a reply. You can send copies (Cc) to others and attachments with the message.

Consolidation

The following tasks will provide you with further email practice.

Outlook/Yahoo! Mail

Build-up task 1

To complete the tasks, work in pairs, swap email addresses with a partner and send each other the following messages. (If you are working at home, then send the email messages to yourself.)

- Spellcheck and proof-read all messages carefully for errors.
- Add your name and centre number to the end of each message.
- Save each message you receive.

1   Compose the following message to your partner:

To:	(your partner's email address)
Subject heading:	EMAIL PRACTICE
Message:	Please let me know if you have received this message and attachment.

    a   Attach the **angel126** image (this can be found on the accompanying CD-ROM.

    b   Send the message.

2   Access your email **Inbox**.

    a   Read the message from your partner.

    b   Save the attachment.

    c   Reply to the message, acknowledging that you have received it.

    d   Forward the message to another member of your group (or to another friend or relative).

3   Compose a new email message to your partner:

Subject heading: EMAIL WITH ATTACHMENT

Message: I am attaching the image you sent me previously to this message.

    a   Attach the image you saved at step **2b**.

    b   Copy the message to your tutor (or another friend or relative).

    c   Send the message.

4   Access and print the attachment saved at step **2b**.

In this task a message is to be deleted from the **Inbox**.

5   Ensure the message with the title **EMAIL PRACTICE** has been saved to disk.
   a   Access the **Inbox**.
   b   Delete the message **EMAIL PRACTICE** from the **Inbox**.

6   Access the **Sent Items** folder and print a copy of the messages sent in this assignment.

7   Close all programs following the correct procedures.

Task Outlook/Yahoo! Mail

Build-up task 2

To complete the tasks, work in pairs, swap email addresses with a partner and send each other the following messages. (If you are working at home, then send the email messages to yourself.)

- Proof-read all messages carefully for errors.

- Add your name and centre number to the end of each message.

- Save each message you receive.

Scenario

You are inviting your partner to an engagement party. Compose a message to your partner inviting him or her to the party. Attach a suitable graphic image to the invitation.

1   Read the message from your partner. Print the message.

2   Save the message and the message attachment to disk.

3   Reply to your partner's message. Thank him or her for the invitation and tell him or her that you will check the date in your diary. Send the message.

4   Compose a new message to your partner. Give your apologies and inform your partner that you will be on holiday on that date.

5   Send a copy of the message to another member of your group.

6   Open the original invitation message from the **Inbox**. Forward the message to another member of your group. Add the following text to the message to be forwarded:

   Message forwarded by (your name).

7   Access the **Sent Items** folder and print a copy of each message you have sent.

8   Close all programs following the correct procedures.

Assignment preparation notes

Classroom situation

Your tutor will have sent the email message you will need to complete the following assignment.

Self-study home user

To enable you to complete the following assignment, you will need to send yourself the following email message with attachment.

1   Access your email account.

2   Compose the following message to yourself (i.e. to your own email address).

To:	(your email address)
Subject:	Shuttle Logo
Message text:	I have attached the first design of the logo for the new shuttle service.

3   Attach the **shuttle.jpg** image from the CD-ROM.

4   Send the message.

When the message has arrived in your **Inbox**, you are ready to start the assignment.

Scenario

A major transport company is in the process of announcing a new train service to add to its existing regular scheduled services. A logo has been designed for the advertising campaign. Several departments within the company are to be kept informed of the progress of the logo design.

- Incoming email messages are to be saved in the departmental user area (to be saved in an area outside the mailbox) and must then be deleted from the mailbox.

- Outgoing messages are to be saved and printed, including header details of the sender, recipient, subject and date to enable departmental colleagues to refer to at a later date if necessary.

- Your personal details (name and centre number) must be shown at the end of every outgoing message.

1.2a 1.2e	**1**	The Design department has sent you an email message. Open and read the message **Shuttle Logo**.
1.3a 1.3b		Add the Design department's email address to the email application's address book facility.
1.1c 1.1g 1.1i 1.1j 1.3c	**2**	The project coordinator is to be informed of the workshop schedules. Following appropriate procedures you are to forward the message **Safety workshops**, with attachment, to the project coordinator at the following email address: [fellow student email address (or friend's email address)] Add the text below to the message to be forwarded: **I am forwarding the new shuttle logo.** Add your personal details at the end of the email message. Check the message carefully for errors and make sure the system you are using saves outgoing messages. Forward the message.
1.1b 1.1e 1.1g 1.1i 1.1j 1.3c	**3**	The Design department requires confirmation that you have received the **Shuttle Logo** message. Prepare to reply to the Design department using the appropriate facility with the following message: **I received the new logo and it looks great.** Add your personal details at the end of the email message. Send a copy of the reply using the appropriate facility to: [another fellow student's (or another friend's) email address] Check the reply carefully for errors. Make sure the system you are using is set to save outgoing messages.
1.2c 1.2d 1.2f	**4**	For security reasons the message is to be stored in the company's filing structure and then deleted from the mailbox. Make a backup copy of the **Shuttle Logo** message and the attachment **shuttle.jpg**. Delete the **Shuttle Logo** message from the mailbox.
1.1a 1.1h 1.1i 1.1j 1.3c	**5**	The new logo has been approved and you have been asked to report back to the project coordinator. Prepare to compose a new email message. You will need to recall the Design department's email address from the address book facility. Give the message the subject heading below: **Shuttle Logo Approval**

Use the following text for the new email message:

The project team is very happy with the new logo. Approval has been given for using this design.

Add your personal details at the end of the email message.

Check the message carefully for errors. Make sure the system you are using is set to save outgoing messages.

1.2b	**6**	The Design team needs a copy of the new logo.
1.3d		Find and print a copy of the file **shuttle.jpg** stored at step 4.

1.1a	**7**	The advertising campaign is to begin as soon as possible. The Marketing team and Administration department need to see the new logo.
1.1d		
1.1f		
1.1g		Using the appropriate facility, prepare a new email message to be sent to the two email addresses below with equal priority (simultaneously).
1.1i		
1.1j		[tutor's (or friend or relative's) email address]
1.3c		[fellow student's (or a different friend or relative's) email address]

Give the message the following subject heading:

New Shuttle Logo

Use the following text in the email message:

I have attached the logo for the new shuttle service.

Find the file **shuttle.jpg**, which you stored at step 4, and attach it to this new email message.

Add your personal details at the end of the email message.

Check the message carefully for errors. Make sure the system you are using is set to save outgoing messages. Send the new message and attachment.

1.3d	**8**	Company procedures state that all email messages must be printed showing header details for the sender, subject, recipient and date.
		Print a copy of the four email messages sent in this assignment. Ensure header details of the messages are shown.

1.3e	**9**	Exit the application following the correct procedures.
1.3f		

Assignment preparation notes

Classroom situation

Your tutor will have sent you the email message you will need to complete the following assignment.

Self-study home user

To enable you to complete the following assignment, you will need to send yourself the following email message with attachment.

1   Access your email account.

2   Compose the following message to yourself (i.e. to your own email address).

To:	(your email address)
Subject:	Safety Workshops
Message text:	I have attached a draft timetable for the Office Safety Workshops.
	It is hoped that the days and times will be suitable for staff to attend at a time which is convenient to them.

3   Attach the **timetable.doc** file from the CD-ROM.

4   Send the message.

When the message has arrived in your **Inbox**, you are ready to start the assignment.

Scenario

In an effort to promote awareness of computer safety, a major organisation has planned a series of safety workshops for staff.

- Incoming email messages are to be saved in the departmental user area (to be saved in an area outside the mailbox) and must then be deleted from the mailbox.

- Outgoing messages are to be saved and printed, including header details of the sender, recipient, subject and date to enable departmental colleagues to refer to at a later date if necessary.

- Your personal details (name and centre number) must be shown at the end of every outgoing message.

1.2a 1.2e	**1**	The Personnel department has sent you an email message. Open and read the message **Safety Workshops**.
1.3a 1.3b		Add the Personnel department's email address to the email application's address book facility.
1.1c 1.1g	**2**	The workshop coordinator is to be informed of the workshop schedules.
1.1i 1.1j 1.3c		Following appropriate procedures, you are to forward the message **Safety workshops**, with attachment, to the workshop coordinator at the following email address: [fellow student's (or friend's) email address] Add the text below to the message to be forwarded: **I am forwarding the safety workshops timetable.** Add your personal details at the end of the email message. Check the message carefully for errors and make sure the system you are using saves outgoing messages. Forward the message.
1.1b 1.1e	**3**	The Personnel department requires confirmation that you have received the **Safety Workshops** message.
1.1g 1.1i 1.1j		Prepare to reply to the Personnel department using the appropriate facility with the following message: **I received the timetable and it looks fine.**
1.3c		Add your personal details at the end of the email message. Send a copy of the reply using the appropriate facility to: [another fellow student's (or another friend's) email address] Check the reply carefully for errors. Make sure the system you are using is set to save outgoing messages.
1.2c 1.2d	**4**	For security reasons the message is to be stored in the company's filing structure and then deleted from the mailbox.
1.2f		Make a backup copy of the **Safety Workshops** message and the attachment **timetable.doc**. Delete the **Safety Workshops** message from the mailbox.
1.1a 1.1h	**5**	The timetable has been approved and you have been asked to report back to the Personnel department.
1.1i 1.1j		Prepare to compose a new email message. You will need to recall the Personnel department's email address from the address book facility. Give the message the subject heading below:
1.3c		**Workshops Timetable**

Use the following text for the new email message:

The timetable for the safety workshops has been approved. This can now be sent to all line managers.

Add your personal details at the end of the email message.

Check the message carefully for errors. Make sure the system you are using is set to save outgoing messages.

1.2b 1.3d	**6**	The line managers need a copy of the workshops timetable. Find and print a copy of the file **timetable.doc** stored at step 4.
1.1a 1.1d 1.1f 1.1g 1.1i 1.1j 1.3c	**7**	The network manager and technicians need to be updated about the safety workshops. Using the appropriate facility, prepare a new email message to be sent to the two email addresses below with equal priority (simultaneously). [tutor's (or friend or relative's) email address] [fellow student's (or a different friend or relative's) email address] Give the message the following subject heading: **Safety Workshops Timetable** Use the following text in the email message: **I have attached the timetable for the staff safety workshops.** Find the file **timetable.doc**, which you stored at step 4, and attach it to this new email message. Add your personal details at the end of the email message. Check the message carefully for errors. Make sure the system you are using is set to save outgoing messages. Send the new message and attachment.
1.3d	**8**	Company procedures state that all email messages must be printed showing header details for the sender, subject, recipient and date. Print a copy of the four email messages sent in this assignment. Ensure header details of the messages are shown.
1.3e 1.3f	**9**	Exit the application following the correct procedures.

Use the Internet for online research

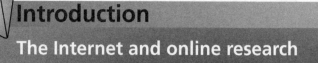

Introduction

The Internet and online research

The world wide web (WWW) can be used simply for browsing and looking around, or it can be used for research – for finding the answers to queries. The Internet is a vast resource of information made up of millions of websites created by individuals or organisations. This information consists mainly of textual information but also includes numerical information, graphical images and even sound and video. Every website has its own home page with hyperlinks, which when selected, take you to further pages within the site and often to other related websites as well. Each page has its own unique address called a URL (Uniform Resource Locator). By using a URL you can directly access that site or alternatively use a search engine which enables you to use keywords to locate the information you are looking for. It is worth noting that since anyone can create a website and upload their pages via their ISP (Internet Service Provider), there is a lot of worthless information on the Internet alongside a wealth of useful websites. Some websites may hold information that is very up to date whilst others may contain information that is a few years old. Sometimes you may try to link to a page and are unable to do so as the page no longer exists. It is not always easy to find the information you are looking for. It is very easy to become distracted by other links that look interesting.

The OCR Internet Technologies award focuses specifically on using the Internet for research.

More and more people are buying computers. Most computers that are sold now are Internet-ready – this means that they have a modem installed in the computer ready for connection to a phone line and, therefore, connection to the Internet.

To access the Internet you must have a modem installed on the computer, an Internet Service Provider (ISP) and a browsing application (software which allows you to move around from one page to another). The two most popular browsers are Internet Explorer and Netscape Navigator. The tasks in this book use the Internet Explorer browser. However, if you use Netscape Navigator, you will find the same tasks on the CD-ROM using Netscape Navigator instead.

There are several techniques you can use to find information on the Internet. The important point to remember is that searching for information on the Internet is very much trial and error – if you don't find the information you require in your first search you simply try again, perhaps with a different search word, or a different search engine.

There are countless search engines available to help you with research or with browsing the web. Some of these, including the web address, are shown below:

- Yahoo!   www.yahoo.co.uk
- Alta Vista   altavista.co.uk
- Ask Jeeves   askjeeves.co.uk
- Google   www.google.com
- Excite   www.excite.co.uk
- Lycos   www.lycos.co.uk

Each task in this element has been designed to guide you through the OCR requirements for Element Two. The tasks will be most beneficial to you if you follow them in the order that they appear.

The syllabus matching chart on page 81 shows which tasks fulfil each of the OCR requirements.

It is important to mention that the screenshots shown in the tasks are only *examples* to demonstrate how to search the Internet for information. As you will be aware, Internet pages are constantly changing. The idea is that you find the requested information by following links. If links to the web pages shown are not available, then choose others that will help you find the information you require.

Each task includes step-by-step instructions for completing it. It is important that you check each of your tasks carefully when you have finished. This is known as self-assessment and will help with your learning process. It is now also a requirement in many educational institutions. The tasks are followed by build-up tasks and two full practice assignments to help consolidate your new skills.

Classroom situation

If you are using this book in a classroom, to further enhance your new skills, OCR has produced a series of practice assignment papers for each element of the award. Your tutor will tell you about this.

Self-study home user

If you are using this book to study at home, then completing the tasks will give you a good grounding in the skills involved, as well as providing the basis for completing Element Two should you decide to enrol at a college to work towards the award.

Syllabus matching chart

Assessment objectives	Task number														
	1	2	3	4	5	6	7	8	9	10	B1	B2	B3	C1	C2
2.1 Navigate the world wide web to access remote data															
a navigate the world wide web using hyperlinks	●	●	●	●	●	●	●	●	●		●	●	●	●	●
b access specified remote web page(s)	●	●	●	●	●	●	●	●	●		●	●	●	●	●
c store URLs in appropriate facility	●	●	●		●	●	●	●	●		●	●	●	●	●
d access web pages from stored URL				●											
2.2 Use online search techniques to retrieve remote data															
a use general web search engine	●	●	●	●	●	●	●	●	●		●	●	●	●	●
b use internal search engine from specified website						●	●	●				●	●	●	●
c retrieve web page containing specified textual information						●	●	●					●	●	●
d retrieve web page containing specified numeric information				●	●							●	●	●	●
e retrieve web page containing information from specified website				●			●		●			●	●	●	●
f retrieve web page containing specified graphical information from specified website							●					●	●	●	●
2.3 Use appropriate software accurately and within regulations															
a select and use appropriate software	●	●	●	●	●	●	●	●	●	●	●	●	●	●	●
b print web page(s), ensuring that content is relevant to the query and within regulations	●	●	●	●	●	●	●	●	●	●	●	●	●	●	●
c enter data as specified ensuring there are no more than 3 data errors in total															
d exit software following correct procedures	●	●	●	●	●	●	●	●	●	●	●	●	●	●	●
e use computer within basic health and safety regulations	●	●	●	●	●	●	●	●	●	●	●	●	●	●	●

Use the Internet for online research

Different ways of searching

Internet Explorer

Search the Internet for information

Objectives

- Load Internet Explorer
- Load Yahoo! home page
- Search for information using Yahoo!
- Save search result
- Print search result
- Return to home page
- Exit Internet Explorer
- Shut down the computer

Scenario

During a school lesson, your seven-year-old niece became fascinated in astronomy. You have told her about a very large and powerful telescope at Jodrell Bank. She has asked if you could find out more about the telescope for her to show her teacher at school.

Loading Internet Explorer

☐ Method

1 *Either* click on: the **ℰ** **Internet Explorer** shortcut icon on the desktop, *or* click on the **Start** button and, from the pop-up menu, select **Programs**, **Internet Explorer**.

The **Internet Explorer** window appears on screen (see Figure 2.1.1-1).

☐ Hint

The first page you see is called the home page. On a home computer this is likely to be that of your ISP.

The Internet Explorer window explained

This is the **Title Bar**. When online, this will show details of the web page you are visiting.

The **Toolbar** contains a number of shortcut buttons to access different facilities (see also Figure 2.1.1-2).

Menu Bar – clicking on an item here will reveal a drop-down menu of options.

Address Bar – this is where you key in the URL (web address) of a website/page.

Figure 2.1.1-1 *The Internet Explorer window*

Reproduced with kind permission from www.virgin.net

The **Back** button takes you back to the last page you viewed. If you click on the down arrow a drop-down menu of the last few pages you have viewed will appear, so you can go back further.

The **Stop** button will stop a page from loading.

The **Home** button will return you to your Internet home page (whichever page loads up automatically when you launch Internet Explorer and connect to the Internet).

The **Favorites** button allows you to add a web page that you visit frequently to your **Favorites** list.

The **Mail** button will reveal several options – you could access your mail account to read your email messages, send email messages or send a link or an Internet web page to someone.

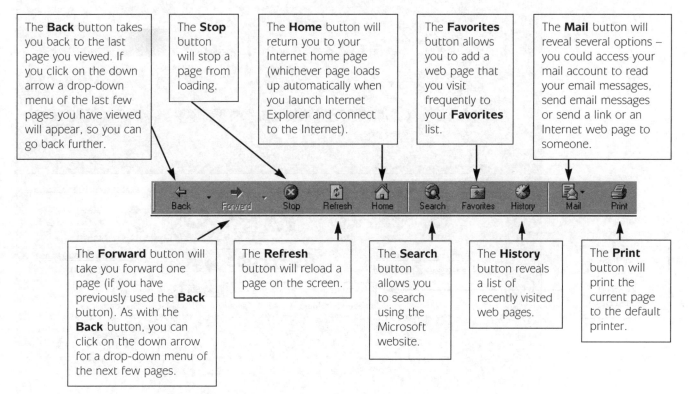

The **Forward** button will take you forward one page (if you have previously used the **Back** button). As with the **Back** button, you can click on the down arrow for a drop-down menu of the next few pages.

The **Refresh** button will reload a page on the screen.

The **Search** button allows you to search using the Microsoft website.

The **History** button reveals a list of recently visited web pages.

The **Print** button will print the current page to the default printer.

Figure 2.1.1-2 *The Internet Explorer toolbar*

Loading Yahoo! home page

☐ Method

1   Unless Yahoo! is your home page (the page that automatically loads up when you launch Internet Explorer and connect to the Internet), then key in the following URL (web address) in the **Address** box at the top of the screen (see Figure 2.1.1-2).

2   Press: **Enter**.

> **Key in the URL in the Address box and press: Enter.**

Figure 2.1.1-3 *Loading Yahoo! home page*

This will load up the **Yahoo! UK & Ireland** home page (see Figure 2.1.1-4).

Searching for information using Yahoo!

In this task, you will be using Yahoo! to search for information about a famous telescope at **Jodrell Bank**.

There are search options in Yahoo! that will allow you to limit your search. In this task, the information you require is in the **UK**.

☐ Method

1   Click to put a dot in the circle next to **UK only**.

2   Click inside the search box and key in **telescopes**.

3   Click on: the **Search** button.

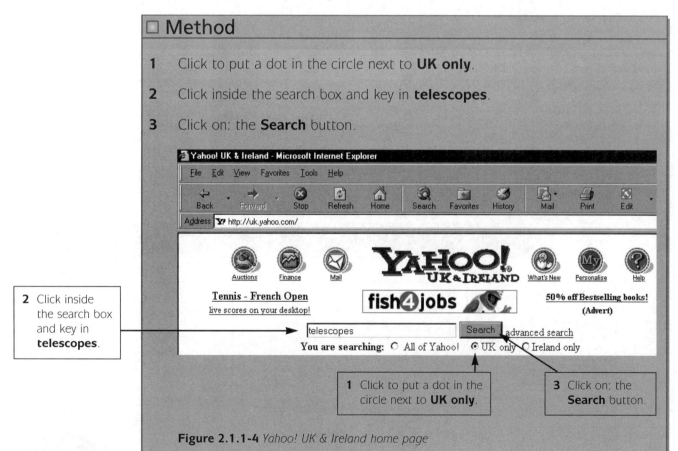

> **2** Click inside the search box and key in **telescopes**.

> **1** Click to put a dot in the circle next to **UK only**.

> **3** Click on: the **Search** button.

Figure 2.1.1-4 *Yahoo! UK & Ireland home page*

The **Search Result** screen appears (see Figure 2.1.1-5). Yahoo! has found many categories matching the criteria you keyed in.

☐ Hint

On screen, the words that are blue and underlined are links (hyperlinks). As you move the mouse pointer over a hyperlink, the pointer changes to a hand. Clicking on a link will take you to another web page. You need to decide which link to follow to find the information you want.

The words with arrows show the location of the links. The example below shows that this link is in England:

Regional>Countries>United Kingdom>England

The Yahoo! Search result shows the sites that match the search criteria. In this example, the link that we will follow is located further down the page, so you need to scroll down to find it.

4   Click on: the down arrow on the scrollbar until you find a link that interests you e.g. the **Jodrell Bank Observatory** link.

5   Click on: the **Jodrell Bank Observatory** link.

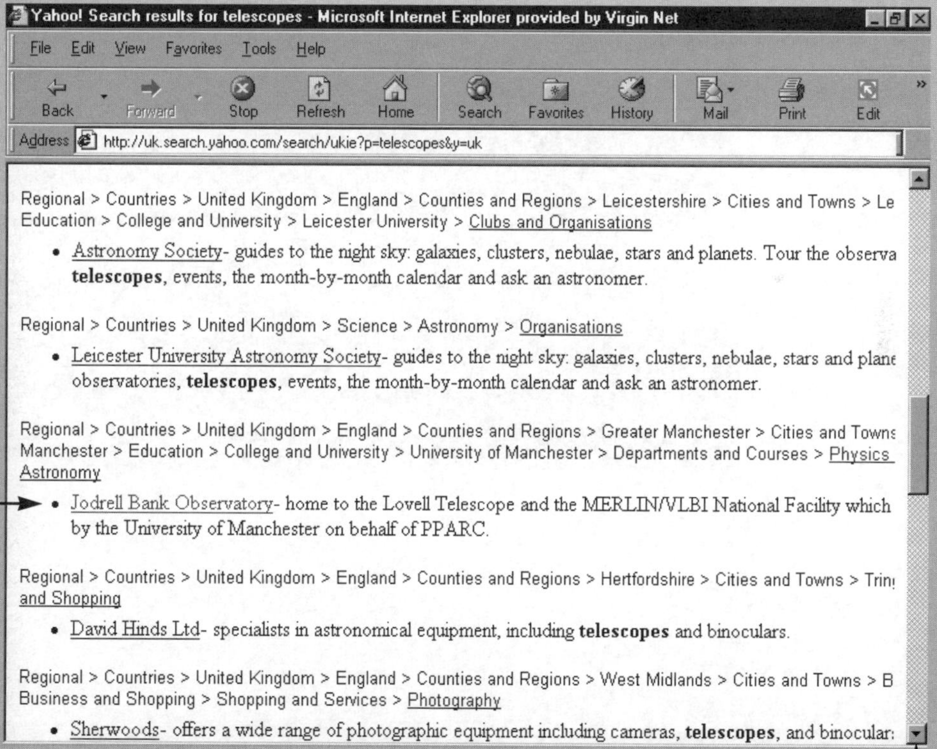

5 Click on: the **Jodrell Bank Observatory** link.

4 Click on: the down arrow on the scrollbar until you find the **Jodrell Bank Observatory** link.

Figure 2.1.1-5 *Search Result screen*

This will take you to the **Jodrell Bank Observatory** home page (see Figure 2.1.1-6). It is a good idea to add this page to the **Favorite** list so that you can easily return to it in the future.

6   From the **Favorites** menu, select **Add to Favorites...** and click on: **OK**. (You will learn more about **Favorites** in Task 2, pages 90–94.)

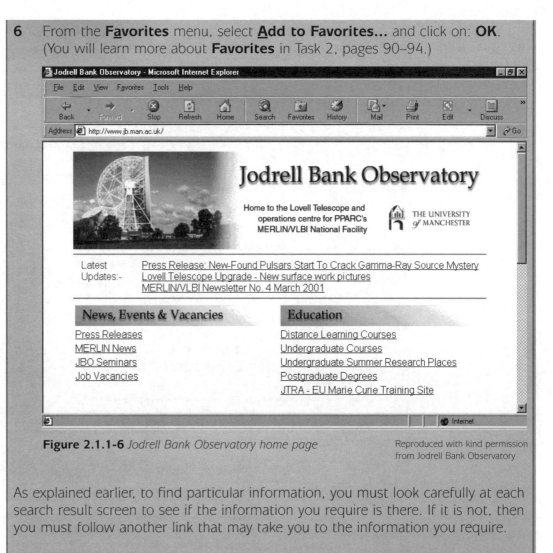

Figure 2.1.1-6 *Jodrell Bank Observatory home page*

As explained earlier, to find particular information, you must look carefully at each search result screen to see if the information you require is there. If it is not, then you must follow another link that may take you to the information you require.

The link you need to follow to find out about Jodrell Bank's most famous telescope is further down the page (see Figure 2.1.1-7).

7   Click on: the down arrow on the scrollbar until you find **The Lovell Telescope** link.

8 Click on: **The Lovell Telescope** link.

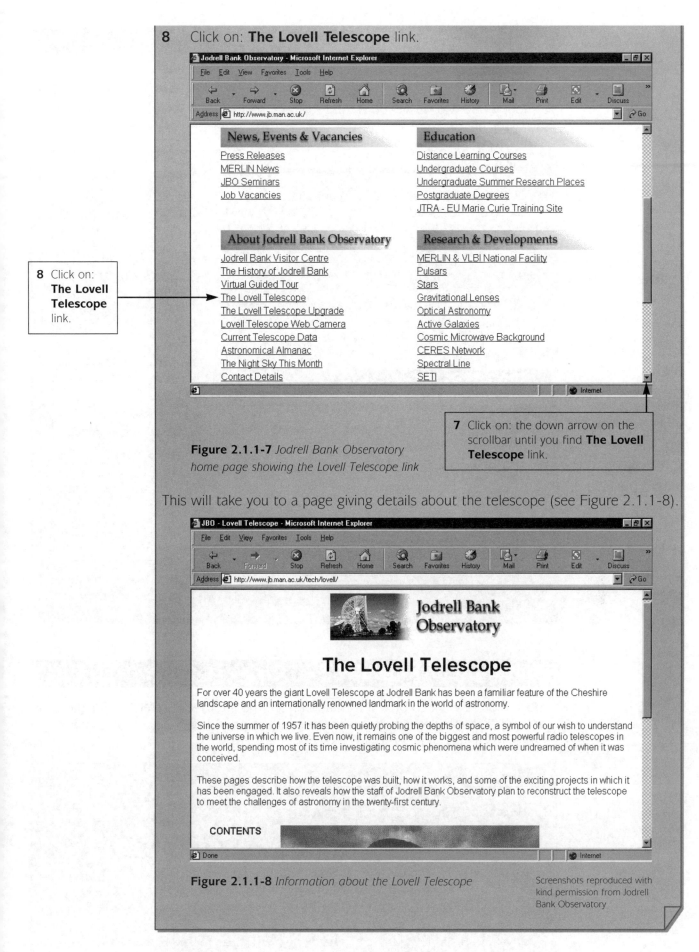

8 Click on:
The Lovell Telescope link.

7 Click on: the down arrow on the scrollbar until you find **The Lovell Telescope** link.

Figure 2.1.1-7 *Jodrell Bank Observatory home page showing the Lovell Telescope link*

This will take you to a page giving details about the telescope (see Figure 2.1.1-8).

Figure 2.1.1-8 *Information about the Lovell Telescope*

Screenshots reproduced with kind permission from Jodrell Bank Observatory

Although there is not actually a lot of text in this search result, it contains all the information required by the search criteria.

Saving search result

Sometimes you may want to save the page to refer back to at a later date, or perhaps when you are offline. In the example shown, the web page is being saved to floppy disk. However, you should save the search result wherever you usually save your files.

☐ Method

1   From the **File** menu, select **Save As...**

The **Save As** dialogue box appears on screen (see Figure 2.1.1-9).

2   Click on the small arrow to the right of the **Save in:** box and select the location to save your files.

3   Click in the **File name:** box and key in: **Jodrell Bank** (followed by your initials).

4   Click on: **Save**.

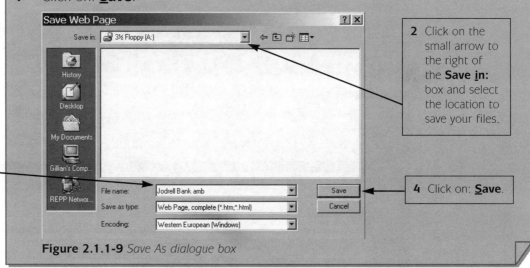

3 Click in the **File name:** box and key in: **Jodrell Bank** (followed by your initials).

2 Click on the small arrow to the right of the **Save in:** box and select the location to save your files.

4 Click on: **Save**.

Figure 2.1.1-9 *Save As dialogue box*

Printing search result

You will often want to print information from the Internet to refer to. For the OCR Internet Technologies award you are required to print a web page that contains details of the original question.

☐ Method

1   From the **File** menu, select: **Print...**

The **Print** dialogue box appears on screen (see Figure 2.1.1-10). It is important to print only the page that contains the information. There is an option in the **Print** dialogue box that allows you to do this. If you do not choose this option, then you may print pages of information that you do not require. It is good practice, therefore, to select this option.

2   Click to put a dot in the circle to the left of **Pages** (in the **Print range** section).

3   Click on: **OK**.

4 Write your name, centre number and task number on the printout.

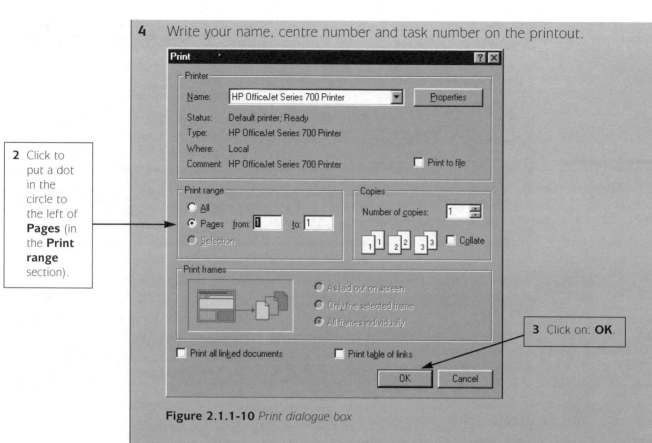

2 Click to put a dot in the circle to the left of **Pages** (in the **Print range** section).

3 Click on: **OK**.

Figure 2.1.1-10 *Print dialogue box*

Although not a requirement, it may be useful to highlight the answer to the question.

5 Use a highlighter pen, pen or pencil to highlight the text **Lovell Telescope** on the printout. This will help you to distinguish between the tasks you are working on.

Returning to home page

☐ Method

1 Click on: the 🏠 Home **Home** button to return you to your home page (the page that is automatically loaded up when you launch Internet Explorer).

If your session is finished you must exit Internet Explorer and shut down the computer using the correct procedures.

Exiting Internet Explorer

☐ Method

1 From the **File** menu, select **Close**.

This will close Internet Explorer.

Shutting down the computer

☐ Method

1 Make sure all other applications are closed.

2 Click on: the **Start** button in the bottom left-hand corner of the screen and, from the pop-up menu, select: **Sh<u>u</u>t Down**.

3 Select: **<u>S</u>hut Down** from the options that appear.

4 Click on: **OK**.

Internet Explorer

Save web address using Favorites

Objectives

- Create a new **Favorite** folder
- Key in a URL (web address)
- Mark a page using **Favorites**
- Print a page

Favorites and Bookmarks are a means of marking pages that you may want to return to. For the OCR Internet Technologies award you are required to store web addresses in the browser's Bookmark/Favorite facility. When you click on an entry you have made using this facility, you will be taken directly to the website, without needing to search or key in the web address.

If you are working at college many students may also be working towards the OCR Internet Technologies award and using the same computers. To save confusion, it would be useful, when storing **Favorites** to save them in a folder of your own. The instructions below will show you how to do this in Internet Explorer.

Creating a new Favorite folder

☐ Method

1 If you do not already have Internet Explorer on screen, then load it (*either* click on: the **Internet Explorer** shortcut icon on the desktop, *or* click on the **Start** button and select: **Programs**, **Internet Explorer**).

2 From the **F<u>a</u>vorites** menu, select **<u>O</u>rganize Favorites...**

The **Organize Favorites** dialogue box appears on screen (see Figure 2.1.2-1).

3 Click on: the **Create Folder** button.

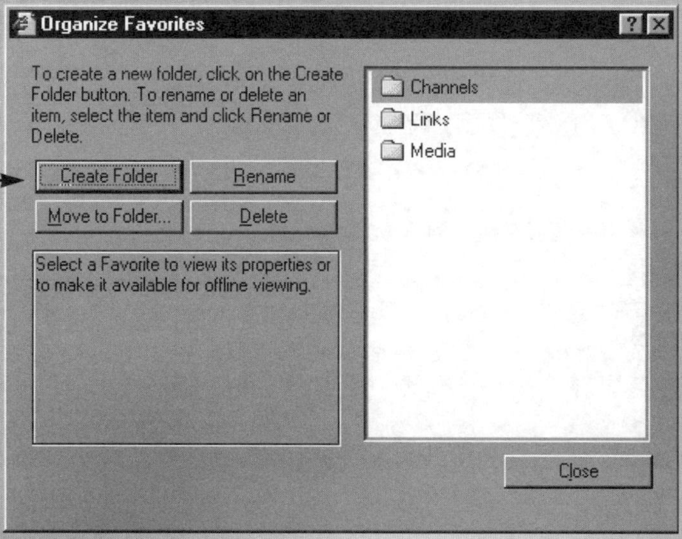

3 Click on: the **Create Folder** button.

Figure 2.1.2-1 *Organize Favorites dialogue box*

A new folder appears. To the right of the folder you will see a highlighted box (see Figure 2.1.2-2). This is where you will key in the name of the new folder. As soon as you begin keying in, the highlight will disappear.

This is where you will key in the name of the new folder. As soon as you begin keying in, the highlight will disappear.

Figure 2.1.2-2 *New Folder*

4 Key in your initials and surname, followed by the day of your class (if you are working at home, then just key in your initials and surname).

5 Click on: **Close**.

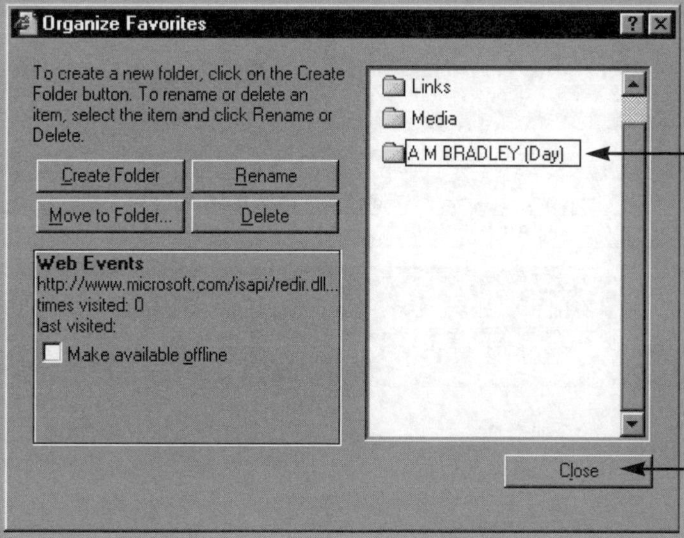

4 Key in your initials and surname, followed by the day of your class (if you are working at home, then just key in your initials and surname).

5 Click on: **Close**.

Figure 2.1.2-3 *Creating a new folder*

You can now check that your new folder has been created.

6 Select the **Favorites** menu to display the drop-down menu.

The new folder you have created with your name and the day of your class will be displayed in the list of folders (see Figure 2.1.2-4).

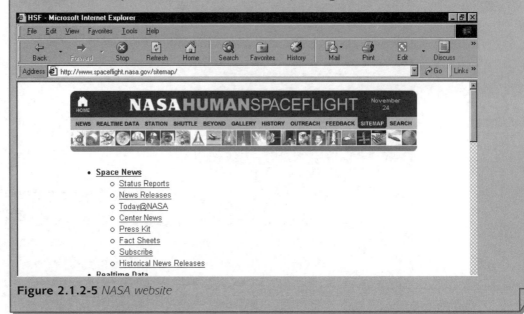

Virgin.net - the number one for entertainment and lei

File   Edit   View   Favorites   Tools   Help

Back   Forward

Address http://w

Add to Favorites...

Organize Favorites...

Channels

Links

Media

A M BRADLEY (Day)

> The new folder you have created with your name and the day of your class will be displayed in the list of folders.

Figure 2.1.2-4 *New folder created*

Keying in a URL (web address)

You will now key in the address of a web page in the **Address:** box in order to load a web page. (You will then add this web page to your new **Favorites** folder.)

☐ Method

1 Key in the following URL in the **Address:** box:

spaceflight.nasa.gov/sitemap/

☐ Hint

If this link does not take you to the web page shown below (Figure 2.1.2-5), then key in: **www.nasa.gov** and, when the **NASA** website has loaded, click on: the **site map** tab at the top of the screen.

2 Press: **Enter**.

This should take you to the **NASA** website (see Figure 2.1.2-5).

HSF - Microsoft Internet Explorer

File   Edit   View   Favorites   Tools   Help

Back   Forward   Stop   Refresh   Home   Search   Favorites   History   Mail   Print   Edit   Discuss

Address http://www.spaceflight.nasa.gov/sitemap/   Go   Links »

NASAHUMANSPACEFLIGHT November 24

NEWS   REALTIME DATA   STATION   SHUTTLE   BEYOND   GALLERY   HISTORY   OUTREACH   FEEDBACK   SITEMAP   SEARCH

- **Space News**
  - Status Reports
  - News Releases
  - Today@NASA
  - Center News
  - Press Kit
  - Fact Sheets
  - Subscribe
  - Historical News Releases
- **Realtime Data**

Figure 2.1.2-5 *NASA website*

Marking a page using Favorites

You will be returning to this website in a later task to search for information, so you need to add it to your **Favorites** folder.

☐ Method

1   From the **Favorites** menu, select **Add to Favorites**.

The **Add Favorite** dialogue box appears on screen (see Figure 2.1.2-6). You now need to select the folder where you want to save the website.

2   Click on: your folder.

3   Click on: **OK**.

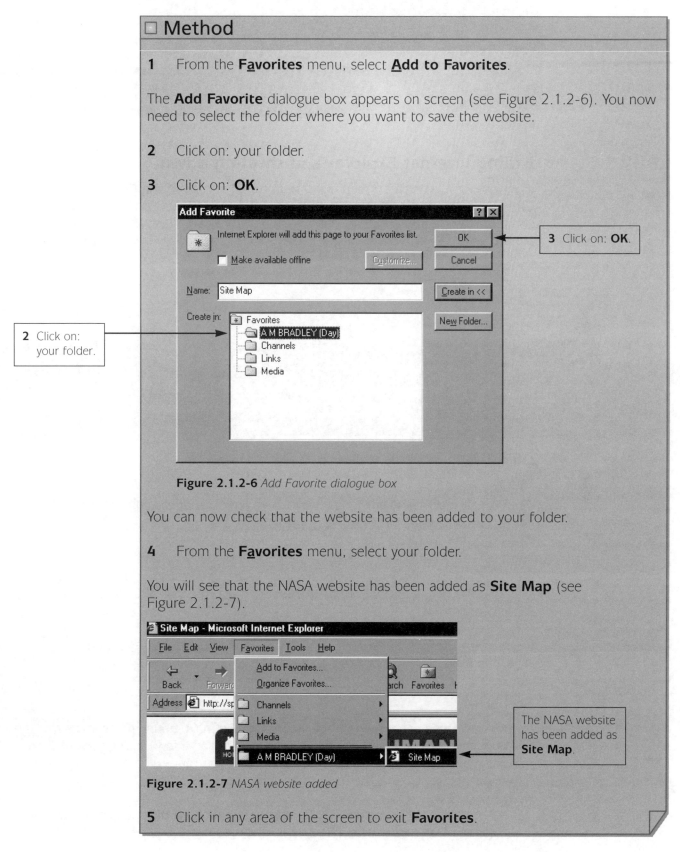

Figure 2.1.2-6 *Add Favorite dialogue box*

You can now check that the website has been added to your folder.

4   From the **Favorites** menu, select your folder.

You will see that the NASA website has been added as **Site Map** (see Figure 2.1.2-7).

Figure 2.1.2-7 *NASA website added*

5   Click in any area of the screen to exit **Favorites**.

Printing a page

☐ Method

1 Print the web page (from the **File** menu, select: **Print** and select the option to print only 1 page).

2 Write your name, date, centre number and task number on the printout.

3 Return to your home page (click on: the **Home** button).

Exiting Internet Explorer and shutting down

If your session is finished, then exit Internet Explorer (from the **File** menu, select **Close** *or* click on: the ✕ cross in the top right-hand corner) and shut down your computer (exit all other applications; click on: the **Start** button; select **Shut Down**; select **Shut Down**; click on: **OK**). Otherwise, move straight on to the next task.

Task 3 Internet Explorer

Search for information using specific URLs

Objectives

- Key in a URL
- Use an internal search engine and links to locate information
- Store web pages in **Favorites** folder
- Print web page

For the OCR Internet Technologies award you are required to access web pages by keying in the URL address in the **Address:** box and then search within the website for information.

If you know the web address it is much easier and quicker to key it in the **Address:** box than to search for the website using a search engine.

Scenario

Sarah, a colleague at your workplace, is retiring. The main retiring present has already been bought, but you have been given the job of finding a few small gifts with the remaining money from the retiring collection. With your private detective hat on, you have managed to find out that her hobbies include reading, music and films.

1 Access the **WH Smith** website (**www.whsmith.co.uk**). Search the website for the **Gone with the Wind** video and find out the price.

2 Access the **HMV** website (**www.hmv.co.uk**). Find the **Hits** CD by Phil Collins and find out the price.

3 Access the **Amazon** website (**www.amazon.co.uk**). Search for a book with the title **The Lord of the Rings** and find out the price.

4 Access the **Comet** electrical store website (**www.comet.co.uk**). Search the website for the least expensive personal CD player.

For each of the searches listed in the scenario above, follow the steps below.

☐ Method

1 If you do not already have Internet Explorer on screen, then load it (*either* click on: the **Internet Explorer** shortcut icon on the desktop, *or* click on the **Start** button and select: **Programs**, **Internet Explorer**).

2 Key in the URL and press: **Enter**.

3 Use the website's internal links and search boxes to locate the required information.

When you have located a page with the required information:

4 Add the web page to your folder in the **Favorites** list (from the **Favorites** menu, select: **Add Favorite**; click on your folder; click on: **OK**).

5 Print the web page (from the **File** menu, select: **Print**; select the option to print only one page; click on: **OK**).

6 Write your name, date, centre number and task number on the printout.

7 Highlight the requested information on the printout.

Exiting Internet Explorer and shutting down

If your session is finished, then exit Outlook (from the **File** menu, select **Exit** *or* click on: the ☒ cross in the top right-hand corner) and shut down your computer (exit all other applications; click on: the **Start** button; select **Shut Down**; select **Shut Down**; click on: **OK**). Otherwise, move straight on to the next task.

Internet Explorer

Load a web page using Favorites

Objectives

- Load a web page from a saved **Favorite**
- Print a web page
- Return to home page

For the OCR Internet Technologies award you are required to access a web page from a stored **Favorite**.

In this task you will load the **Jodrell Bank** web page that you stored in Task 1.

Loading a web page from a saved Favorite

□ Method

1 If you do not already have Internet Explorer on screen, then load it (*either* click on: the **Internet Explorer** shortcut icon on the desktop, *or* click on the **Start** button and select: **Programs**, **Internet Explorer**).

2 From the **Favorites** menu, select the **Jodrell Bank** page that you saved in Task 1 (*remember*, you didn't put this in your folder, so it should just be at the bottom of the **Favorites** menu).

You will automatically be taken to the **Jodrell Bank** web page.

Printing a web page

□ Method

1 Print the web page (from the **File** menu, select: **Print**; select the option to print only one page; click on: **OK**).

2 Write your name, date, centre number and task number on the printout.

3 Highlight the requested information on the printout.

Returning to home page

□ Method

1 Return to your home page (click on: the **Home** button).

Exiting Internet Explorer and shutting down

If your session is finished, then exit Internet Explorer (from the **File** menu, select **Close** *or* click on: the ☒ cross in the top right-hand corner) and shut down your computer (exit all other applications; click on: the **Start** button; select **Shut Down**; select **Shut Down**; click on: **OK**). Otherwise, move straight on to the next task.

Use the Internet for online research

Finding information

Internet Explorer

Use search facility to find information

Objectives

- Search a website for numeric information
- Store pages using **F_avorites**
- Print pages

For the OCR Internet Technologies award you are required to find different types of information. For this task you will use a search engine to find numeric information.

Scenario

You are doing a project on the history of the royal family. You need to find out answers to the following questions:

1 In which year were the Crown Jewels first used?

2 What are the Honours of Scotland?

3 In which year did Queen Victoria come to the throne?

4 How many Royal Palaces are there?

5 Who was the last British monarch to fight in battle and when?

6 Follow links to find out the official titles and dates of birth of each of the Queen's children.

☐ Hint

The answers to the above questions can all be found at the same website.

For each of the questions, follow the steps below.

☐ Method

1 If you do not already have **Internet Explorer** on screen, then load it (*either* click on: the **Internet Explorer** shortcut icon on the desktop, *or* click on the **Start** button and select: **Programs, Internet Explorer**).

2 Use a search engine to find the answers to each question.

3 For each question, store the web page containing the answer in your **Favorites** folder.

4 For each question, print the web page containing the information. Write your name, date, centre number and task number on the printouts and highlight the required information on each printout.

5 When you have finished, use the **Back** button to return to your home page.

Exiting Internet Explorer and shutting down

If your session is finished, then exit Internet Explorer (from the **File** menu, select **Close** *or* click on: the ☒ cross in the top right-hand corner) and shut down your computer (exit all other applications; click on: the **Start** button; select **Shut Down**; select **Shut Down**; click on: **OK**). Otherwise, move straight on to the next task.

Internet Explorer

Use internal search facility to find information

Objectives

- Use an internal (or local) search engine
- Store pages in **Favorites** folder
- Save pages
- Print pages

In this task, you will access a website and use its own internal (or local) search engine to find information within the site.

Scenario

You recently started a new job inputting data into a computer. You feel you need to know more about the rules and regulations relating to working on a computer and decide to research this.

1 Find information about:
   a RSI (Repetitive Strain Injury)
   b display screen regulations
   c general office safety regulations.

2 Find three possible causes of headaches associated with using a VDU.

3 Find and print the images for the following safety signs:
   a Fire Exit   **b** Electrical Hazard.

4 Find a diagram that shows working with VDUs/Display Screen Equipment guidelines.

5 What is British Health and Safety law based on?

☐ Method

1 If you do not already have Internet Explorer on screen, then load it (*either* click on: the **Internet Explorer** shortcut icon on the desktop, *or* click on the **Start** button and select: **Program, Internet Explorer**).

2 Using a search engine, begin a search with the subject **Health and Safety**. Follow appropriate links to locate the **Health and Safety Executive** website.

3 Using the internal search facility on the website, locate the information listed in the scenario above.

4 For each piece of information, add the web page to your folder in the **Favorites** list (from the **Favorites** menu, select: **Add Favorite**; click on your folder; click on: **OK**).

5 For each piece of information, print the web page and highlight the required information on the printout. Put the information printouts in numerical order (as listed in the scenario above).

Exiting Internet Explorer and shutting down

If your session is finished, then exit Internet Explorer (from the **File** menu, select **Close** *or* click on: the ☒ cross in the top right-hand corner) and shut down your computer (exit all other applications; click on: the **Start** button; select **Shut Down**; select **Shut Down**; click on: **OK**). Otherwise, move straight on to the next task.

Task 7 Internet Explorer

Search for graphical information

Objectives

- Search specific website for graphical information
- Add pages containing information to **Favorites**
- Printing a web page containing graphical information

For the OCR Internet Technologies award you are required to search a website to find graphical information. In this task you will be shown how to search the Met Office website to find a graph showing details of monthly sunshine for 2000. You will then be asked to find another graph from the same website.

Search a specific website for graphical information

□ Method

1 If you do not already have **Internet Explorer** on screen, then load it (*either* click on: the **Internet Explorer** shortcut icon on the desktop, *or* click on the **Start** button and select: **Program, Internet Explorer**).

2 Key in the following URL in the **Address** box:

www.metoffice.com

3 Press the **Enter** key on the keyboard, or click on the **Go** button to the right of the **Address** box.

This should load the Met Office homepage (Figure 2.2.7-1).

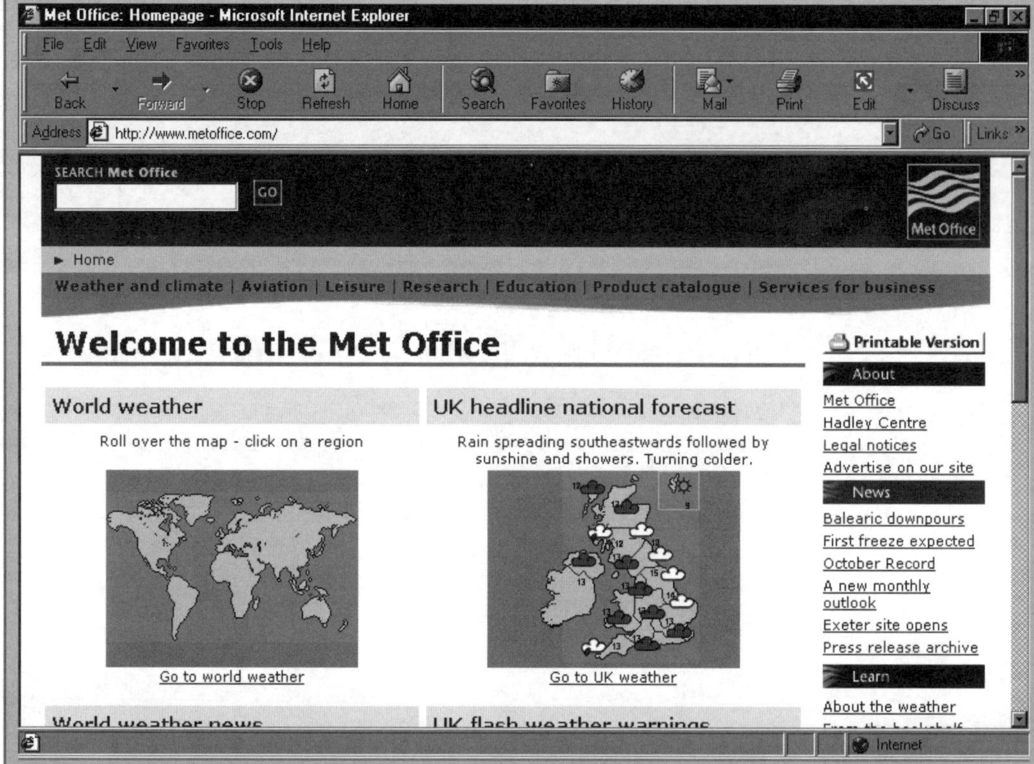

Figure 2.2.7-1 *Met Office homepage* © Crown, Met Office

As mentioned previously, you will be searching this site to find a graph showing details of the monthly sunshine for 2000. You will first need to conduct a search for the information you require. You will do this by keying in search criteria. In this example you will use the word **sunshine** (Figure 2.2.7-2).

4   Click in the box below **Search Met Office** and key in: **sunshine**. Click on
the **Go** button to the right of the Search box, or press the **Enter** key on the
keyboard.

Figure 2.2.7-2 *Met Office website internal search screen*

The results of the search appear on screen (see Figure 2.2.7-3). You will need to
scroll down to find the link you need to follow.

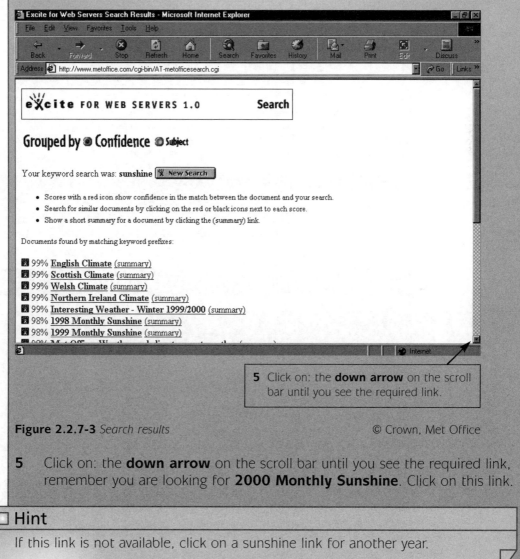

> **5** Click on: the **down arrow** on the scroll
> bar until you see the required link.

Figure 2.2.7-3 *Search results*   © Crown, Met Office

5   Click on: the **down arrow** on the scroll bar until you see the required link,
remember you are looking for **2000 Monthly Sunshine**. Click on this link.

☐ Hint

If this link is not available, click on a sunshine link for another year.

This should load the graph for **Monthly Sunshine 2000**, the information you were required to find. You now need to mark the page by adding it to your personal folder in the **Favorites** list.

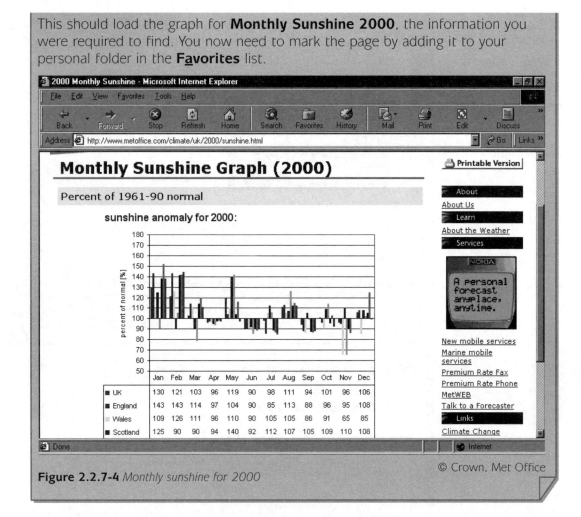

Figure 2.2.7-4 *Monthly sunshine for 2000*

© Crown, Met Office

Add the page containing information to F**a**vorites list

☐ Method

1   From the **menu bar**, select **F**a**vorites**.

2   Click on: **A**dd to Favorites**. Select your folder.

3   Click on: **OK**.

Printing the web page containing graphical information

For the OCR Internet Technologies award, you are required to print the page containing the graphical information.

☐ Method

1   From the **File** menu, select **Print** to print the page.

Write your name, date, centre number and task number on the printout.

Further graphical information search practice

☐ Method

1 Search the Met Office website and follow links to locate and print the following graphs:

   a global climate predictions

   b stratosphere.

☐ Hint

If a link does not take you to the page containing the information, click on: the **Back** button on the toolbar and try another link.

2 Add the pages containing the graphical information to your personal folder in the **Favorites** list, print the pages and write your name, date, centre number and task number on the printout.

3 When you have found the requested information, return to your home page.

Exiting Internet Explorer and shutting down

If your session is finished, then exit Internet Explorer (from the **File** menu, select **Close** *or* click on: the ☒ cross in the top right-hand corner) and shut down your computer (exit all other applications; click on: the **Start** button; select **Shut Down**; select **Shut Down**; click on: **OK**). Otherwise, move straight on to the next task.

Objectives

- Search for websites
- Use internal search engines to search for information
- Save page containing information
- Print page containing information

The following exercise is designed to help consolidate the searching skills you have learnt in previous tasks. This exercise focuses specifically on using search engines within websites to find the information you want. For each piece of information, save and print the page containing the information. Write your name, date, centre number and task number on each printout and highlight the information requested on the printout.

Scenario

You are arranging a weekend day out for you and your fellow workers to celebrate your birthday. You feel like doing something a little different from the usual celebratory meal.

1   You haven't been skating for years. Find details of times available at a skating rink in your area.

2   You've never been bowling. Find details of a bowling alley in your area.

3   Find the website of your nearest cinema and search for information on films being shown next Sunday.

4   Find the website for your nearest fitness/leisure centre. Search the site for information on the swimming facilities available.

☐ **Hint**

If you do not already have Internet Explorer on screen, then load it (*either* click on: the **Internet Explorer** shortcut icon on the desktop, *or* click on the **Start** button and select: **Programs**, **Internet Explorer**).

You will need to use a search engine to find the websites. You may be able to link to the relevant websites from a web guide about your area or from a local council page.

Remember to close Internet Explorer and shut down the computer following correct procedures if your session is finished.

Internet Explorer

Find information using saved Favorite

Objectives

- Load web page from saved **Favorite**
- Follow links in the site to find information
- Add the new page containing information to the **Favorite** folder
- Print information

For the OCR Internet Technologies award you are required to load a web page saved in the **Favorite** facility and follow links within the website to find further information.

In this task, you will load the NASA web page (**site map**) that you added to the **Favorite** menu in Task 2 and follow links within the website to find information on the subject of **space history**. You will then mark the page containing the information. Write your personal details on each printout and highlight the requested information on the printout.

> ### ☐ Hint
> You are looking for details of a lunar landing and an Apollo mission. There were lots of Apollo missions, so you need to take care to select the correct one.

Scenario

You have been asked to prepare an inter-departmental quiz, the proceeds of which will be donated to a local charity. You need to use the Internet to find the answers to the following questions:

1 What date did a man first land on the moon?

2 Who was the first man to set foot on the moon?

3 What were the famous words he said?

4 Who followed him?

> ### ☐ Hint
> If you do not already have Internet Explorer on screen, then load it (*either* click on: the **Internet Explorer** shortcut icon on the desktop, *or* click on the **Start** button and select: **Programs**, **Internet Explorer**).
>
> From the **Favorites** menu, select your folder and then **site map**.
>
> Click on: the **SEARCH** button and use the internal search engine to look for the required information.
>
> *Remember* to close Internet Explorer and shut down the computer following correct procedures if your session is finished.

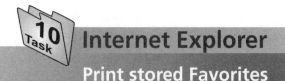
Objectives

- Export, save and print your **F<u>a</u>vorites** folder
- Access your **F<u>a</u>vorites** folder
- Take a screen shot of your **F<u>a</u>vorites** folder
- Paste screen shot into Microsoft Word
- Save **F<u>a</u>vorites** list
- Print **F<u>a</u>vorites** list

For the OCR Internet Technologies award you are required to provide evidence that you have stored requested web pages in the **F<u>a</u>vorite** facility. You can get your tutor to check this. However, there is a way you can provide a printout of the list. This will show the websites that you visited on the Internet (and stored in your **F<u>a</u>vorites** folder) during the course of your research.

Export and save your F<u>a</u>vorites folder

In this task you will **export** your Favorites folder, save the folder where you save your files, and then access and print the exported file.

☐ Method

1   If you do not already have Internet Explorer on screen, then load it (*either* click on: the **Internet Explorer** shortcut icon on the desktop, *or* click on the **start** button and select: **Programs, Internet Explorer**).

2   From the **File** menu select **Import and Export**.

The **Import/Export Wizard** dialogue box appears on screen (Figure 2.2.10-1).

3   Click on: **Next**.

Figure 2.2.10-1 *Import/Export wizard dialogue box*

You will then be required to select the action you wish to perform (Figure 2.2.10-2).

4 Select **Export Favorites**. Click on: **Next**.

4 Select **Export Favorites**.

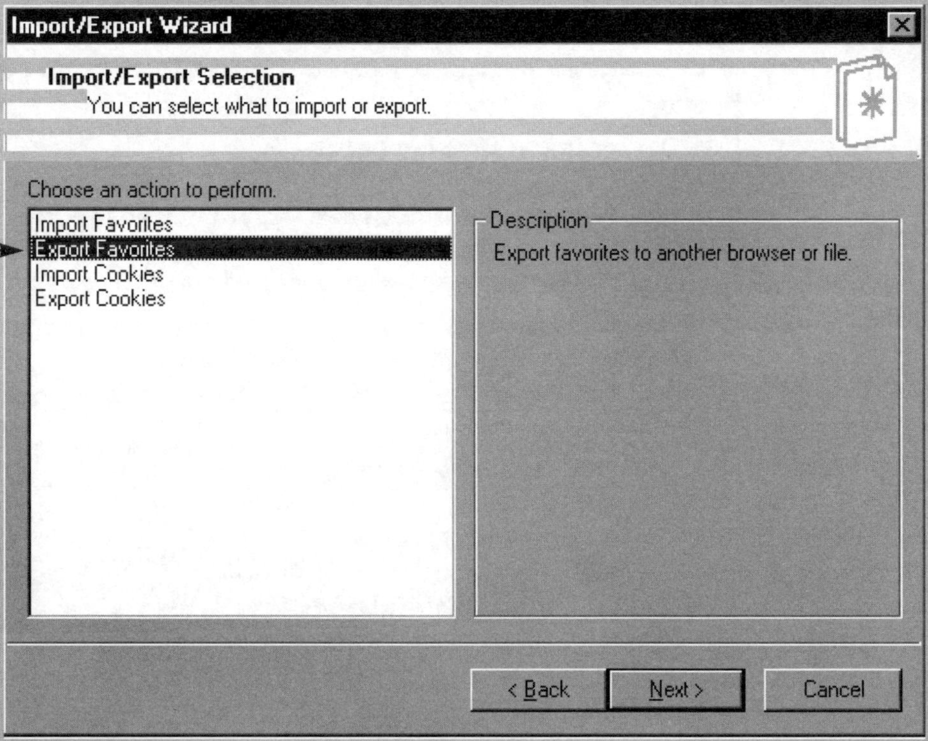

Figure 2.2.10-2 *Export Favorites*

You will then need to select the folder you wish to export from (see Figure 2.2.10-3).

5 Select your personal folder. Click on: **Next**.

5 Select your personal folder.

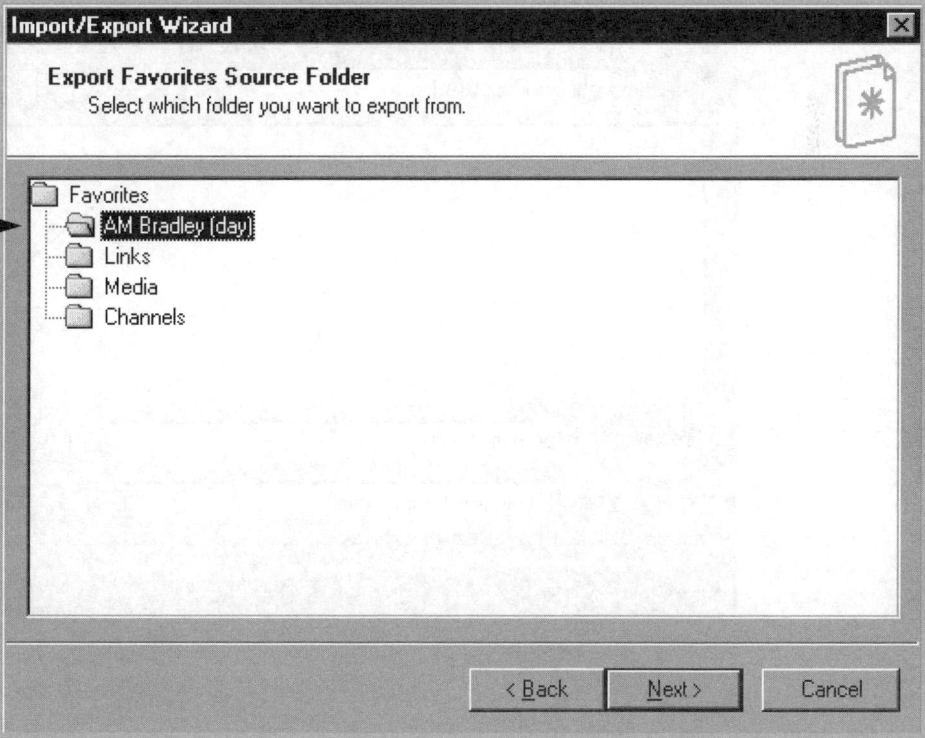

Figure 2.2.10-3 *Export Favorites source folder*

You now need to select the location you wish to export the favorites to (see Figure 2.2.10-4).

6 Click on: the **Browse** button.

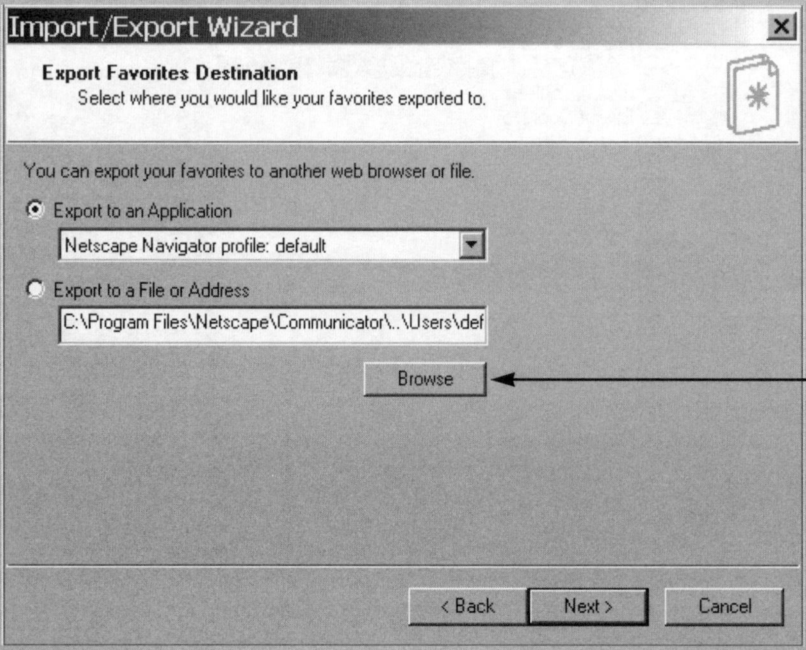

Import/Export Wizard ☒

Export Favorites Destination
Select where you would like your favorites exported to.

You can export your favorites to another web browser or file.

◉ Export to an Application

Netscape Navigator profile: default ▼

○ Export to a File or Address

C:\Program Files\Netscape\Communicator\..\Users\def

Browse ◀———————————— **6** Click on: the **Browse** button.

< Back | Next > | Cancel

Figure 2.2.10-4 *Export Favorites destination*

The **Select Bookmark File** dialogue box appears on screen (Figure 2.2.10-5).

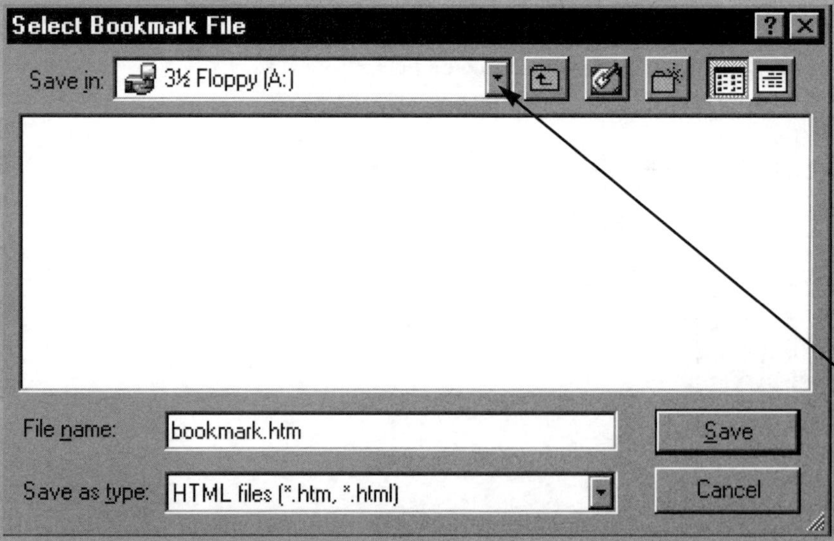

Select Bookmark File ? ☒

Save in: 3½ Floppy (A:) ▼

File name: bookmark.htm | Save | **7** Click on the arrow to the right of the **Save in** box and select the location to save the file.

Save as type: HTML files (*.htm, *.html) ▼ | Cancel

Figure 2.2.10-5 *Select Bookmark File dialogue box*

7 Click on: the arrow to the right of the **Save in** box and select the location where you want to save your files. The suggestion in the **File name** box is fine, so click on: **Save**.

You will be returned to the **Import/Export Wizard** dialogue box. The box below **Export to a File or Address** will give you confirmation of where the file has been saved (Figure 2.2.10-6).

8 Click on: **Next**.

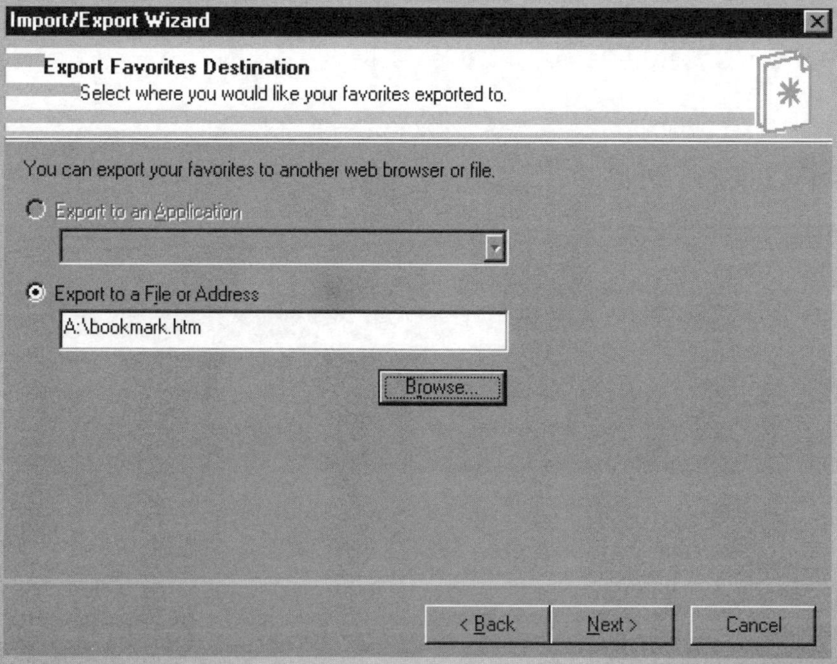

Figure 2.2.10-6 *Location of exported file*

The final dialogue box confirms that you have successfully completed the **Import/Export Wizard** and shows details of the location of the **Exported favorites** (Figure 2.2.10-7).

Figure 2.2.10-7 *Completion of the Import/Export wizard*

9 Click on: **Finish**.

One further dialogue box will appear on the screen to tell you that you have successfully exported your favorites.

10 Click on: **OK**.

11 Exit your browser (from the **File** menu, select **Close**).

Access and print your exported favorites

☐ Method

You will now access and print the exported favorites file from **My Computer**.

12 Double-click on: the ▣ **My Computer** icon on the desktop and open the folder where you saved the file.

13 Double-click on: the **bookmark.htm** file to open it.

This will load the file into the browser.

14 From the **File** menu, select **Print** to print the bookmarks.

Write your name, centre number and task number on the printout.

Exiting Internet Explorer and shutting down

If your session is finished, then exit Internet Explorer (from the **File** menu, select **Close** or click on: the ▣ cross in the top right-hand corner) and shut down your computer (exit all other applications; click on: the **Start** button; select **Shut Down**; click on: **OK**). Otherwise, move straight on to the next task.

Accessing your Favorites folder; taking a screen shot and pasting it into Paint

There is no facility in Internet Explorer to print the **Favorite** list. What you will do in this task, therefore, is access your list, then take a screen shot of what appears on the screen and paste this picture into Paint, where you can add your personal details and save and print the list.

☐ Method

1 If you do not already have Internet Explorer on screen, then load it (*either* click on: the **Internet Explorer** shortcut icon on the desktop, *or* click on the **Start** button and select: **Programs, Internet Explorer**).

2 From the **Favorites** menu, select your folder so that the drop-down list of the **Favorites** you have added is displayed.

3 Press: **Print Scrn** (this key is usually located at the top right-hand side of the keyboard, to the right of the **F** keys). This will store a picture of what is on the screen in the computer's memory.

4 Load **Windows Paint**. Click on: the **Start** button and select **Programs, Accessories, Paint**).

5 From the **Edit** menu, click on: **Paste**. An image of your Favorites should appear on screen.

Saving Favorites list in Paint

☐ Method

1 From the **File** menu, select **Save**.

The **Save As** dialogue box appears on screen (see Figure 2.2.10-8).

2 From the **Save in:** box, select the location to save the document.

3 Click in the File name: box, delete the suggested name for the file and key in: **favorite list** (followed by your initials).

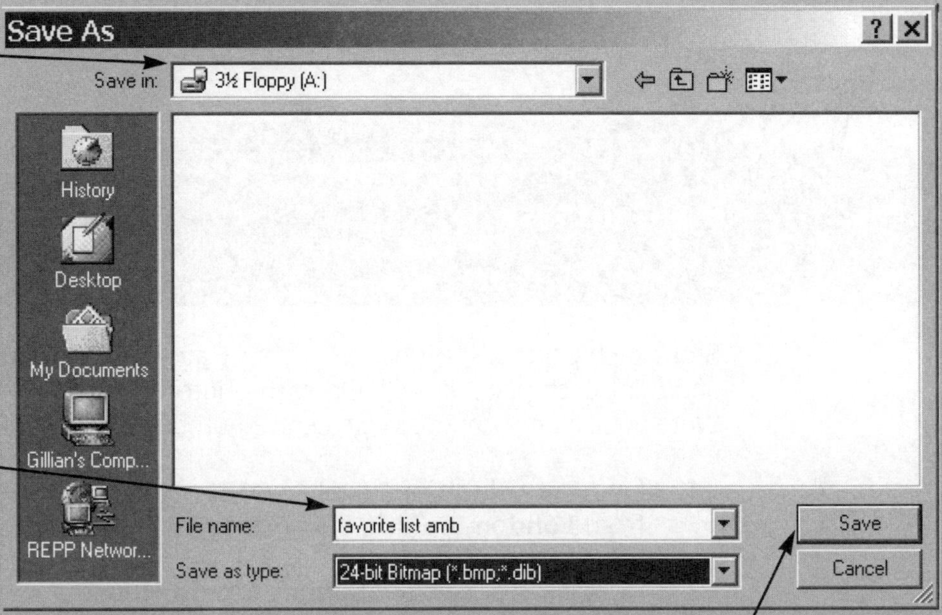

Figure 2.2.10-8 *Save As dialogue box*

4 Click on: **Save**.

2 From the **Save in:** box, select the location to save the document.

3 Click in the **File name:** box, delete the suggested name for the file and key in: **favorite list** (followed by your initials).

4 Click on: **Save**.

Printing Favorites list from Paint

☐ Method

1 From the **File** menu, select **Print**.

Write your name, date, centre number and task number on the printout.

2 Close the document (from the **File** menu, select: **Close**).

3 Exit Microsoft Word (from the **File** menu, select: **Exit**).

Exiting Internet Explorer and shutting down

If your session is finished, then exit Internet Explorer (from the **File** menu, select **Close** or click on: the ⊠ cross in the top right-hand corner) and shut down your computer (exit all other applications; click on: the **Start** button; select **Shut Down**; click on: **OK**). Otherwise, move straight on to the next task.

Use the Internet for online research

Consolidation

The following tasks will help consolidate the skills you have learnt in the previous tasks.

Task

Internet Explorer/Netscape

Build-up task 1

Store each page of information in your **F<u>a</u>vorites/Bookmarks** folder and save and print each page as well. On each printout, highlight the information requested. Write your name, date, college centre number and task number on each printout.

1   Find the website of a passenger train company. Find out the times of trains from **London** to **Paris** next **Friday**.

2   In which year was the **Sydney Opera House** built and completed?

3   Locate a picture of the **Houses of Parliament**. Save the image to disk.

4   Follow links to find general information about the **Statue of Liberty**.

Task

Internet Explorer/Netscape

Build-up task 2

Follow appropriate links to find the information. Use at least two different search engines. Store each page of information in your **F<u>a</u>vorites/Bookmarks** folder and save and print each page as well. On each printout, highlight the information requested. Write your name, date, centre number and task number on each printout.

You are looking for an unusual gift for a friend's fortieth birthday. You have a few ideas but can't decide which to choose.

1   Search the Internet for a company (in your area if possible) that provides helicopter trips.
    a   Print details of the location and brief details about the company.
    b   If possible find out the cost.

2   Search for a flying club supplying flying lessons.
    a   Print the location and details of the company.
    b   Print the cost if available.

3 Your friend has always wanted a Persian cat.

    a Carry out a general search for Persian cats (why not try the Cats Protection League or RSPCA first).

    b Print details of the search result.

    c Print the cost if possible.

4 Your friend loves London and is a big fan of musicals and shows.

    a Access the timetable of a passenger train company – you will be travelling after 1 pm on Friday.

    b Find out the performances and prices for a current West End musical.

    c Find reasonably priced overnight accommodation.

Internet Explorer/Netscape

Build-up task 3

Follow appropriate links to find the information. Use at least two different search engines. Store each page of information in your **Favorites/Bookmarks** folder and save and print each page as well. On each printout, highlight the information requested.

Write your name, date, centre number and task number on each printout.

1 Perform a general search for the following information.

    a How many Spanish pesetas are there to the British pound?

    b What is the unit of currency in Iceland?

2 Access the following website:

    www.dfee.gov.uk

    a Store the page in your **Favorites/Bookmarks** folder.

    b Print the page.

3 Search for information on Emperor Penguins.

    a What unique role does the male play?

    b Where can they be found?

4 Load the page you added to your **Favorites/Bookmarks** list at step 2 and search the site for the following information.

    a What is **learndirect**?

    b Find the contact number for enquiries.

    c What is **New Deal**?

Scenario

You are the project coordinator for Freedom Travel Services. A team-briefing meeting is planned in a few days' time and there are still some topics in the agenda for the meeting you have to find out.

2.1a 2.1b	**1**	The transport manager requires details of local train timetables for the meeting.
2.1c		Find a website that lists the major passenger train companies.
2.3a		Follow appropriate links in the website to locate a timetable showing local weekday services in your area and mark the page containing the information using the Favorites/Bookmarks application.
2.1a 2.1c	**2**	The catering manager requires details of companies that specialise in providing business uniforms.
2.2a 2.2c		Use a web-based search engine to find a web page containing the appropriate information.
2.3b		Favorite/Bookmark the page containing the information
		Print the page containing the information
2.1a 2.1c 2.2a	**3**	The personnel officer is planning a quiz night for staff to reward them for the hard work they have put into the project. She has asked you to help come up with questions for the quiz and needs to know when the Flying Scotsman was built.
2.2c 2.3b		Use a web-based search engine to find a web page containing the appropriate information.
		Mark the web page using the Favorites/Bookmarks facility.
		Print a copy of the page containing the information.
		Return to your Internet home page.
2.1a 2.1b	**4**	The transport manager wants to predict future passenger numbers, so he has asked you to research population growth in the surrounding area.
2.1c		Load the following web page:
2.2b		**www.progress-media.co.uk**
2.2f 2.3b		Use the local search facilities to locate the web page displaying the graph of Population Growth in a Medium City.
		Mark the web page using the Favorites/Bookmarks facility.
		Print the page containing the information.

2.1a	**5**	When the project is completed you plan to have a break for a few days. You use this opportunity to find out train times. You are travelling from London to Edinburgh on Friday after 1 pm.
2.1c		
2.2b		
2.2e		Load the web page marked at step 1.
2.3b		Follow appropriate links in the website to find the required information.
		Mark the web page using the Favorites/Bookmarks facility.
		Print the page containing the information.
2.1a	**6**	Load the web page marked at step 1.
2.1c		Follow links in the site to find the company's environmental policy.
2.2b		
2.2e		Mark the page containing the information.
2.2f		Print a copy of the page containing the information.
2.3b	**7**	Access the Favorites/Bookmarks facility and ask your tutor to observe the stored URLs.
2.1c		
2.3c	**8**	Exit the browsing application following correct procedures.
2.3d		

Internet Explorer/Netscape

Consolidation assignment 2: Search for information related to weather

Scenario

Some friends have been given a project at college to research meteorology. They do not have access to the Internet and they have asked for your help. The Met Office would probably be the best place to start.

2.1a	**1**	Load the Met Office web page at:
2.1b		
2.1c		**www.metoffice.com**
2.3a		Follow the link to the Weather and Climate page listed. Mark the page using the Favorites/Bookmarks facility.
2.1a	**2**	You have been asked to find out what El Niño is.
2.1c		
2.2a		Use the internal search engine to find a web page containing the appropriate information.
2.2c		
2.3b		
		Favorite/Bookmark the page containing the information.
		Print the page containing the information.

2.1a 2.1c 2.2a 2.2d 2.3b	**3**	The project is to include research on ozone layer depletion. Use the internal search engine to find a web page containing the appropriate information. Favorite/Bookmark the page containing the information. Print the page containing the information.
2.1a 2.1b 2.1c 2.2b 2.2f 2.3b	**4**	You and your friend decide to take a break from the research and carry out some recreational research. Your friend is keen on kite flying and you don't know a thing about flying a kite. However, you know a website that may help. Load the following web page: **www.progress-media.co.uk** Use the website's internal search facility to find the web page displaying the graph of Kite Sizes and Wind Strengths. Favorite/Bookmark the page. Print the page containing the information.
2.1a 2.1c 2.2b 2.2e 2.3b	**5**	It is necessary to include diagrams of the stratosphere in the meteorology project. A friend has accessed this information before and tells you that it can be found on the Met Office website. Use the website's internal search facility to locate the web page displaying information on the stratosphere. Favorite/Bookmark the page. Print the page containing the information.
2.1a 2.1c 2.1d 2.3b	**6**	You have also been asked to find out about the history of weather forecasts on television. Recall the Weather and Climate page marked at step 1. Follow the links About Met Office and History to find a web page containing the date of the first televised weather forecast by the BBC. Favorite/Bookmark the page. Print the page containing the information.
2.1c	**7**	Access the Favorite/Bookmark facility and ask your tutor to observe the stored URLs.
2.3c 2.3d	**8**	Exit the browsing application following correct procedures.

Publish information on a website

Introduction

Web page design and HTML

Having used the internet to send emails and to search for information from web pages, you will now design some web pages. Each page is created and saved as a separate file and then linked together by the creation of hyperlinks. Before doing this, it is important to discuss HTML.

What is HTML?

HTML (Hypertext Mark-up Language) is the code from which every web page is made. This includes the text formatting, e.g. bold, italic, alignment, graphics, pictures, etc.

For the OCR Internet Technologies award you need to know about the following HTML codes.

HTML	The code that every web page begins with
HEAD	Contains details of the document
BODY BG COLOR	Refers to the background colour in a web page
FONT SIZE	The size of the text in a web page
<p>	Indicates a new paragraph
<b>	Text formatted to bold
<i>	Text formatted to italic
A HREF	Indicates a hyperlink in a web page either to a web page or file
ALIGN	The alignment of items in a web page
IMG SRC	Details of graphic image(s) in a web page

Task 10 in this element will show you how to view and print the HTML code in a web page that you have produced. A description of the code used in the formatting of the web page will also be given in this task to help you understand HTML coding.

In previous years, you would have produced a web page using a text editor such as Windows Notepad or WordPad. In these programs, you would key in every code used in a web page – for example, formatting a word to bold, or italic has its own HTML code. As you can imagine, for a novice, this could be quite tricky, as well as time consuming.

The popularity of the Internet and web page design has grown immensely in recent years. Having a web page designed for you as an individual, or as a company, can be very expensive. This has given rise to more and more HTML editing software.

These packages can help you produce a very professional and interesting web page. The most important function of these packages is that they put all the HTML code in the web page for you. They can be so easy to use that you almost feel as if you are doing ordinary word processing.

There are numerous HTML editing packages available, some of which are shown below:

- Netscape (Page) Composer
- Microsoft FrontPage
- Coolpage
- Dreamweaver
- Microsoft Word.

Even though these packages insert the HTML code for you, it is hoped that you try to understand the basic functions of HTML.

The tasks in this book take you through step by step, using Microsoft FrontPage 2000 and Microsoft Word. However, if you want to use Netscape Page Composer 6, then the tasks are also provided on the CD-ROM with instructions for this software package.

The editing options available in these packages are more than sufficient for you to work through the OCR objectives for this element.

The software matching guide shows formatting commands in the three HTML packages used.

If, on completion of the tasks in this element and after you have achieved the award, you would like to develop more elaborate web pages, you could try one of the other packages mentioned above.

HTML software matching guide

Assessment objective	Microsoft Word 2000	FrontPage 2000	Netscape Composer 6
3.1a Create a new document	Click on: **New** button.	Click on: New Web Page button.	Click on: **Create a New Composer Page** button.
3.1b Insert image in document	Click on: **Insert Picture** button. In the **Insert Picture** dialogue box, select location of image; select image; click on: **Insert**.	Click on: **Insert Picture from file** button. In the **Insert Picture** dialogue box, select location of image; select image; click on: **OK**.	Click on: **Image** button; click on: **Choose file**; key in alternative text; click on: **OK**.
3.1c Use 3 different font sizes	Click at beginning of text to be formatted; from `Normal` **Style** drop-down menu, select required style. **OR** Highlight text; select required size from **font size** drop-down menu `11`	Click at beginning of text to be formatted; from `Normal` **Style** drop-down menu, select required style. **OR** Highlight text; select required size from **font size** drop-down menu `11`	Click at beginning of text to be formatted; from `Body Text` **Paragraph Format** drop-down menu, select required style. **OR** Highlight text; click on **smaller font size** or **larger font size** as required `-a +a`

Assessment objective	Microsoft Word 2000	FrontPage 2000	Netscape Composer 6
3.1d **Embolden text**	Highlight text; click on **B** **Bold** button.	Highlight text; click on **B** **Bold** button.	Highlight text; click on **B** **Bold** button.
3.1e **Italicise text**	Highlight text; click on *I* **Italics** button.	Highlight text; click on *I* **Italics** button.	Highlight text; click on *I* **Italics** button.
3.1f **Align page items**	Highlight text; click on: appropriate alignment button:	Highlight text; click on: appropriate alignment button:	Highlight text; click on: appropriate alignment button:
3.1g **Change background colour**	From **Format** menu, select: **Background**; from drop-down menu, select colour.	From **Format** menu, select: **Background**; in **Page Properties** dialogue box; from **Background** box, select colour; click on: **OK**.	Click on: white button; choose colour for background. *Or:* From **Format** menu, select **Page Colors and Background**; click on: **Background** box; click on: colour; click on: **OK**; click on: **OK** again.
3.2a **3.2b** **3.2c** **Link web pages**	Highlight text to link; click on: **Insert Hyperlink** button. In **Insert Hyperlink** dialogue box, click on: **File** button. In **Link to File** dialogue box select location of file; select file; click on: **OK**.	Highlight text to link; click on: **Hyperlink** button; click on: **Make a hyperlink to a file** button; select location of file; select file; click on: **OK**.	Highlight text to link; click on: **Link** button; click on: **Choose file**; select location of file; click on: **Open**; click on **OK**.
3.2d **Link text to email address**	Highlight text to link; click on: **Insert Hyperlink** button. In **Insert Hyperlink** dialogue box, click on: E-mail Address **E-mail Address** button; key in email address; click on: **OK**.	Highlight text to link; click on: **Hyperlink** button. In **Insert Hyperlink** dialogue box, click on: **Email Hyperlink** button. In **Create E-mail link** dialogue box, key in email address; click on: **OK**.	Highlight text to link; click on: **Link** button; in **Link to** box, key in **mailto:** followed by email address; click on: **OK**.
3.2e **Link text to URL**	Highlight text to link; click on: **Insert Hyperlink** button; key in URL (web address) below **Type the file**; click on: **OK**.	Highlight text to link; click on: **Hyperlink** button; key in URL (web address) in box to right of **URL**; click on: **OK**.	Highlight text to link; click on: **Link** button; key in URL (web address) in box below **Link Location**; click on: **OK**.

Assessment objective	Microsoft Word 2000	FrontPage 2000	Netscape Composer 6
3.2f **Test** **hyperlinks**	Load web page; click on: **Web Page Preview** button; click on: link to test. This should load linked web page.	Load web page; click on: **Preview in Browser** button; click on: link to test. This should load linked web page.	Load web page; click on: **Browse** button; click on: link to test. This should load linked web page.
3.3d **Print source code for** **web pages**	**View** Load page into browser; from **View** menu, select **Source**. This will load source code into Windows Notepad; move to top of document; press Enter twice; key in your personal details; key in **SOURCE CODE** followed by name of web page. **Save** It is important to save the source code using a different name to the web page. From the **File** menu, select **Save As**. **Print** From the **File** menu, select **Print**.	**View** Load page into browser; from **View** menu, select **Source**. This will load source code into Windows Notepad; move to top of document; press Enter twice; key in your personal details; key in **SOURCE CODE** followed by name of web page. **Save** It is important to save the source code using a different name to the web page. From the **File** menu, select **Save As**. **Print** From the **File** menu, select **Print**.	**View** Load page into browser; from **View** menu, select **Page Source**. **Highlight source** (press: **Ctrl + A**). Copy source (press: **Ctrl + V**). **Paste source into Notepad** Click on: **Start** button; select **Programs, Accessories, Notepad**. From **Edit** menu, select **Paste**. Move to top of document; press Enter twice; key in your personal details; key in **SOURCE CODE** followed by name of web page. **Save** It is important to save the source code using a different name to the web page. From the **File** menu, select **Save As**. **Print** From the **File** menu, select **Print**.

Objectives

What you will achieve in this element

This element is divided into three sections:

1 Compose and edit a web page

2 Create a web structure

3 Consolidation.

Each task in this element has been designed to guide you through the OCR requirements for Element Two. It is important that you complete the tasks in the order shown.

The syllabus matching chart on page 122 shows which tasks fulfil each of the OCR requirements.

Each task includes step-by-step instructions for completing it. It is important that you check each of your tasks carefully when you have finished. This is known as self-assessment and will help with your learning process. It is now also a requirement in many educational institutions. The tasks are followed by build-up tasks and two full practice assignments to help consolidate your new skills.

Classroom situation

If you are using this book in a classroom, to further enhance your new skills, OCR has produced a series of practice assignment papers for each element of the award. Your tutor will tell you about this.

Self-study home user

If you are using this book to study at home, then completing the tasks will give you a good grounding in the skills involved, as well as providing the basis for completing Element Three should you decide to enrol at a college to work towards the award.

Syllabus matching chart

Assessment objectives	Task number																								
	1	2	3	4	5	6	7	8	9	10	11	12	13	14	15	16	17	18	19	20	B1	B2	B3	C1	C2
3.1 Compose and edit a web page																									
a create a new document											●				●			●			●	●		●	●
b insert image in document as specified		●											●	●	●			●			●	●		●	●
c use 3 different font sizes as specified	●			●									●					●			●	●	●	●	●
d embolden specified text	●			●									●	●				●			●	●		●	●
e italicise specified text	●			●									●	●				●			●	●	●	●	●
f align page items as specified	●			●									●					●			●			●	●
g change background colour of specified document			●		●									●							●	●		●	●
3.2 Create a web structure																									
a link existing pages as specified						●	●									●					●	●		●	●
b link new page to existing pages as specified																					●	●	●	●	●
c link existing page to new page as specified																●					●	●		●	●
d link specified text to email address									●												●	●		●	●
e link specified text to specified URL																	●	●			●	●	●	●	●
f test hyperlinks								●								●				●	●	●	●	●	●
g store website pages as specified	●	●	●		●	●	●	●	●	●	●	●	●	●		●			●	●	●	●	●	●	●
3.3 Use appropriate software accurately and within regulations																									
a select and use appropriate software	●	●		●	●	●	●	●	●	●	●	●	●	●	●	●	●	●	●	●	●	●	●	●	●
b enter data as specified ensuring there are no more than 3 data entry errors in total												●				●		●			●	●	●		●
c print web pages as specified	●	●	●	●	●	●	●	●	●	●	●	●	●	●	●	●	●	●	●	●	●	●	●	●	●
d print source code for all web pages	●	●	●	●	●	●	●	●	●	●	●	●	●	●	●	●	●	●	●	●	●	●	●	●	●
e exit software following correct procedures	●	●	●	●	●	●	●	●	●	●	●	●	●	●	●	●	●	●	●	●	●	●	●	●	●
f use computer within basic health and safety regulations	●	●	●	●	●	●	●	●	●	●	●	●	●	●	●	●	●	●	●	●	●	●	●	●	●

Publish information on a website

Compose and edit a web page using Microsoft FrontPage

FrontPage

Format text and alignment

Objectives

- Load Microsoft FrontPage
- Load prepared web page
- Format headings
- Emphasise text
- Align text
- Add personal details
- Save amended web page
- Print amended web page
- Exit FrontPage
- Shut down computer

Scenario

You are a personal trainer at the Anderson Fitness Club. As you are the only member of staff with computer skills, the manager has asked if you would consider designing a simple web page to promote the club.

The text for this web page is provided on the CD-ROM.

In this task, you will format the text and alignment in the Anderson Fitness Club home page.

Loading Microsoft FrontPage

☐ Method

1   *Either* click on: the ▣ **Microsoft FrontPage** shortcut icon on the desktop, *or* click on: the **Start** button at the bottom left-hand side of the screen and, from the pop-up menu, select: **Programs**, **Microsoft FrontPage**.

The FrontPage window explained

FrontPage has a blue title bar, menu bar, toolbar and formatting toolbar very much like that of the Microsoft Word window. However, most of the options from the drop-down menus and most of the buttons on the toolbar are specifically for web page design (rather than word processing).

The buttons on the toolbar are shortcut buttons. Move the mouse over the buttons and the function that the button performs will be displayed.

The **Title Bar** tells you that you are working in Microsoft FrontPage.

The **Menu Bar** has categories similar to that of Microsoft Word. As an example, select the **View** menu. You will see that most of the options available are specifically for web page design. Move to the other categories and look at the options available.

The **Views** bar contains shortcut buttons. Move the mouse over each of these buttons. Now select the **View** menu. You will notice that the options available from the **View** menu are the same as the shortcut buttons on the **Views** bar.

The **Formatting Toolbar** has formatting options similar to that of Microsoft Word. Move the mouse over each of the buttons to see what function they perform.

Clicking the **HMTL** tab will show the HTML source code in the web page (you will learn more about this on pages 156–59).

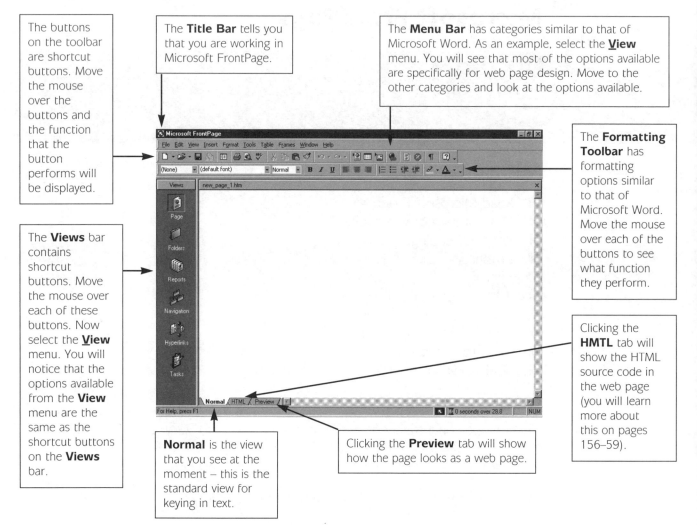

Normal is the view that you see at the moment – this is the standard view for keying in text.

Clicking the **Preview** tab will show how the page looks as a web page.

Figure 3.1.1-1 *The FrontPage window*

In the tasks that follow you will only use the **Page** and the **Hyperlinks** options from the **Views** bar. As these options are also available from the **View** menu, you can choose not to show the **Views** bar.

Hide Views bar

1   From the **View** menu, select **Views Bar** to remove the tick next to it.

The bar should now be removed from the screen.

Loading prepared web page

This web page has been partly prepared for you. The document can be found on the accompanying CD-ROM. The example below shows the document being opened from the floppy drive. You should open it either from the CD-ROM or from wherever your tutor has saved the files.

☐ Method

1   Click on: the 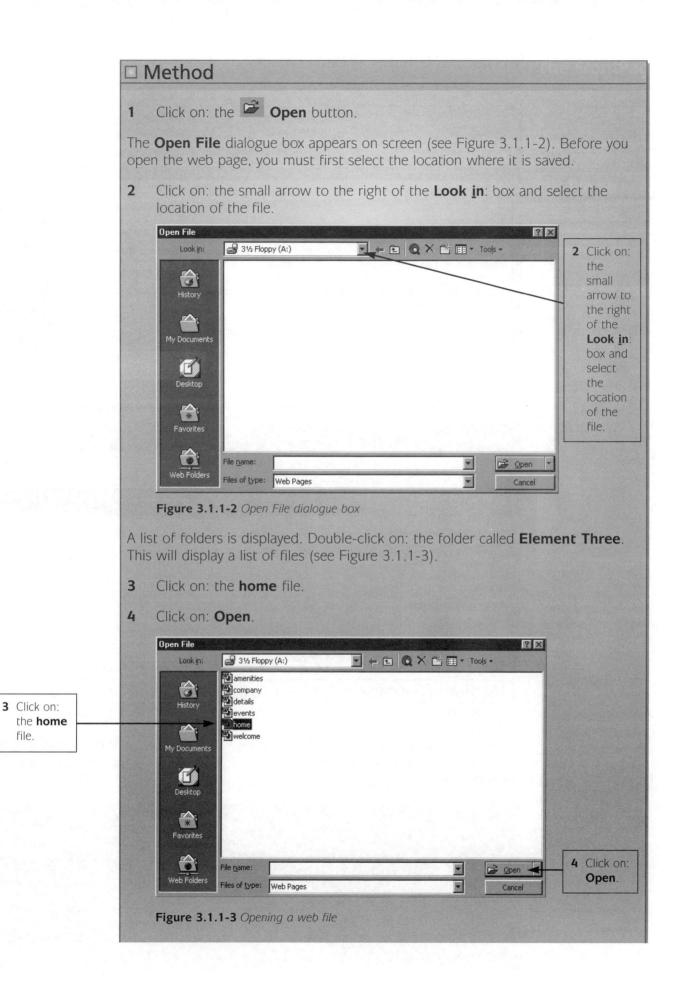 **Open** button.

The **Open File** dialogue box appears on screen (see Figure 3.1.1-2). Before you open the web page, you must first select the location where it is saved.

2   Click on: the small arrow to the right of the **Look in**: box and select the location of the file.

> **2** Click on: the small arrow to the right of the **Look in**: box and select the location of the file.

Figure 3.1.1-2 *Open File dialogue box*

A list of folders is displayed. Double-click on: the folder called **Element Three**. This will display a list of files (see Figure 3.1.1-3).

3   Click on: the **home** file.

4   Click on: **Open**.

> **3** Click on: the **home** file.

> **4** Click on: **Open**.

Figure 3.1.1-3 *Opening a web file*

The Anderson Fitness Club home page will now be displayed on screen (see Figure 3.1.1-4).

The location and name of the file you are working on is displayed here.

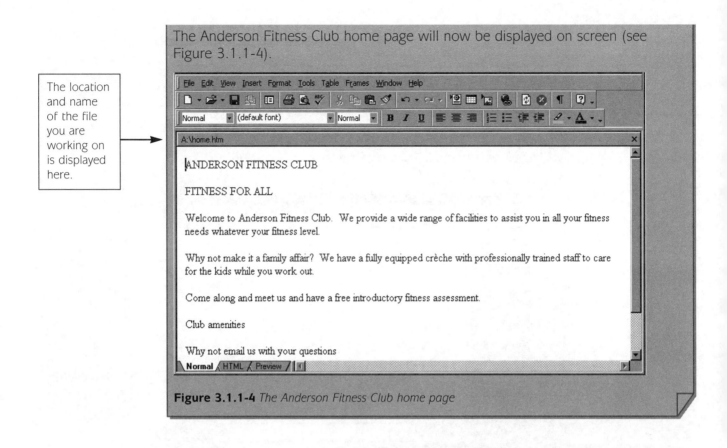

Figure 3.1.1-4 *The Anderson Fitness Club home page*

Formatting text

As you can see, at the moment, this is simply a page of text. You will now begin to format and enhance the look of the web page.

For the OCR Internet Technologies award you are required to format text in a web page using three different font sizes. The examples below show which font sizes to use for the font size required in Microsoft FrontPage:

Large font size	Main heading	Size 6 (24 pt)
Medium font size	Subheading	Size 4 (14 pt)
Small font size	Body text	Size 3 (12 pt)

The main body text can remain the same. As you will be formatting the headings in this document, you will have three different font sizes within the web page. It is important not to change the body text.

☐ Method

1   Move the mouse slightly to the left of the first (main) heading and, when the **I** shape changes to a white arrow, click once. This will highlight the heading.

2   Click on: the small arrow to the right of the **Font size** box.

A drop-down menu of styles appears (see Figure 3.1.1-5). The first heading is to be formatted to a large font size.

3 Select: **Font size 6**.

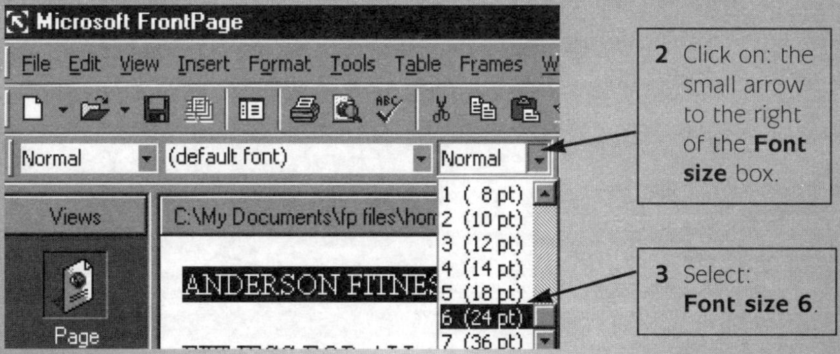

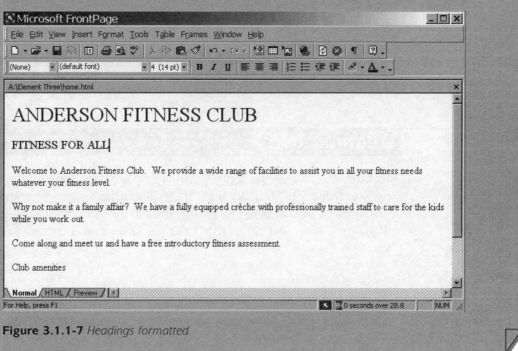

Figure 3.1.1-5 *Selecting a font size*

The first heading should now look like the one shown below (see Figure 3.1.1-6). You can see that it looks much better and stands out from the rest of the text on the page.

Figure 3.1.1-6 *First heading formatted*

4 Click in a blank area of the screen to remove the highlight from the heading.

5 Using the same method as before, highlight the second (sub) heading and select **Size 4** (medium font size) from the **Font size** box.

6 Click in a blank area of the screen to remove the highlight.

The headings should now appear larger and more prominent. At this stage, the web page should look like the one shown below (see Figure 3.1.1-7).

Figure 3.1.1-7 *Headings formatted*

Emphasising text

To make important parts of the text stand out you can apply further formatting to emphasise text in the web page using **Bold** and *Italic*.

☐ Method

1 In the first paragraph of the body text, highlight the words **wide range** (see Figure 3.1.1-8).

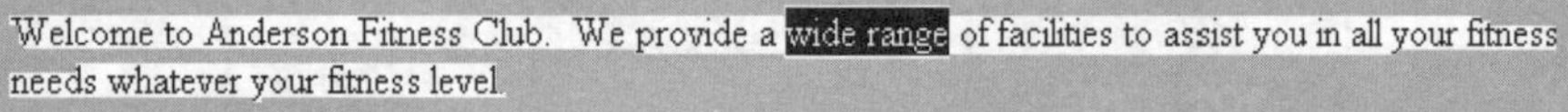

> Welcome to Anderson Fitness Club. We provide a wide range of facilities to assist you in all your fitness needs whatever your fitness level.

Figure 3.1.1-8 *Highlighting text*

☐ Hint

Move the cursor to the beginning of **wide**. When the mouse pointer changes to an **I** shape, click and, holding down the mouse button, drag the mouse to the right until both the words are highlighted. Release the mouse button.

2 Click on: the **B** **Bold** button.

☐ Info

There is another method you can use to highlight text. Click at the beginning of the words you want to highlight, hold down the **Shift** key and, at the same time, press the right arrow key until the text is highlighted. Release the keys when the required words are highlighted.

3 In the second paragraph of the body text highlight the words **family affair**.

4 Click on: the *I* **Italic** button.

5 Also in the second paragraph, highlight the word **crèche** and format it to bold and italic (click on: the **B** **Bold** button and then on the *I* **Italic** button).

6 In the third paragraph, highlight the word **free** and format it to bold (click on: the **B** **Bold** button).

Aligning text

To further enhance the look of the web page, you can change the alignment of the text on the page. To align all of the text on the page, the text must first be highlighted. In this task, all of the text will be centred on the page. If you want to highlight all the text on a page, there is an option available that will do this for you.

Method

1 From the **Edit** menu, select: **Select All**.

When highlighted, the page should look like the one shown below (see Figure 3.1.1-9).

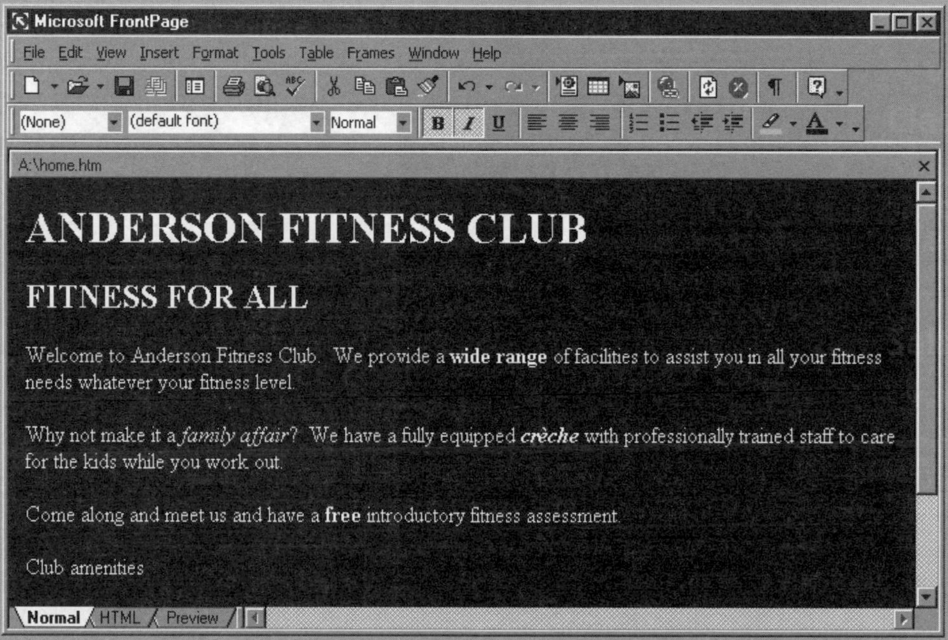

Figure 3.1.1-9 *All text highlighted*

2 Click on: the **Center** button.

3 Click in a blank area of the screen to remove the highlight.

All of the text should now be centred on the page.

Adding personal details

It is important to add your personal details to each page you produce.

Method

1 Key in your name, date, centre number and task number after the text: **This web page designed by:**.

Hint

There should be one space after the colon (:) before you key in your personal details.

□ Info

There is a facility in FrontPage that allows you to key in a header or footer. A header is text that will appear within the top margin of the page. A footer is text that will appear within the bottom margin of the page. Because you have already keyed in your details in the web page it is not necessary to use this function. However, if you want to use this function, you could key in a header showing the task number and your name.

1 From **File** menu, select: **Page Setup...**

The **Print Page Setup** dialogue box appears on screen (see Figure 3.1.1-10)

2 Click inside the **Header:** box and key in the task number followed by your name.

3 Click on: **OK**.

2 Click inside the **Header:** box and key in the task number followed by your name.

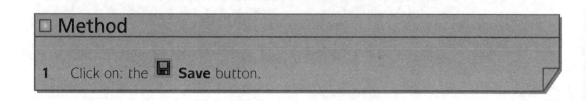

Print Page Setup   ? ✕

Header: | Task 1F Anne-Marie Bradley |

Footer: | Page &P |

Margins:

Left: 20   Top: 20

Right: 20   Bottom: 20

Options...   OK   Cancel

3 Click on: **OK**.

Figure 3.1.1-10 *Print Page Setup dialogue box*

Saving amended web page

This web page already has a name, so it is not necessary to use the **Save As** facility. It is important not to change the name of the web page, as this would cause confusion when you create hyperlinks in later tasks.

□ Hint

If you opened the file directly from the CD-ROM, then you will need to use the **Save As** facility to save it where you usually save your files. *Remember* to keep the same filename.

□ Method

1 Click on: the 💾 **Save** button.

Printing amended web page

☐ Method

1 Click on: the 🖨 **Print** button.

If your session is finished you need to exit FrontPage and shut down the computer following the correct procedures (otherwise, leave them open and move on to the next task).

Exiting FrontPage

☐ Method

1 Close the document (from the **File** menu, select: **Close**).

2 Exit FrontPage (from the **File** menu, select: **Exit**).

Shutting down computer

☐ Method

1 Make sure all other programs are closed.

2 Click on: the **Start** button.

3 From the pop-up menu, select: **Shut Down**.

4 Select: **Shut Down** from the options that appear.

5 Click on: **OK**.

FrontPage

Insert a graphic image

Objectives

🔖 Insert a graphic
🔖 Save amended web page
🔖 Preview web page
🔖 Print web page from browser
🔖 Close browser

The formatting for the **home** web page is almost complete. Inserting an image will further enhance the look of the page.

The **fitness** image for this task can be found on the accompanying CD-ROM or your tutor may have placed it on the network for you.

Inserting a graphic

☐ Method

1 If you do not already have Microsoft FrontPage on screen, then load it (*either* click on: the **Microsoft FrontPage** shortcut icon on the desktop, *or* click on the **Start** button and select: **Programs**, **Microsoft FrontPage**).

2 Open the **home** file (click on: the 🗁 **Open** button; from the **Look in**: box, select the location of the file; click on: the **home** file; click on: **OK**).

The Anderson Fitness Club **home** page that you formatted in Task 1 will now be displayed on screen.

The image in this task is to appear above the first heading. Before you can insert the image into the web page you must first make space for it.

3 Click at the beginning of the first heading.

4 Press: **Enter**.

A new space will appear above the heading (see Figure 3.1.2-1).

5 Click in the space you have created.

> **5** Click in the space you have created.

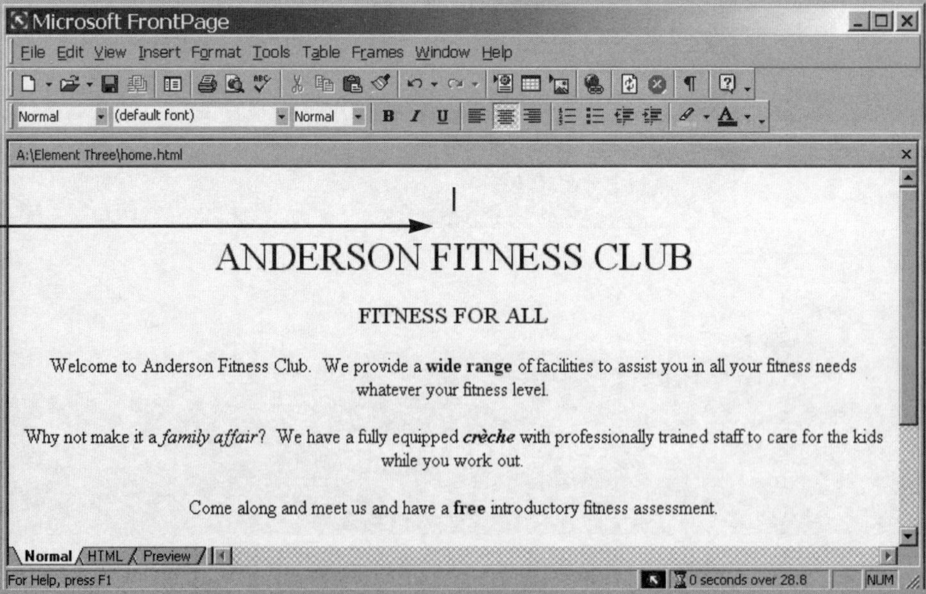

Figure 3.1.2-1 *Space added above heading*

The **fitness** image you are going to insert can be found on the accompanying CD-ROM.

6 Click on: the 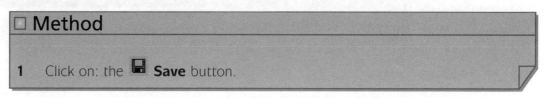 **Insert Picture from File** button.

The **Select File** dialogue box appears on screen (see Figure 3.1.2-2).

7 Click on: the small arrow to the right of the **Look in**: box and select the location of the graphic.

8 Click on: the **fitness** file.

9 Click on: **OK**.

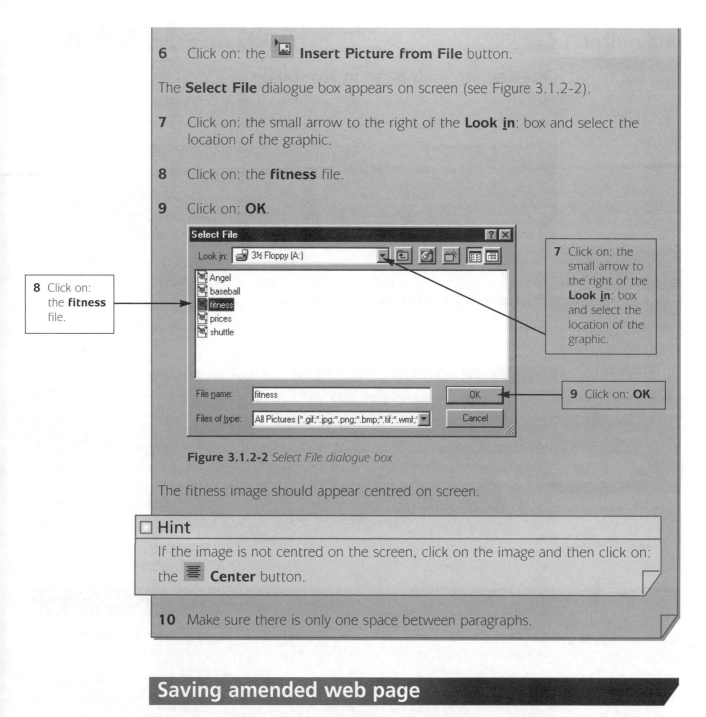

8 Click on: the **fitness** file.

7 Click on: the small arrow to the right of the **Look in**: box and select the location of the graphic.

9 Click on: **OK**.

Figure 3.1.2-2 *Select File dialogue box*

The fitness image should appear centred on screen.

☐ Hint

If the image is not centred on the screen, click on the image and then click on: the ☰ **Center** button.

10 Make sure there is only one space between paragraphs.

Saving amended web page

It is important to save the changes you make to tasks. This web page already has a name, so it is not necessary to use the **Save As** facility. In the **This web page designed by:** section, change the task number to **2** and change the date if necessary (if you keyed in a header in Task 1, you will need to change this information here as well).

☐ Method

1 Click on: the ▣ **Save** button.

Previewing web page

Previewing web page in FrontPage

Now that you have inserted the image in the web page you can see how the web page will look if it were loaded on the Internet by clicking on the **Preview** tab.

☐ Method

1   Click on: the **Preview** tab at the bottom of the FrontPage window.

2   Click on: the **Normal** tab to return to your web page.

Previewing web page in browser

You can also preview the web page in your browser software (probably either Internet Explorer or Netscape).

☐ Method

1   Click on: the ▣ **Preview in Browser** button.

This will load the web page into the browser.

You will know you are in the browser by looking at the buttons on the toolbar – **Back**, **Forward**, **Home**, etc. – these buttons are used for navigating the world wide web.

Printing web page from browser

For the OCR Internet Technologies award you are required to print the web page from the browser.

☐ Method

1   Click on: the browser's **Print** button.

Closing browser

To prevent confusion in having different programs open at the same time, it is good practice to close the browser when you have printed the web page.

□ Method

1 From the **File** menu, select: **Close**.

You will be returned to the web page in Microsoft FrontPage.

Exiting FrontPage and shutting down

If your session is finished, then close the document (from the **File** menu, select: **Close**), exit FrontPage (from the **File** menu, select: **Exit**) and shut down the computer (exit all other applications; click on: the **Start** button, select **Shut Down**; select **Shut Down**; click on: **OK**). Otherwise, move straight on to the next task.

FrontPage

Change background colour

Objectives

- Change background colour
- Save amended web page
- Print web page from browser

In this task, to further enhance the look of the **home** page, you will change the background colour.

Changing background colour

□ Method

1 If you do not already have Microsoft FrontPage on screen, then load it (*either* click on: the **Microsoft FrontPage** shortcut icon on the desktop, *or* click on the **Start** button and select: **Programs**, **Microsoft FrontPage**).

2 Open the **home** file (click on: the 📂 ▾ **Open** button; from the **Look in:** box, select the **home** file; click on: **Open**).

3 From the **Format** menu, select: **Background**).

The **Page Properties** dialogue box appears on screen (see Figure 3.1.3-1). Make sure the **Background** tab is selected. You will see that there are many options for changing the colour of various properties of the web page. At the moment, you are only concerned with changing the background colour of the web page.

4   Click on the small arrow next to the **Ba<u>c</u>kground:** box.

> **4** Click on the small arrow next to the **Background:** box.

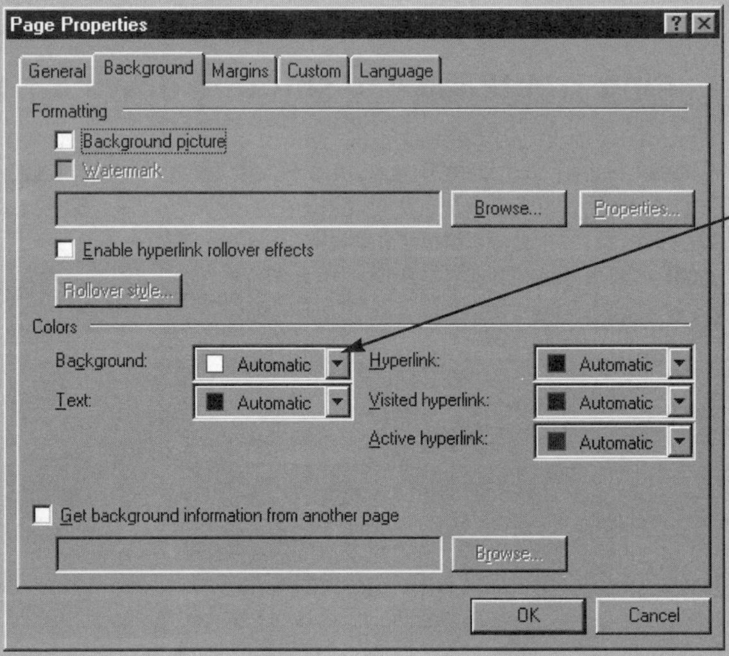

Figure 3.1.3-1 *Page Properties dialogue box*

5   From the drop-down menu of colours, select a colour.

> **5** From the drop-down menu of colours, select a colour.

> **6** Click on: **OK**.

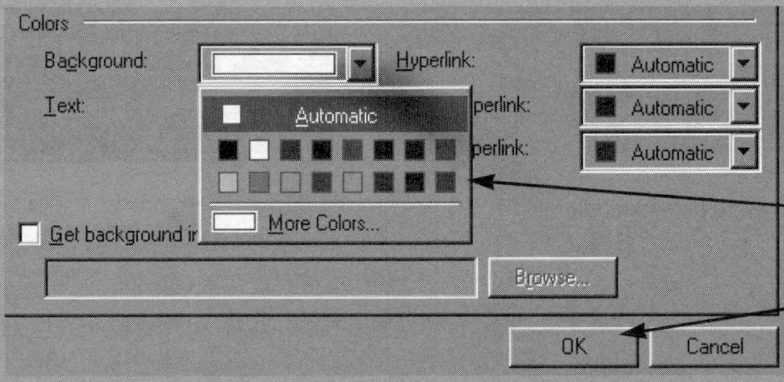

Figure 3.1.3-2 *Selecting a colour*

☐ **Hint**

Select a light colour, as your text is black. If you were to select a dark colour, it would be very difficult to read the text.

If you want to select a different colour to the few that are displayed in the drop-down menu, then click on **More Colors...**. The **More Colors** dialogue box appears on screen (see Figure 3.1.3-3). This gives you a much wider selection of colours.

1   Click on a colour.

A preview of the colour you have chosen will be shown in the **New:** box.

2   Click on: **OK**.

This will return you to the **Page Properties** dialogue box.

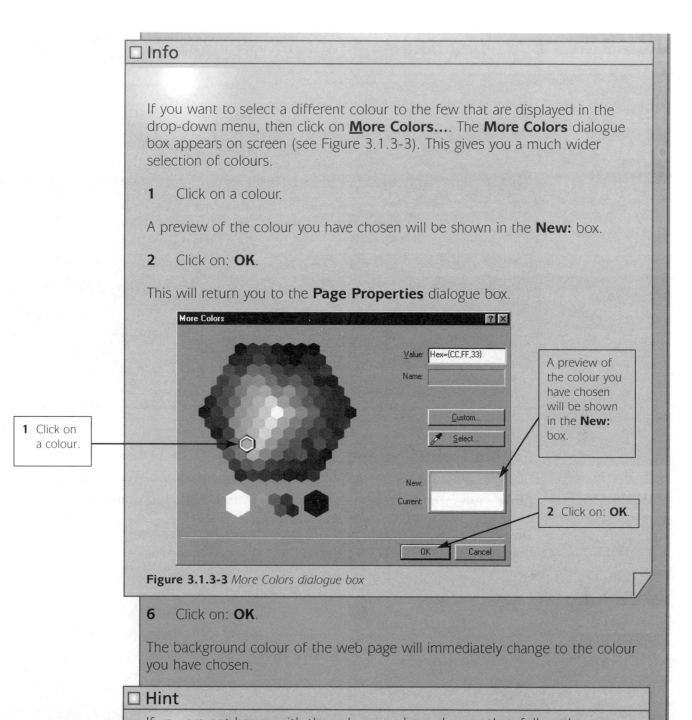

1 Click on a colour.

A preview of the colour you have chosen will be shown in the **New:** box.

2 Click on: **OK**.

Figure 3.1.3-3 *More Colors dialogue box*

6   Click on: **OK**.

The background colour of the web page will immediately change to the colour you have chosen.

If you are not happy with the colour you have chosen, then follow the steps again and select a different colour.

Saving amended web page

It is important to save the changes you have made to the web page.

In the **This web page designed by:** section, change the task number to **3** and change the date if necessary (if you set a header for the document in Task 1, then you will need to change these details here as well).

1   Click on: the 🖫 **Save** button.

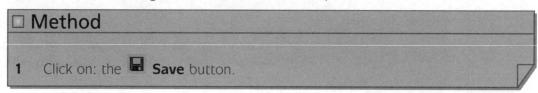

Printing web page from browser

As mentioned previously, for the OCR Internet Technologies award you are required to print the web page from the browser.

☐ Method

1   Click on: the 🔍 **Preview in Browser** button.

This will load the web page into your browser.

2   Click on: the browser's **Print** button.

Don't worry if, when printed, the web page does not show the background colour. What you must remember is that you are not working on an ordinary document; this is a web page. The background colour you selected will be shown in the HTML code of the web page. It might be useful to write the colour you selected on the printout for your tutor's reference.

3   Exit the browser (from the **File** menu, select: **Close**).

Exiting FrontPage and shutting down

If your session is finished, then close the document (from the **File** menu, select: **Close**), exit FrontPage (from the **File** menu, select: **Exit**) and shut down the computer (exit all other applications; click on: the **Start** button, select **Shut Down**; select **Shut Down**; click on: **OK**). Otherwise, move straight on to the next task.

Task 4 FrontPage

Format text and alignment

Objectives
- 📁 Format headings
- 📁 Emphasise text
- 📁 Align text
- 📁 Save amended web page
- 📁 Print amended web page from browser

Scenario

Your line manager was very impressed with the web page you designed. So much so, that she has asked if you would design another page to link to the first one. She assures you that your hard work in promoting the club will be rewarded!

In the previous three tasks, you formatted and edited the Anderson Fitness Club **home** page. In this task, you will format the text and alignment in the new Anderson Fitness Club **amenities** web page. The text for this web page has been prepared for you and can be found on the CD-ROM.

Formatting headings

☐ Method

1 If you do not already have Microsoft FrontPage on screen, then load it (*either* click on: the **Microsoft FrontPage** shortcut icon on the desktop, *or* click on the **Start** button and select: **Programs**, **Microsoft FrontPage**).

2 Open the **amenities** file (click on: the ☞ ▾ **Open** button; from the **Look in:** box, select the location of the file; click on: the **amenities** file; click on: **OK**).

The Anderson Fitness Club **amenities** web page will be displayed on screen. As mentioned previously, for the OCR Internet Technologies award you are required to use at least three different font sizes when formatting a web page. A reminder of the font sizes in Microsoft FrontPage is shown below.

Large font size	Main heading	Size 6 (24 pt)
Medium font size	Subheading	Size 4 (14 pt)
Small font size	Body text	Size 3 (12 pt)

3 Highlight the first (main) heading.

4 From the **Font size** box, select **Size 6** (see Figure 3.1.4-1).

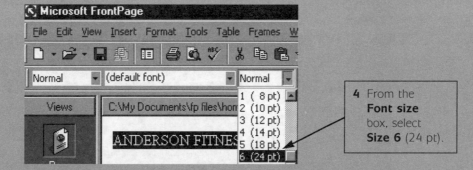

Figure 3.1.4-1 *Formatting headings*

The first heading should now appear larger and more prominent.

5 Highlight and format the second (sub) heading to **Size 4**.

Make sure there is only one clear line space between paragraphs.

☐ Hint

If there is a large gap between the headings click at the beginning of the second heading and press ← (backspace) until there is only one clear line between the headings.

Emphasising text

To make important parts of the text stand out, you can apply further formatting to the web page using **Bold** and *Italic*.

☐ Method

1   In the first paragraph, highlight and format the words **modern equipment** to bold (click on: the **B** **Bold** button).

2   In the first paragraph, highlight and format the words **formal** and **informal** to bold (click on: the **B** **Bold** button).

3   In the first paragraph, highlight and format the words **lakeside view** to italic (click on: the *I* **Italic** button).

4   In the second paragraph, highlight and format the words **personal advisor** to bold *and* italic (click on: the **B** **Bold** button then click on: the *I* **Italic** button).

Aligning text

The text in this web page will be aligned using different alignment options. The web page may not look quite right, but the purpose of this is for you to learn to use the different alignment options available.

☐ Method

The first heading is to be right aligned on the web page.

1   Click at the beginning of the first heading.

2   Click on: the ☰ **Align Right** button.

The second heading can stay left aligned.

The list of amenities would stand out more if it were centred.

3   Highlight the list of amenities (click before **Our amenities** and, holding down the mouse button, drag down and to the right until the list is highlighted; release the mouse button) (see Figure 3.1.4-2).

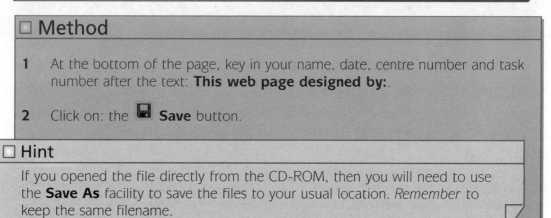

After a brief introduction to the club, and a **free** fitness
negotiate a fitness regime with you. Your personal adv

Our amenities:

Modern up-to-date equipment

Mixed and single sex gymnasiums

Circuit training

Swimming pool

Aerobics\aqua aerobics

Jacuzzi

Sauna

Sunbeds

Dining facilities

Figure 3.1.4-2 *Highlighting list*

4   Click on: the ☰ **Center** button.

The list should now be centred on the page.

Saving amended web page

☐ Method

1   At the bottom of the page, key in your name, date, centre number and task number after the text: **This web page designed by:**.

2   Click on: the 💾 **Save** button.

☐ Hint

If you opened the file directly from the CD-ROM, then you will need to use the **Save As** facility to save the files to your usual location. *Remember* to keep the same filename.

Printing amended web page from browser

☐ Method

1   Click on: the 🔍 **Preview in Browser**.

This will load the web page in the browser.

2   Click on: the browser's **Print** button.

3   Close the browser (from the **File** menu, select **Close**).

Exiting FrontPage and shutting down

If your session is finished, then close the document (from the **File** menu, select: **Close**), exit FrontPage (from the **File** menu, select: **Exit**) and shut down the computer (exit all other applications; click on: the **Start** button, select **Shut Down**; select **Shut Down**; click on: **OK**). Otherwise, move straight on to the next task.

FrontPage

Insert graphic image and change background colour

Objectives

- 📁 Insert graphic image
- 📁 Change background colour
- 📁 Save amended web page
- 📁 Print amended web page from browser

In this task, you will insert a graphic into the **amenities** page and change the background colour. Refer to instructions in Tasks 2 and 3 when necessary.

Inserting graphic image

☐ Method

1   If you do not already have Microsoft FrontPage on screen, then load it (*either* click on: the **Microsoft FrontPage** shortcut icon on the desktop, *or* click on the **Start** button and select: **Programs**, **Microsoft FrontPage**).

2   Open the **amenities** web page (click on: the 📂 ▾ **Open** button; select the location of the file; click on: the **amenities** file; click on: **OK**).

The graphic is to appear centred between the first and second headings. Before you can insert the image you must make room for it.

3 Click at the beginning of the second heading.

4 Press: **Enter**.

5 Click on: the **Insert Picture from File** button (*or* from the **Insert** menu, select: **Picture**, **From File**).

The **Insert File** dialogue box appears on screen. The **fitness** image can be found on the accompanying CD-ROM.

6 From the **Look in:** box, select the location of the graphic image.

7 Click on: the **fitness** image.

8 Click on: **OK**.

You will be returned to the web page with the newly inserted image.

9 Centre the image and make sure there is still only one clear line space between paragraphs.

Changing background colour

To complete the formatting of the **amenities** web page, you will now change the background colour of the page.

☐ Method

1 From the **Format** menu, select **Background**.

2 From the **Background:** box, select a colour (choose a different one to that of the **home** web page, but make sure it is still a *light* colour).

3 Click on: **OK**.

The background colour of the web page will have changed to the colour you chose.

Saving amended web page

☐ Method

1 Change the task number to **5** and the date if necessary.

2 Click on: the **Save** button.

Printing amended web page from browser

☐ Method

1   Click on: the 🔍 **Preview in Browser** button.

This will load the web page in the browser.

2   Click on: the browser's **Print** button.

3   Close the browser (from the **File** menu, select **Close**).

Exiting FrontPage and shutting down

If your session is finished, then close the document (from the **File** menu, select: **Close**), exit FrontPage (from the **File** menu, select: **Exit**) and shut down the computer (exit all other applications; click on: the **Start** button, select **Shut Down**; select **Shut Down**; click on: **OK**). Otherwise, move straight on to the next task.

Publish information on a website

Create a web structure using Microsoft FrontPage

FrontPage

Create hyperlink from home page to amenities page

Objectives

- Create hyperlink
- Save amended web page
- Print amended web page from browser

Now that you have formatted the Anderson web pages, in this task you will create a hyperlink that will take you from the **home** page to the **amenities** page.

What is a hyperlink?

A link in a web page can be text or an image. Clicking on a link will take you to another web page. A text link is usually blue and underlined. You will know you have moved to a link when the mouse pointer changes to a hand: ☝.

Creating hyperlink

☐ Method

1 If you do not already have Microsoft FrontPage on screen, then load it (*either* click on: the **Microsoft FrontPage** shortcut icon on the desktop, *or* click on the **Start** button and select: **Programs, Microsoft FrontPage**).

2 Open the Anderson **home** page (click on: the 📂 ▾ **Open** button; select the location of the file; click on: the **home** file; click on: **Open**).

To create a hyperlink, you must first highlight the text you are going to use for the link.

3 At the bottom of the page, highlight the words **Club amenities** (see Figure 3.2.6-1).

> Come along and meet us and have a **free** introductory fitness assessment.
>
> Club amenities

Figure 3.2.6-1 *Highlight Club amenities*

4 Click on: the 🖳 **Insert Hyperlink** button.

The **Create Hyperlink** dialogue box appears on screen (see Figure 3.2.6-2). The first step to linking two web pages is to select the location of the file you want to link to.

5 From the **Look in:** box, select the location of the **amenities** file.

6 Click on: the **amenities** file.

7 Click on: **OK**.

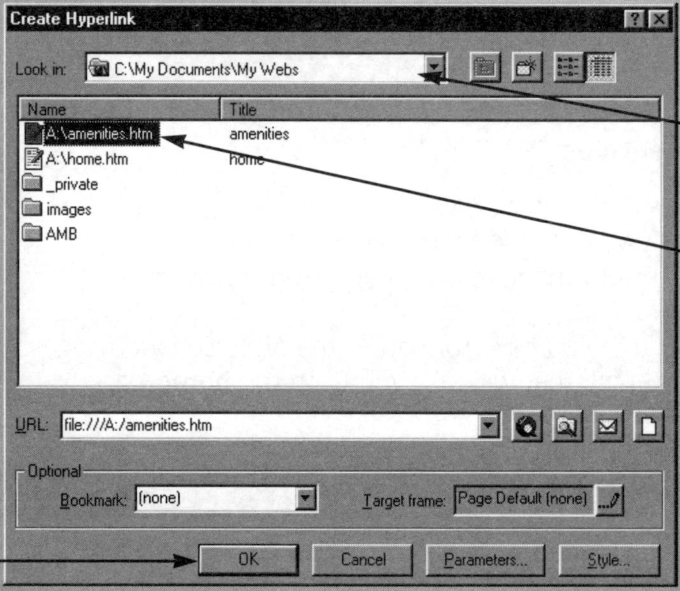

> **5** From the **Look in:** box, select the location of the **amenities** file.

> **6** Click on: the **amenities** file.

> **7** Click on: **OK**.

Figure 3.2.6-2 *Create Hyperlink dialogue box*

☐ Info

If you are unable to locate the file using the method above, you may need to use the following method instead.

1 In the **Create Hyperlink** dialogue box, click on: the **Make a hyperlink to a file on your computer** button (see Figure 3.2.6-3).

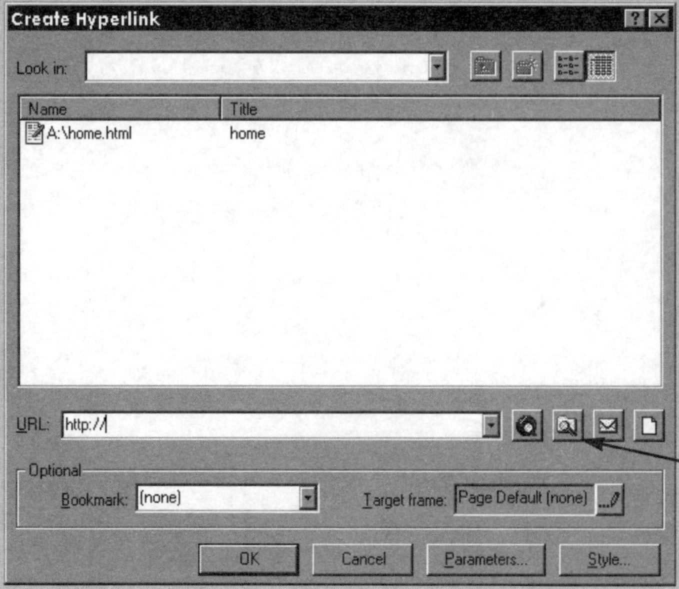

> Click on: the **Make a hyperlink to a file on your computer** button.

Figure 3.2.6-3 *Create Hyperlink dialogue box*

The **Select File** dialogue box appears on screen (see Figure 3.2.6-4).

2   From the **Look in:** box, select the location of the file.

3   Click on: the **amenities** file.

4   Click on: **OK**.

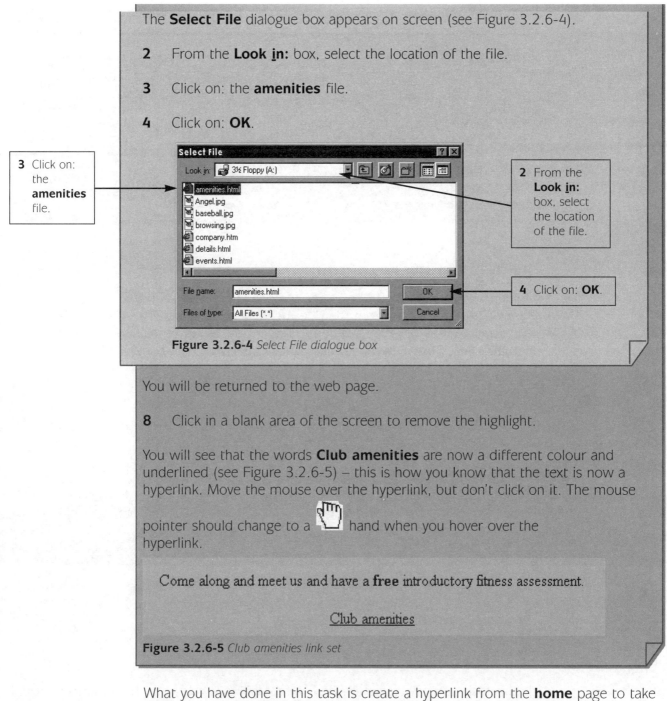

3 Click on: the **amenities** file.

2 From the **Look in:** box, select the location of the file.

4 Click on: **OK**.

Figure 3.2.6-4 *Select File dialogue box*

You will be returned to the web page.

8   Click in a blank area of the screen to remove the highlight.

You will see that the words **Club amenities** are now a different colour and underlined (see Figure 3.2.6-5) – this is how you know that the text is now a hyperlink. Move the mouse over the hyperlink, but don't click on it. The mouse pointer should change to a ✋ hand when you hover over the hyperlink.

Come along and meet us and have a **free** introductory fitness assessment.

Club amenities

Figure 3.2.6-5 *Club amenities link set*

What you have done in this task is create a hyperlink from the **home** page to take you to the **amenities** page. This means that, when you click the hyperlink you created, the **amenities** page will automatically be loaded on to the screen. This will become clearer when you test the hyperlink in Task 8.

Saving amended web page

☐ Method

1   Change the task number to **6** and the date if necessary.

2   Click on: the 💾 **Save** button.

Printing amended web page from browser

☐ Method

1 Click on: the 🔍 **Preview in Browser**.

This will load the web page in the browser.

2 Click on: the browser's **Print** button.

3 Close the browser (from the **File** menu, select **Close**).

Exiting FrontPage and shutting down

If your session is finished, then close the document (from the **File** menu, select: **Close**), exit FrontPage (from the **File** menu, select: **Exit**) and shut down the computer (exit all other applications; click on: the **Start** button, select **Shut Down**; select **Shut Down**; click on: **OK**). Otherwise, move straight on to the next task.

FrontPage

Create hyperlink from amenities page to home page

Objectives

- 📁 Create hyperlink
- 📁 Save amended web page
- 📁 Print amended web page from browser

In this task, you will create a hyperlink that will take you from the **amenities** page back to the **home** page.

Creating hyperlink

☐ Method

1 If you do not already have Microsoft FrontPage on screen, then load it (*either* click on: the **Microsoft FrontPage** shortcut icon on the desktop, *or* click on the **Start** button and select: **Programs**, **Microsoft FrontPage**).

2 Open the Anderson **amenities** web page (click on: the 📂 ▾ **Open** button; select the location of the file; click on: the **amenities** file; click on: **Open**.

To create a hyperlink, you must first highlight the text you want to use as the link.

3 At the bottom of the page, highlight the words **Back to home page** (see Figure 3.2.7-1).

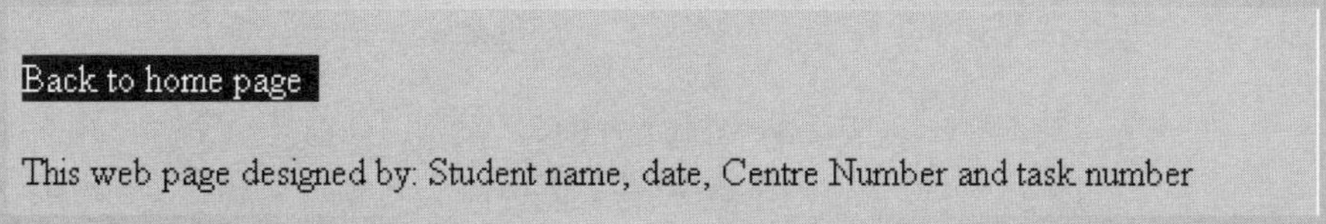

Back to home page

This web page designed by: Student name, date, Centre Number and task number

Figure 3.2.7-1 *Highlight Back to home page*

4 Click on: the 🖼 **Hyperlink** button.

The **Create Hyperlink** dialogue box appears on screen (see Figure 3.2.7-2). The first step to linking two web pages is to select the location of the file you want to link to.

5 From the **Look in:** box, select the location of the **home** file.

6 Click on: the **home** file.

7 Click on: **OK**.

5 From the **Look in:** box, select the location of the **home** file.

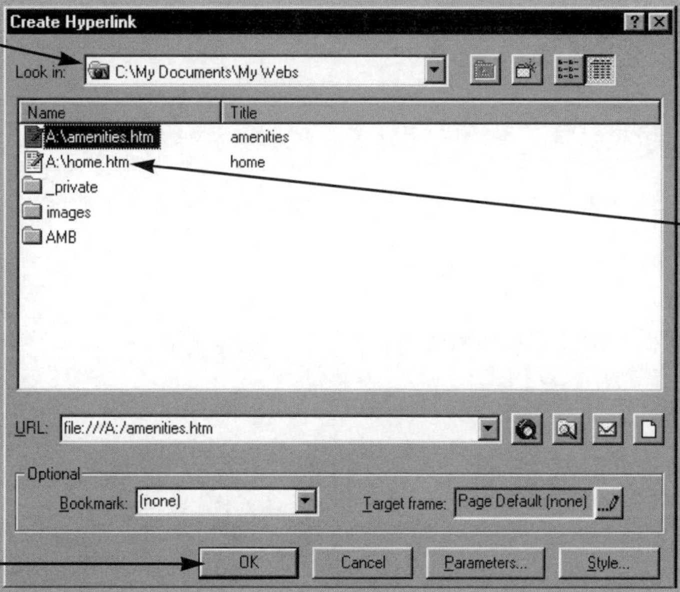

6 Click on: the **home** file.

7 Click on: **OK**.

Figure 3.2.7-2 *Create Hyperlink dialogue box*

□ Info

If you are unable to locate the file using the method above, you may need to use the following method instead.

1   In the **Create Hyperlink** dialogue box, click on: the **Make a hyperlink to a file on your computer** button (see Figure 3.2.7-3).

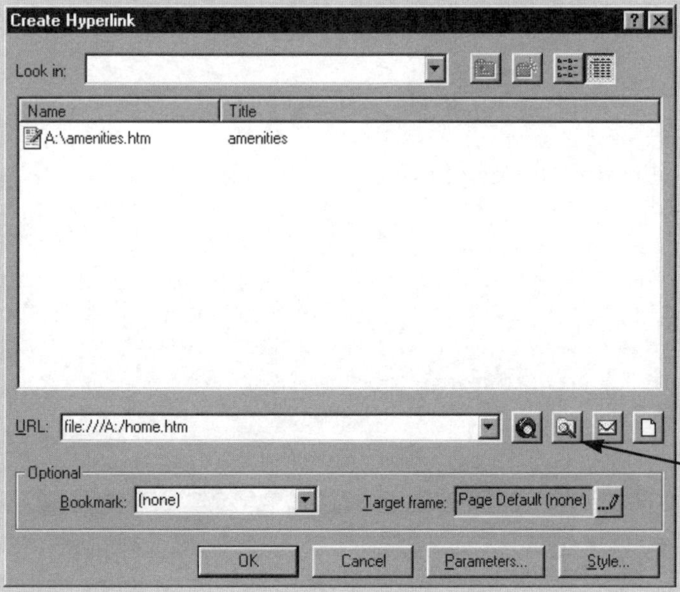

Click on: the **Make a hyperlink to a file on your computer** button.

Figure 3.2.7-3 *Create Hyperlink dialogue box*

The **Select File** dialogue box appears on screen (see Figure 3.2.7-4).

2   From the **Look in:** box, select the location of the file.

3   Click on: the **home** file.

4   Click on: **OK**.

2 From the **Look in:** box, select the location of the file.

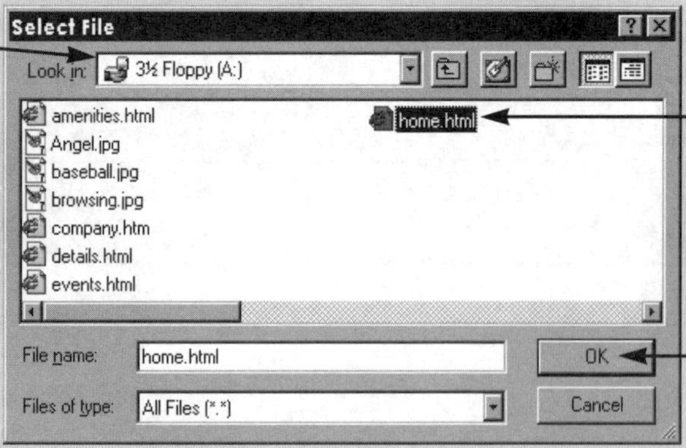

3 Click on: the **home** file.

4 Click on: **OK**.

Figure 3.2.7-4 *Select File dialogue box*

You will be returned to the web page.

8   Click in a blank area of the screen to remove the highlight.

You will see that the words **Back to home page** are now a different colour and underlined (see Figure 3.2.7-5) – this is how you know that the text is now a hyperlink. Move the mouse over the hyperlink, but don't click on it. The mouse pointer should change to a ⬚ hand when you hover over the hyperlink.

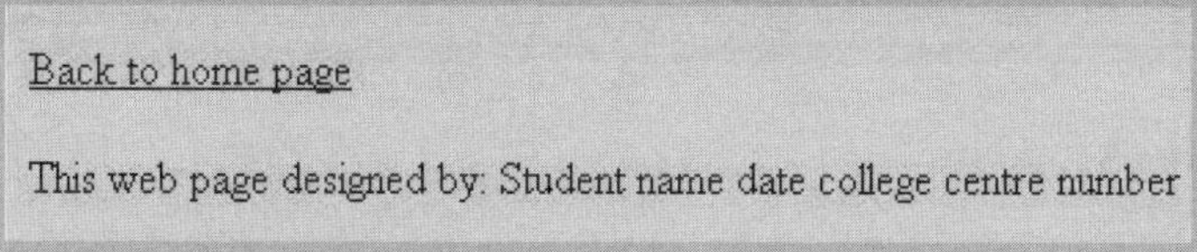

Back to home page

This web page designed by: Student name date college centre number

Figure 3.2.7-5 *Back to home page link set*

What you have done in this task is create a hyperlink from the **amenities** page to take you to the **home** page. This means that, when you click the hyperlink you created, the **home** page will automatically be loaded on to the screen. This will become clearer when you test the hyperlink in Task 8.

Saving amended web page

☐ Method

1   Change the task number to **7** and the date if necessary.

2   Click on: the 🖫 **Save** button.

Printing amended web page from browser

☐ Method

1   Click on: the 🔍 **Preview in Browser**.

This will load the web page in the browser.

2   Click on: the browser's **Print** button.

3   Close the browser (from the **File** menu, select **Close**).

Exiting FrontPage and shutting down

If your session is finished, then close the document (from the **File** menu, select: **Close**), exit FrontPage (from the **File** menu, select: **Exit**) and shut down the computer (exit all other applications; click on: the **Start** button, select **Shut Down**; select **Shut Down**; click on: **OK**). Otherwise, move straight on to the next task.

Objectives

- Preview in browser
- Test hyperlinks

Now it's time to see if the links work. In this task, you will test the hyperlinks that you created in the formatted Anderson web pages.

☐ Info

If the hyperlinks don't work, go back to the tasks in which you created the hyperlinks and make sure you followed each step correctly.

Previewing in browser

☐ Method

1   If you do not already have Microsoft FrontPage on screen, then load it (*either* click on: the **Microsoft FrontPage** shortcut icon on the desktop, *or* click on the **Start** button and select: **Programs, Microsoft FrontPage**).

2   Open the Anderson **home** page (click on: the 📂 ▾ **Open** button; select the location of the file; click on: the **home** file; click on: **Open**).

3   Click on: the 🔍 **Preview in Browser** button.

Testing hyperlinks

You should now be looking at the **home** page in your web browser.

☐ Method

1   Click on: the **Club amenities** link that you created.

This should take you to the Anderson Fitness Club **amenities** page.

2   Click on: the **Back to home page** link you created.

This should take you back to the Anderson Fitness Club **home** page.

3   Close the browser (from the **File** menu, select **Close**).

Exiting FrontPage and shutting down

You should now be looking at the **home** page in your web browser.
If your session is finished, then close the document (from the **File** menu, select: **Close**), exit FrontPage (from the **File** menu, select: **Exit**) and shut down the computer (exit all other applications; click on: the **Start** button, select **Shut Down**; select **Shut Down**; click on: **OK**). Otherwise, move straight on to the next task.

FrontPage

Create email link

Objectives

- Create email hyperlink
- Save amended web page
- Print amended web page from browser
- Test email link

For the OCR Internet Technologies award you are required to create a hyperlink to an email address. Many web pages on the Internet have email links, clicking on which will take you to an email application to compose and send an email message. This will be addressed automatically to a contact at that site.

In this task, you will be loading the **home** web page you worked on previously and creating an email link within the web page.

Creating email hyperlink

☐ Method

1   If you do not already have Microsoft FrontPage on screen, then load it (*either* click on: the **Microsoft FrontPage** shortcut icon on the desktop, *or* click on the **Start** button and select: **Programs, Microsoft FrontPage**).

2   Open the Anderson **home** page (click on: the ☞ ▾ **Open** button; select the location of the file; click on: the **home** file; click on: **Open**).

3   Highlight the text **Why not email us with your questions?**

4   Click on: the 🌐 **Hyperlink** button.

The **Create Hyperlink** dialogue box appears on screen (see Figure 3.2.9-1).

In previous tasks you have linked web pages by choosing a file to link to. Creating an email link is different. In some software packages you would key in **mailto:** followed by the email address you are linking to. Microsoft FrontPage has a facility that will enter the **mailto:** part for you.

5 Click on: the **Make a hyperlink that sends email** button.

5 Click on: the **Make a hyperlink that sends email** button.

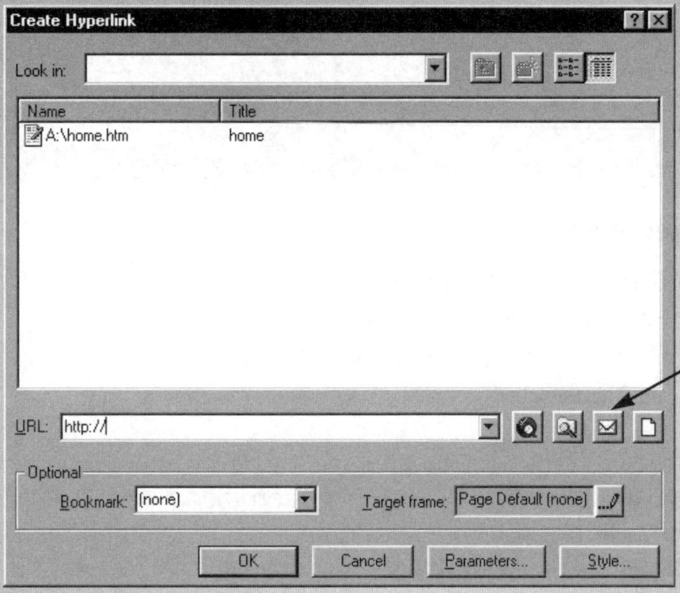

Figure 3.2.9-1 *Create Hyperlink dialogue box*

The **Create E-mail Hyperlink** dialogue box appears on screen (see Figure 3.2.9-2). You now need to key in the email address you want to link to.

6 Key in your email address in the white box under **Type an E-mail address**.

☐ **Info**

It is very important that you key in your email address accurately, otherwise the link will not work.

7 Click on: **OK**.

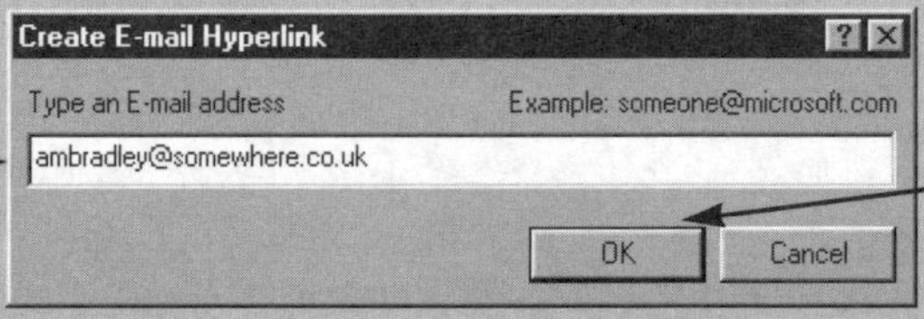

6 Key in your email address.

7 Click on: **OK**.

Figure 3.2.9-2 *Create E-mail Hyperlink dialogue box*

You will be returned to the **Create Hyperlink** dialogue box (see Figure 3.2.9-3). If you look in the URL box you will see that FrontPage has put **mailto:** in front of the email address for you.

8 Click on: **OK**.

FrontPage has put **mailto:** in front of the email address for you.

8 Click on: **OK**.

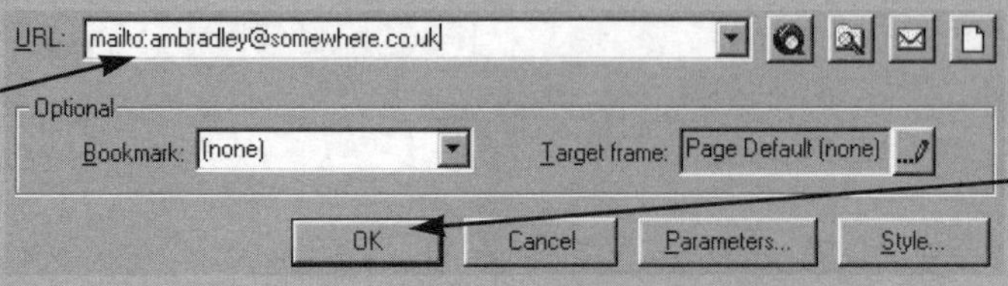

Figure 3.2.9-3 *E-mail address inserted in URL box*

This will return you to the web page.

9 Click on a blank area of the screen to remove the highlight.

The text that you highlighted, **Why not email us...** is now a different colour and underlined. This is now an email hyperlink.

Saving amended web page

☐ Method

1 Change the task number to **9** and the date if necessary.

2 Click on: the 🖫 **Save** button.

Printing amended web page from browser

☐ Method

1 Click on: the 🔍 **Preview in Browser** button.

This will load the web page in the browser.

2 Click on: the browser's **Print** button.

Testing email link

☐ Method

1 Click on: the email link that you have just created.

An email application **Message** window appears on screen (see Figure 3.2.9-4).

2 Click on: the ☒ cross in the top right-hand corner of the **Message** window to close the email application.

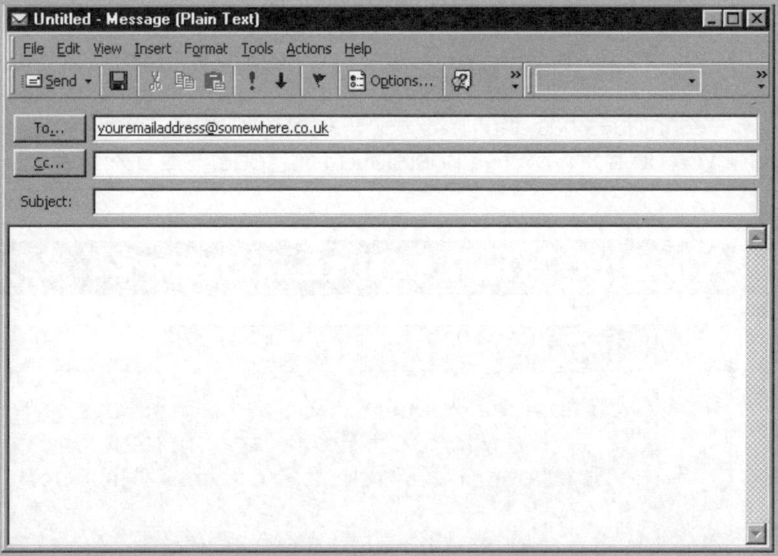

Figure 3.2.9-4 *Message window*

3 If you see the following prompt box (or a similar one), asking if you want to keep the draft of the message, then click on: **No**.

Click on: **No**.

Figure 3.2.9-5 *Save draft message prompt box*

4 Close the browser (from the **File** menu, select: **Close**).

Exiting FrontPage and shutting down

If your session is finished, then close the document (from the **File** menu, select: **Close**), exit FrontPage (from the **File** menu, select: **Exit**) and shut down the computer (exit all other applications; click on: the **Start** button, select **Sh<u>u</u>t Down**; select **<u>S</u>hut Down**; click on: **OK**). Otherwise, move straight on to the next task.

Task **10**

FrontPage

Print HTML source code

Objectives

- View HTML source code
- Print source code

For the OCR Internet Technologies award you are required to print the HTML codes used to format the web page. When you formatted the alignment, text, changed the background colour, inserted an image and set links, each one of these formatting techniques has an HTML code attached to it. This is called the *source code*. Whilst you do not have to understand this code, it is useful to take some time to look at it.

Viewing HTML source code

☐ Method

1 If you do not already have Microsoft FrontPage on screen, then load it (*either* click on: the **Microsoft FrontPage** shortcut icon on the desktop, *or* click on the **Start** button and select: **Programs**, **Microsoft FrontPage**).

2 Open the Anderson **home** page (click on: the 🗁 ▾ **Open** button; select the location of the file; click on: the **home** file; click on: **Open**).

To view the HTML source code used in formatting the page, you must first view the web page in the browser. Although there is a facility in FrontPage in which you can view the HTML source code, it is a requirement of the OCR Internet Technologies award that you print the code from the browser.

3 Click on: the 🔍 **Preview in Browser** button.

This will load the web page into the browser.

4 From the **View** menu, select: **Source**.

This will load the HTML code into Windows Notepad (see Figure 3.2.10-1).

Don't panic! A page of text that looks like a foreign language will be on the screen. This page is showing the HTML codes used in formatting the web page. You can see that, as mentioned in the introduction, the web page begins with the code <html>, followed by the code <head> which contains the details of the document. When you produce web pages in Microsoft FrontPage, there is a lot of HTML code produced. However, you do not need to worry about most of this – the important code you need to look at is further down the document.

```
🗐 home - Notepad                                    _□×
File   Edit   Search   Help
<html>

<head>
<meta http-equiv="Content-Language" content="en-gb">
<meta http-equiv="Content-Type" content="text/html;
charset=windows-1252">
<meta name="GENERATOR" content="Microsoft FrontPage 4.0">
<meta name="ProgId" content="FrontPage.Editor.Document">
<title>ANDERSON FITNESS CLUB</title>
</head>
```

Figure 3.2.10-1 *Source code in Notepad*

The first code you need to find is the code that gives the background colour of the web page.

5 Click on: the down arrow on the scrollbar until you see **<body bgcolour=**.

This HTML code is giving details about the background colour of the web page. To the right of the text **body bgcolor** you will see the code for the background colour of the web page (the code you see here is for green – yours may be different if you chose a different colour).

<body bgcolor="#00FF00">

6 Now look for this code:

** <img border="0" src="fitness.jpg" width= "158", height="126"> **

This HTML code gives details of the graphic – the name and size of the image and that the image has been centred on the web page.

7 Click on: the down arrow on the scrollbar until you see the line beginning **h1**.

** <font size="6">ANDERSON FITNESS CLUB</font> **

The HTML code used here tells you that the main heading has been formatted to **Size 6** (large font size) and centred on the web page.

8 Look for this code:

** <font size="4">FITNESS FOR ALL</font> **

This HTML code tells you that the second (sub) heading has been formatted to **Size 4** (medium font size) and centred on the web page.

9   Look for this code:

> **<p align ="center">Welcome to Anderson Fitness Club. We provide a wide range of facilities to assist you in all your fitness needs whatever your fitness level. </p>**

This is the body text of the web page. The **<p** at the beginning tells you that this is a new paragraph. If you look at the beginning and end of the words **wide range** you will see **** and **** – these are the HTML codes used for **bold**.

10 Look for this code:

> **<p align ="center">Why not make it a <i>family affair</i>? We have a**

At the beginning and end of the words **family affair** you will see **<i>** and **</i>**. If you remember, you formatted these words to italic in the web page – these are the HTML codes for italic. If you remember, also, you formatted the word **crèche** to bold and italic. Look for the word **crèche** and you will see **<i>** and **</i>** – this is how HTML codes up bold and italic.

11 Look for this code:

> ** <a href="amenities.html">Club amenities</a> **

The **href** in this HTML code tells you that the text **Club amenities** has been linked to the **amenities** web page.

12 Look for this code:

> ** <a href="mailto:amb@somewhere.co.uk">Why not email us with your questions</a> **

The **href** in this HTML code tells you that the text **Why not e-mail us...** is an email link to the email address shown.

□ Info

These brief explanations of HTML codes were designed to give you a little background knowledge of HTML. Formatting a web page using HTML code can be quite difficult and time consuming, which is why you have used Microsoft FrontPage. When you produce a web page in FrontPage, the codes are automatically put in for you.

Although there are many HTML editors available, there are still people who prefer to key in the codes in packages such as Windows Notepad. If you inserted the HTML codes using Notepad, the web pages would look the same as the ones you have produced.

Printing source code

□ Method

1   From the **File** menu, select: **Print**.

2   From the **File** menu, select **Exit** to close Notepad.

Look at the HTML code on the printout. It may be useful to go through and highlight the formatting that you did in the tasks.

3   Look for and highlight the following:
   ● the background colour
   ● the graphic image you inserted
   ● the headings you formatted
   ● each time you used bold and italic
   ● the links you created.

4   Exit Notepad (from the **File** menu, select: **Exit**).

5   Close the browser (from the **File** menu, select: **Close**).

Exiting FrontPage and shutting down?

If your session is finished, then close the document (from the **File** menu, select: **Close**), exit FrontPage (from the **File** menu, select: **Exit**) and shut down the computer (exit all other applications; click on: the **Start** button, select **Shut Down**; select **Shut Down**; click on: **OK**). Otherwise, move straight on to the next task.

FrontPage

Create and save welcome page

Objectives

● Key in text in new web page
● Spellcheck and proof-read
● Save new web page
● Print new web page

Now that you have completed the Anderson Fitness Club tasks, you will create a new website from scratch. In this task and Task 12, you will key in and save text for the two Maryhill Little League Baseball Club web pages in preparation for editing and formatting in later tasks.

Keying in text in new web page; spellchecking and proof-reading

☐ Method

1   If you do not already have Microsoft FrontPage on screen, then load it (*either* click on: the **Microsoft FrontPage** shortcut icon on the desktop, *or* click on the **Start** button and select: **Programs**, **Microsoft FrontPage**).

You should have a blank page on screen (if not, from the **File** menu, select: **New**).

☐ Info

Keying-in reminders

The following points are important when keying in new text:
- One space after a comma (,).
- Two spaces after a full stop (.).
- One clear space between paragraphs.

2   Key in the following text, using size 12 font. Retain upper case and lower case as shown. The line endings do not have to be the same as those shown. Add your personal details after the text **This web page designed by:**

> MARYHILL LITTLE LEAGUE BASEBALL CLUB
>
> OPEN DAY
>
> We are having an Open Day on Saturday 11 July to help raise funds for our club. This will be a wonderful opportunity for you to meet the teams and the coaching staff. There will be a short presentation by a member of our twinned American Little League baseball club, Wyndford County, to introduce you to the game of baseball, after which why not try a game or two!
>
> Come along and join us.
>
> The fun starts at 2.30 pm and will finish approximately 4.30 pm.
>
> Click here to see the events planned for the day.
>
> This web page designed by:

3   Spellcheck the document and make any necessary amendments (from the **Tools** menu, select **Spelling and Grammar...**).

4   Proof-read the text carefully for any errors that the **Spellcheck** might have missed.

Saving new web page

☐ Method

1   From the **File** menu, select: **Save As...**

2   From the **Save in:** box, select the location where you usually save your files. In the **File name:** box, delete the suggested name for the file and key in **welcome**.

3   Click on: **Save**.

Printing new web page

☐ Method

1   Click on: the 🖶 **Print** button.

Exiting FrontPage and shutting down

If your session is finished, then close the document (from the **File** menu, select: **Close**), exit FrontPage (from the **File** menu, select: **Exit**) and shut down the computer (exit all other applications; click on: the **Start** button, select **Shut Down**; select **Shut Down**; click on: **OK**). Otherwise, move straight on to the next task.

FrontPage

Create and save events web page

Objectives

- 📁 Key in text in new web page
- 📁 Spellcheck and proof-read
- 📁 Save new web page
- 📁 Print new web page

Now that you have created the Maryhill Little League Baseball Club **welcome** web page, in this task you will key in and create the Maryhill Little League **events** web page.

Keying in text in new web page; spellchecking and proof-reading

☐ Method

1   If you do not already have Microsoft FrontPage on screen, then load it (*either* click on: the **Microsoft FrontPage** shortcut icon on the desktop, *or* click on the **Start** button and select: **Programs**, **FrontPage**).

You should have a blank page on screen (if not, from the **File** menu, select: **New**).

Remember to follow the keying-in reminders from Task 11.

2   Key in the following text, using size 12 font. Retain upper case and lower case as shown. The line endings do not have to be the same as those shown. Add your personal details after the text **This web page designed by:**

MARYHILL LITTLE LEAGUE BASEBALL CLUB

OPEN DAY

EVENTS FOR THE DAY

As you can see, we have planned a day of fun for the whole family.
Contributions to the toy and bookstall would be very much appreciated.
The proceeds from the day will help towards uniforms for the teams.
Please come along and support us.

Events

Bouncy Castle, no adults allowed!

Book stall

Toy stall

Hot Dog and Hamburger stall

Cake stall (Bring and Buy of course!)

Treasure Hunt

Children v Parents baseball tournament

AND MUCH MORE!

Back to welcome page

Email us for further information

This web page designed by:

3   Spellcheck the document and make any necessary amendments (from the **Tools** menu, select **Spelling and Grammar...**).

4   Proof-read the text carefully for any errors that the **Spellcheck** might have missed.

Saving new web page

☐ Method

1   From the **File** menu, select: **Save As**.

2   From the **Save in:** box, select the location where you usually save your files. In the **File name:** box, delete the suggested name for the file and key in **events**.

3   Click on: **Save**.

Printing new web page

☐ Method

1   Click on: the 🖨 **Print** button.

Exiting FrontPage and shutting down

If your session is finished, then close the document (from the **File** menu, select: **Close**), exit FrontPage (from the **File** menu, select: **Exit**) and shut down the computer (exit all other applications; click on: the **Start** button, select **Shut Down**; select **Shut Down**; click on: **OK**). Otherwise, move straight on to the next task.

FrontPage

Task 13

Format welcome page

Objectives

- 📁 Format headings
- 📁 Format body text
- 📁 Align text
- 📁 Save amended web page
- 📁 Print amended web page

In this task, you will format the Maryhill Little League Baseball Club **welcome** page that you created in Task 11.

Formatting headings

For the OCR Internet Technologies award you are required to format headings and text in three different font sizes.

☐ Method

1   If you do not already have Microsoft FrontPage on screen, then load it (*either* click on: the **Microsoft FrontPage** shortcut icon on the desktop, *or* click on the **Start** button and select: **Programs**, **Microsoft FrontPage**).

2   Open the **welcome** page that you created in Task 11 (click on: the 📂 ▾ **Open** button; select the location of the file; click on: the **welcome** file; click on: **Open**).

The Maryhill Little League Baseball Club **welcome** page will appear on screen.

3   Highlight the first (main) heading and format it to **Size 6 (24 pt)** (large font size).

4   Highlight the second (sub) heading and format it to **Size 4 (14 pt)** (medium font size).

Formatting body text

The main text in the web page is known as the *body text*. You will now emphasise important points in the text using the **bold** and *italic* formatting options.

☐ Method

1 In the first paragraph of the body text, highlight and format the words **Open Day** to bold (click on: the **B** **Bold** button).

2 Highlight and format the words **Saturday 11 July** to bold.

3 Highlight and format the words **short presentation** to bold.

4 Highlight and format the word **twinned** to italic (click on: the *I* **Italic** button).

5 Highlight and format the words **why not try a game or two** to bold and italic.

6 In the third paragraph, highlight and format the words **2.30 pm** and **4.30 pm** to bold.

Aligning text

There are a number of alignment styles available to choose from. In this page, the text will be centred. Text to be aligned must first be highlighted.

☐ Method

1 Centre all of the text on the web page (from the **Edit** menu, select: **Select All**; click on: the ☰ **Center** button).

Saving amended web page

☐ Method

1 Change the task number to **13** and the date if necessary.

2 Click on: the 🖫 **Save** button.

Printing amended web page

☐ Method

1 Click on: the 🖨 **Print** button.

Exiting FrontPage and shutting down

If your session is finished, then close the document (from the **File** menu, select: **Close**), exit FrontPage (from the **File** menu, select: **Exit**) and shut down the computer (exit all other applications; click on: the **Start** button, select **Shut Down**; select **Shut Down**; click on: **OK**). Otherwise, move straight on to the next task.

FrontPage

Insert graphic image and change background colour

Objectives

- Insert graphic image
- Change background colour
- Save amended web page
- Preview web page in browser
- Print amended web page from browser
- Close browser

In this task, to further enhance the look of the web page, you will insert a graphic image and change the background colour of the web page.

Inserting graphic image

The baseball image can be found on the accompanying CD-ROM.

□ Method

1   If you do not already have Microsoft FrontPage on screen, then load it (*either* click on: the **Microsoft FrontPage** shortcut icon on the desktop, *or* click on the **Start** button and select: **Programs, Microsoft FrontPage**).

2   Open the Maryhill Little League **welcome** page that you formatted in Task 13 (click on: the ☞ ▾ **Open** button; select the location of the file; click on: the **welcome** file; click on: **Open**).

3   Make a space for the image above the first heading (click at beginning of heading; press: **Enter**).

4   Click in: the space you have created and click on: the 🖾 **Insert Picture from File** button.

5   From the **Look in**: box, select the location of the file.

6   Click on: the **baseball** file.

7   Click on: **Insert** and make sure that the image is centred.

Changing background colour

☐ Method

1   From the **Format** menu, select **Background**.

2   From the **Background:** box, select a light colour.

3   Click on: **OK**.

Saving amended web page

☐ Method

1   Click on: the 🖫 **Save** button.

Previewing web page in browser

☐ Method

1   Click on: the 🔍 **Preview in Browser** button.

Printing web page from browser

☐ Method

1   Click on: the browser's **Print** button.

Closing browser

☐ Method

1   From the **File** menu, select: **Close**.

Exiting FrontPage and shutting down

If your session is finished, then close the document (from the **File** menu, select: **Close**), exit FrontPage (from the **File** menu, select: **Exit**) and shut down the computer (exit all other applications; click on: the **Start** button, select **Shut Down**; select **Shut Down**; click on: **OK**). Otherwise, move straight on to the next task.

FrontPage

Format events page

Objectives

- Open **events** web page
- Format and align text
- Insert graphic image
- Change background colour
- Save amended web page
- Preview amended web page in browser
- Print amended web page from browser
- Close browser

In this task, you will open the Maryhill Little League Baseball Club **events** page that you created in Task 12.

Opening events web page

☐ Method

1   If you do not already have Microsoft FrontPage on screen, then load it (*either* click on: the **Microsoft FrontPage** shortcut icon on the desktop, *or* click on the **Start** button and select: **Programs, Microsoft FrontPage**).

2   Open the Maryhill Little League Baseball Club **events** page that you created in Task 13 (click on: the 📂 ▾ **Open** button; select the location of the file; click on: the **events** file; click on: **Open**).

The Maryhill Little League Baseball Club **events** web page will appear on screen.

Formatting and aligning text

For the OCR Internet Technologies award you are required to format headings and text in different font sizes.

☐ Method

1   Format the main heading to large font size and the subheading to medium font size and choose two different alignment options.

2   Select important points of the body text and emphasise them using the bold and italic formatting options.

3   Format the body text to alignment options of your choice, using at least two different alignment styles.

Inserting graphic image

☐ Method

1 Insert the **baseball** image in a place of your choice (this is available on the accompanying CD-ROM.

Changing background colour

☐ Method

1 Select a background colour for the web page (choose a different colour to that of the **welcome** page).

Saving amended web page

☐ Method

1 Click on: the 🖫 **Save** button.

Previewing amended web page in browser

☐ Method

1 Click on: the 🔍 **Preview in Browser** button.

Printing amended web page from browser

☐ Method

1 Click on: the browser's **Print** button.

Closing browser

☐ Method

1 From the **File** menu, select: **Close**.

Exiting FrontPage and shutting down

If your session is finished, then close the document (from the **File** menu, select: **Close**), exit FrontPage (from the **File** menu, select: **Exit**) and shut down the computer (exit all other applications; click on: the **Start** button, select **Shut Down**; select **Shut Down**; click on: **OK**). Otherwise, move straight on to the next task.

FrontPage

Create hyperlinks

Objectives
- Link **welcome** page to **events** page
- Link **events** page to **welcome** page
- Test hyperlinks

In this task, you will create links between the Maryhill Little League Baseball Club web pages and then test them.

Linking welcome page to events page

☐ Method

1 If you do not already have Microsoft FrontPage on screen, then load it (*either* click on: the **Microsoft FrontPage** shortcut icon on the desktop, *or* click on the **Start** button and select: **Programs**, **Microsoft FrontPage**).

2 Open the Mayhill Little League Baseball Club **welcome** web page.

3 Highlight the whole of the line: **Click here to see...**

4 Create a hyperlink to the **events** web page.

5 Save the amended web page.

Linking events page to welcome page

☐ Method

1 Open the **events** web page.

2 Highlight the text: **Back to welcome page**.

3 Create a hyperlink to the **welcome** web page.

4 Save the amended web page.

Testing hyperlinks

□ Method

1 View the web page in the browser.

2 Print the **events** web page.

3 Click on the link you have just created.

This should take you to the **welcome** web page.

4 Print the **welcome** web page.

5 Click on the link: **Click to see...**

This should take you to the **events** web page.

□ Hint

If the links did not work, then check that you have followed the procedure correctly and try again. (Look back at Tasks 6 and 7 – pages 205–11 – if you need a reminder of the steps.)

6 Close the browser.

7 Close the **events** file.

8 Close the **welcome** file.

Exiting FrontPage and shutting down

If your session is finished, then exit FrontPage and shut down the computer following the correct procedures. Otherwise, move straight on to the next task.

FrontPage

Create external hyperlink

Objectives

- Create external hyperlink
- Save amended web page
- View and print amended web page in browser
- Test hyperlink

For the OCR Internet Technologies award you are required to create an external hyperlink to a published page already on the Internet. This is often done to provide links to other relevant sites on a similar theme. In this task, you will load the Maryhill Little League Baseball Club **welcome** web page, add new text to the web page and link the new text to a page on the Internet.

Creating external hyperlink

☐ Method

1   If you do not already have Microsoft FrontPage on screen, then load it.

2   Open the Maryhill Little League Baseball Club **welcome** web page.

3   Make a space below the text: **Click here to...**

4   Key in the following text, ensuring there is one clear line space between paragraphs:

   Link to British Baseball Federation

5   Highlight the new text

6   Click on: the 🌐 **Hyperlink** button.

The **Create Hyperlink** dialogue box appears on screen.

7   In the **URL:** box, after **http://**, key in the following URL:

   www.bbf.org

8   Click on: **OK**.

Saving amended web page

☐ Method

1   Save the amended web page.

Viewing and printing amended web page in browser

☐ Method

1   View the amended page in the web browser.

2   Print the amended web page from the browser.

Testing hyperlink

☐ Method

1   Click on the link you have just created.

This should take you to the **British Baseball Federation** web page on the Internet.

2   Close the browser.

3   Close the **welcome** file.

Exiting FrontPage and shutting down

If your session is finished, then exit FrontPage and shut down the computer following the correct procedures. Otherwise, move straight on to the next task.

FrontPage

Create new hyperlinks

Objectives

- Link Baseball Club **welcome** page to Anderson Fitness Club **home** page
- Link Anderson Fitness Club **home** page to Baseball Club **welcome** page
- Test new hyperlinks

The Maryhill Little League Baseball Club is being sponsored by nearby Anderson Fitness Club. As a gesture of goodwill it would be nice to link the Baseball Club's website to the Fitness Club's website. In this task, you will create a link from the **welcome** page of the Baseball Club to the **home** page of the Fitness Club and then create another link back from the **home** page of the Fitness Club to the **welcome** page of the Baseball Club.

Linking Baseball Club welcome page to Anderson Fitness Club home page

☐ Method

1 If you do not already have Microsoft FrontPage on screen, then load it.

2 Open the Maryhill Little League **welcome** web page.

3 On a separate line above your personal details, key in the following text:

Sponsored by Anderson Fitness Club

4 Create a link, with this new text, to the Anderson Fitness Club **home** page.

5 Save the amended page.

6 Close the **welcome** page.

172

Linking Anderson Fitness Club home page to Baseball Club welcome page

☐ Method

1 Open the Anderson Fitness Club **home** web page.

2 On a new line below the text: **Why not email us...** and above your personal details, key in the following text:

We sponsor Maryhill Little League Baseball Club.

3 Create a link, with this new text, to the Maryhill Little League **welcome** page.

4 Save the amended page.

5 Close the **home** page.

Testing new hyperlinks

Now that the links between the two pages are complete you should test the links in the browser and print the amended web pages.

☐ Method

1 Preview the Anderson Fitness Club **home** page in the browser.

2 Print the amended **home** page from the browser.

3 Click on the new link you created: **We sponsor Maryhill Little League Baseball Club.**

This will load the Maryhill Little League **welcome** web page.

4 Print the amended Baseball Club **welcome** page.

5 Click on the new link you created: **Sponsored by Anderson Fitness Club**.

This will load the Anderson Fitness Club **home** page.

6 Close the browser.

7 Close the **home** page.

Exiting FrontPage and shutting down

If your session is finished, then exit FrontPage and shut down the computer following the correct procedures. Otherwise, move straight on to the next task.

Objectives

- Key in text
- Format text and alignment
- Insert image
- Create links
- Test links

This task will help consolidate the skills you have learnt in previous tasks. You will create a demo web page which will be formatted using a variety of heading and alignment styles. The links in the page will be to an existing file, an email address and a published web page (a page that exists on the Internet). The **angel** image can be found on the accompanying CD-ROM.

Keying in text

☐ Method

1. If you do not already have Microsoft FrontPage on screen, then load it and ensure you have a new blank document on screen.

2. Key in the following text, making sure there is one clear line between paragraphs:

    > MAIN HEADING – LARGE FONT AND LEFT ALIGNED
    >
    > SUBHEADING – MEDIUM FONT AND CENTRE ALIGNED
    >
    > This text and the image will appear centred on the page.
    >
    > This is the main body text and this line will appear centred and underlined on the page.
    >
    > This is a new paragraph and will be italic and bold and right aligned on the page.
    >
    > This is a link to another file.
    >
    > This is a link to an email address.
    >
    > This is a link to a published web page.
    >
    > This web page designed by:

3. Add your personal details after the text: **This web page designed by:**.

4. Spellcheck the document, making any necessary amendments.

5. Proof-read the document carefully, checking for any errors the **Spellcheck** might have missed.

Formatting text and alignment

☐ Method

1   Format the document according to the text – for example, the main heading will be a large font size and left aligned, the sub heading will be medium font size and centred, etc.

2   Change the background colour of the page.

Inserting image

☐ Method

1   Insert the **angel** image below the subheading.

2   Centre the image.

3   Save the document as a web page, using the filename: **demohtml**.

4   Print the document.

Creating links

☐ Method

1   With the text: **This is a link to another file.**, create a link to the **amenities** web page.

2   With the text: **This is a link to an email address.**, create a link to your own email address.

3   With the text: **This is a link to a published web page.**, create a link to the following web page:

    http://www.heinemann.co.uk

4   Save the changes.

Testing links

☐ Method

1   Preview the page in the browser.

2   Print the page from the browser.

3   Test all the links that you inserted.

4   Close the browser.

5   Close the **demohtml** file.

Exiting FrontPage and shutting down

If your session is finished, then exit FrontPage and shut down the computer following the correct procedures. Otherwise, move straight on to the next task.

FrontPage

Print HTML source codes

Objectives

View, save and print HTML codes

For the OCR Internet Technologies award you are required to load web pages that you have formatted into the browser and view and print the HTML source codes used in formatting the pages. Instructions on how to do this were given in Task 10 (pages 156–59).

Refer back to these instructions when necessary and view and print the HTML codes used for formatting the following web pages:

- Anderson Fitness Club **amenities**
- Maryhill Little League **welcome** and **events**
- **demohtml** web page.

☐ **Info**

If your browser is **Internet Explorer**, when you view the HTML source code, it will immediately be loaded into Windows Notepad.

If your browser is **Netscape**, when you view the source code, you will need to highlight the code (**Ctrl + A**); copy the source code (**Ctrl + C**) and paste the code (**Ctrl + V**) into Windows Notepad.

When you have printed the HTML codes, highlight the formatting you used, e.g. font sizes, alignment styles, bold, italic, hyperlinks, etc.

Publish information on a website

Compose and edit a web page using Microsoft Word

Word

Format text and alignment

Objectives

- Load Microsoft Word
- Load prepared web page
- Format headings
- Check paragraph spacing
- Emphasise text
- Aligning text
- Add personal details
- Save amended web page
- Print amended web page
- Exit Word
- Shut down computer

Scenario

You are a personal trainer at the Anderson Fitness Club. As you are the only member of staff with computer skills, the manager has asked if you would consider designing a simple web page to promote the club.

The text for this web page is provided on the CD-ROM.

In this task, you will format the text and alignment in the Anderson Fitness Club home page.

Loading Microsoft Word

☐ Method

1   *Either* click on: the **W** **Microsoft Word** shortcut icon on the desktop *or* click on: the **Start** button at the bottom left-hand side of the screen and, from the pop-up menu, select: **Programs**, **Microsoft Word**.

Loading prepared web page

This web page has been partly prepared for you. The document can be found on the accompanying CD-ROM. The example below shows the document being opened from the floppy drive. You should open it either from the CD-ROM or from wherever your tutor has saved the files.

☐ Method

1 Click on: the 📂 **Open** button.

The **Open** dialogue box appears on screen (see Figure 3.3.1-1). Before you open the web page, you must first select the location where it is saved.

2 Click on: the small arrow to the right of the **Look in**: box and select the location of the file.

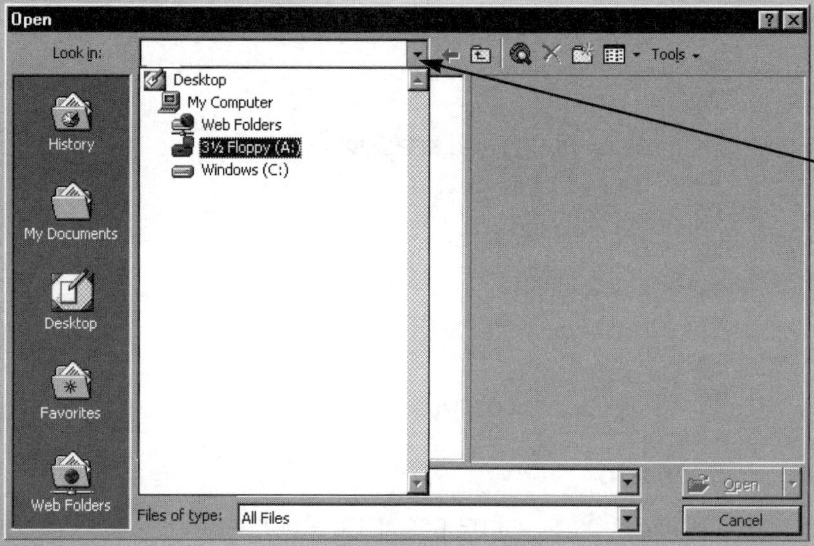

> **2** Click on: the small arrow to the right of the **Look in**: box and select the location of the file.

Figure 3.3.1-1 *Open dialogue box step 1*

This will display a list of folders (see Figure 3.3.1-2).

3 Double-click on: the **Element Three** folder.

> **3** Double-click on: the **Element Three** folder.

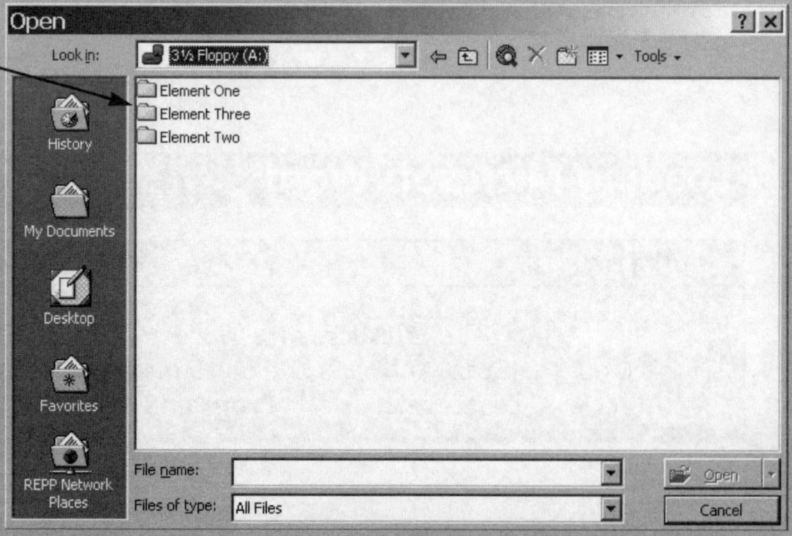

Figure 3.3.1-2 *Opening dialogue box step 2*

This will display a list of files (see Figure 3.3.1-3).

4 Click on: the **home** file.

5 Click on: **Open**.

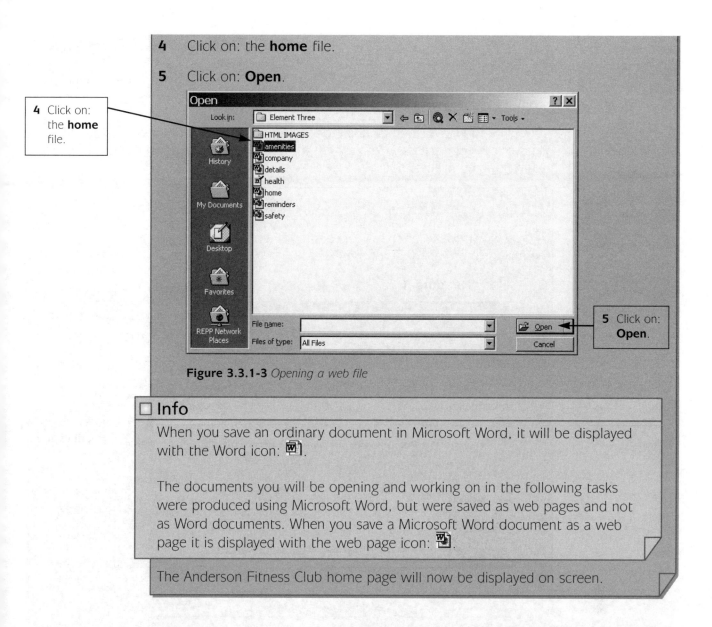

4 Click on: the **home** file.

5 Click on: **Open**.

Figure 3.3.1-3 *Opening a web file*

☐ Info

When you save an ordinary document in Microsoft Word, it will be displayed with the Word icon: 📄.

The documents you will be opening and working on in the following tasks were produced using Microsoft Word, but were saved as web pages and not as Word documents. When you save a Microsoft Word document as a web page it is displayed with the web page icon: 📄.

The Anderson Fitness Club home page will now be displayed on screen.

Formatting headings

As you can see, at the moment, this is simply a page of text. You will now begin to format and enhance the look of the web page.

For the OCR Internet Technologies award you are required to format headings in a web page using three different font sizes. The examples below show which heading to use for the font size required in Microsoft Word:

Large font size	Heading 1
Medium font size	Heading 2
Small font size	Heading 3

The main body text can remain the same. As you will be formatting the headings in this document, you will have three different font sizes within the web page.

Method

1 Click at the beginning of the first (main) heading.

Hint

Move the mouse to the beginning of the first heading; click when you see an **I** shape. It is not necessary to highlight the text before formatting if you are only formatting one line of text.

2 Click on: the small arrow to the right of the **Style** box.

A drop-down menu of styles appears (see Figure 3.3.1-4). The first heading is to be formatted to a large font size.

3 Select: **Heading 1**.

2 Click on: the small arrow to the right of the **Style** box.

3 Select: **Heading 1**.

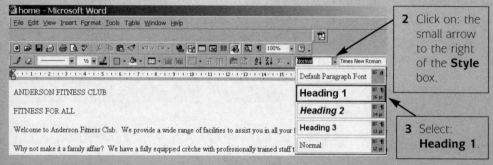

Figure 3.3.1-4 *Selecting a heading style*

The first heading should now look like the one shown below (see Figure 3.3.1-5). You can see that it looks much better and stands out more from the rest of the text on the page.

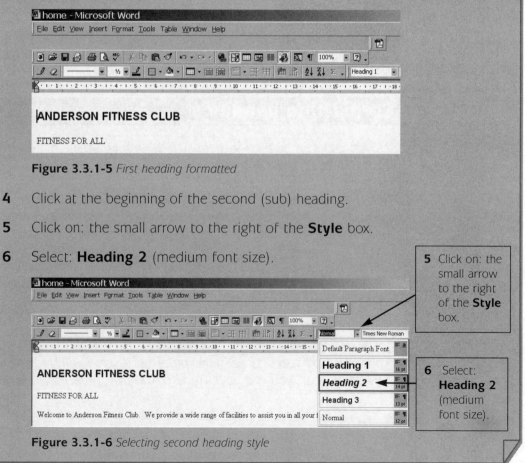

Figure 3.3.1-5 *First heading formatted*

4 Click at the beginning of the second (sub) heading.

5 Click on: the small arrow to the right of the **Style** box.

6 Select: **Heading 2** (medium font size).

5 Click on: the small arrow to the right of the **Style** box.

6 Select: **Heading 2** (medium font size).

Figure 3.3.1-6 *Selecting second heading style*

Checking paragraph spacing

For the OCR Internet Technologies award there must be one clear line space between paragraphs. Because you have formatted the headings, extra spaces will have appeared.

To check spacing in a document it is useful to use the ¶ **Show/Hide** function. This will show the spaces between paragraphs and words. Look for one dot between words, one dot after a comma, and two dots after a full stop.

You will see that there is quite a large gap between the first and second headings (see Figure 3.3.1-7). A space will need to be deleted between the headings.

This line space needs to be deleted.

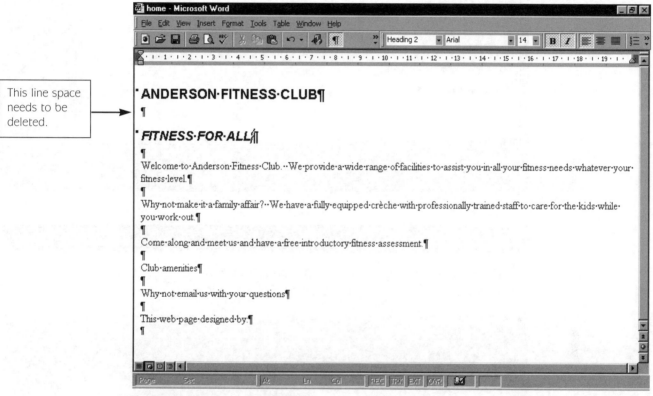

Figure 3.3.1-7 *Space between paragraphs*

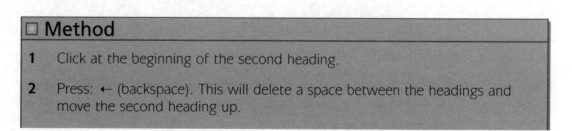

☐ Method

1   Click at the beginning of the second heading.

2   Press: ← (backspace). This will delete a space between the headings and move the second heading up.

The headings should now appear larger and more prominent. At this stage, the web page should look like the one shown below (see Figure 3.3.1-8).

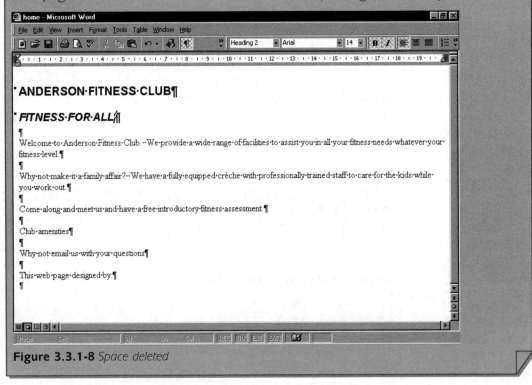

Figure 3.3.1-8 *Space deleted*

Emphasising text

To make important parts of the text stand out you can apply further formatting to emphasise text in the web page using **Bold** and *Italic*.

☐ Method

1   In the first paragraph of the body text, highlight the words **wide range** (see Figure 3.3.1-9).

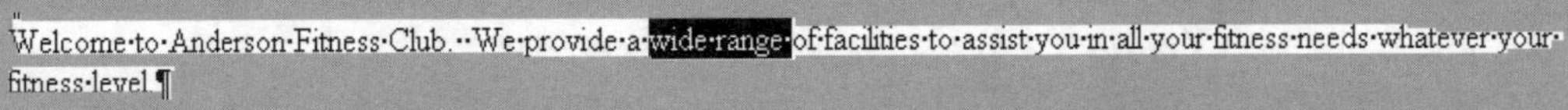

Welcome·to·Anderson·Fitness·Club.··We·provide·a·wide·range·of·facilities·to·assist·you·in·all·your·fitness·needs·whatever·your·
fitness·level.¶

   Figure 3.3.1-9 *Highlighting text*

☐ Hint

Move the cursor to the beginning of **wide**. When the mouse pointer changes to an **I** shape, click and, holding down the mouse button, drag the mouse to the right until both words are highlighted. Release the mouse button.

2   Click on: the **B** **Bold** button.

☐ Info

There is another method you can use to highlight text. Click at the beginning of the words you want to highlight, hold down the **Shift** key and, at the same time, press the right arrow key until the text is highlighted. Release the keys when the required words are highlighted.

3 In the second paragraph of the body text highlight the words **family affair**.

4 Click on: the *I* **Italic** button.

5 Also in the second paragraph, highlight the word **crèche** and format it to bold and italic (click on: the **B** **Bold** button and then on the *I* **Italic** button).

6 In the third paragraph, highlight the word **free** and format it to bold (click on: the **B** **Bold** button).

Aligning text

To further enhance the look of the web page, you can change the alignment of the text on the page. To align all of the text on the page, the text must first be highlighted. In this task, all of the text will be centred on the page. If you want to highlight all the text on a page, there is an option available that will do this for you.

☐ Method

1 From the **Edit** menu, select: **Select All**.

When highlighted, the page should look like the one shown below (see Figure 3.3.1-10).

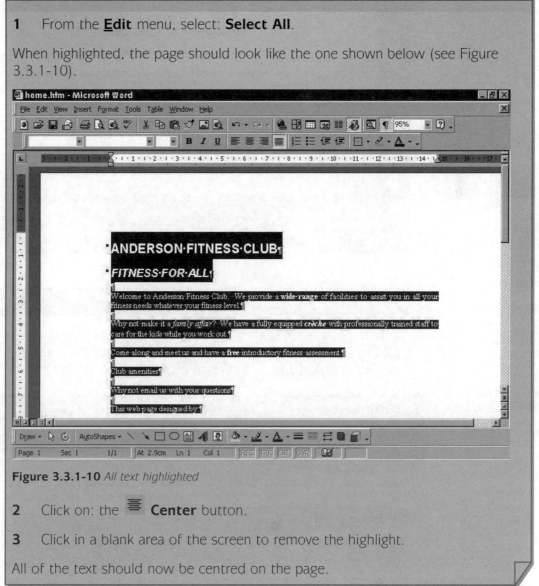

Figure 3.3.1-10 *All text highlighted*

2 Click on: the ≡ **Center** button.

3 Click in a blank area of the screen to remove the highlight.

All of the text should now be centred on the page.

Adding personal details

It is important to add your personal details to each page you produce.

☐ Method

1 Key in your name, date, college centre number and task number after the text: **This web page designed by:**.

☐ Hint

There should be one space after the colon (:) before you key in your personal details.

The page should now look like the one shown below (see Figure 3.3.1-11).

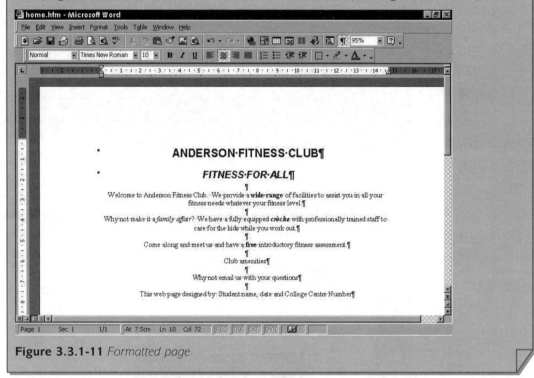

Figure 3.3.1-11 *Formatted page*

Saving amended web page

This web page already has a name, so it is not necessary to use the **Save As** facility. It is important not to change the name of the web page, as this would cause confusion when you create hyperlinks in later tasks.

☐ Hint

If you opened the file directly from the CD-ROM, then you will need to use the **Save As** facility to save it where you usually save your files. *Remember* to keep the same filename.

☐ Method

1 Click on: the 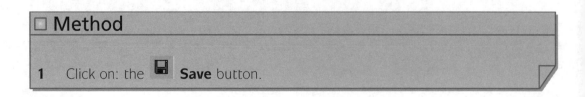 **Save** button.

Printing amended web page

☐ Method

1   Click on: the 🖨 **Print** button.

Exiting Word

If your session is finished you need to exit Word and shut down the computer following the correct procedures (otherwise, leave them open and move on to the next task).

☐ Method

1   Close the document (from the **File** menu, select: **Close**).

2   Exit Word (from the **File** menu, select: **Exit**).

Shutting down computer

☐ Method

1   Make sure all other programs are closed.

2   Click on: the **Start** button.

3   From the pop-up menu, select: **Shut Down**.

4   Select: **Shut Down** from the options that appear.

5   Click on: **OK**.

Task 2 Word

Insert a graphic image

Objectives

- Insert a graphic
- Save amended web page
- Preview web page in browser
- Print web page from browser
- Close browser

The formatting for the **home** web page is almost complete. Inserting an image will further enhance the look of the page.

The **fitness** image for this task can be found on the accompanying CD-ROM or your tutor may have placed it on the network for you.

Inserting a graphic

☐ Method

1 If you do not already have Microsoft Word on screen, then load it (*either* click on: the **Microsoft Word** shortcut icon on the desktop, *or* click on the **Start** button and select: **Programs**, **Microsoft Word**).

2 Open the **home** file (click on: the 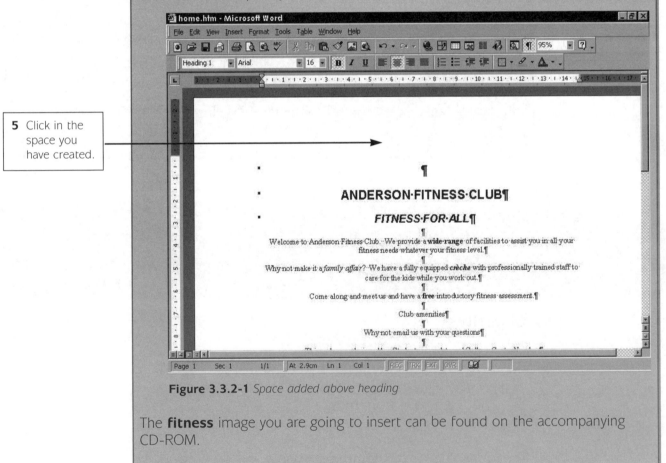 **Open** button; from the **Look in**: box, select the location of the file; click on: the **home** file; click on: **Open**).

The Anderson Fitness Club **home** page that you formatted in Task 1 will now be displayed on screen.

The image in this task is to appear above the first heading. Before you can insert the image into the web page you must first make space for it.

3 Click at the beginning of the first heading.

4 Press: **Enter**.

A new space will appear above the heading (see Figure 3.3.2-1).

5 Click in the space you have created.

> **5** Click in the space you have created.

Figure 3.3.2-1 *Space added above heading*

The **fitness** image you are going to insert can be found on the accompanying CD-ROM.

6   Click on: the 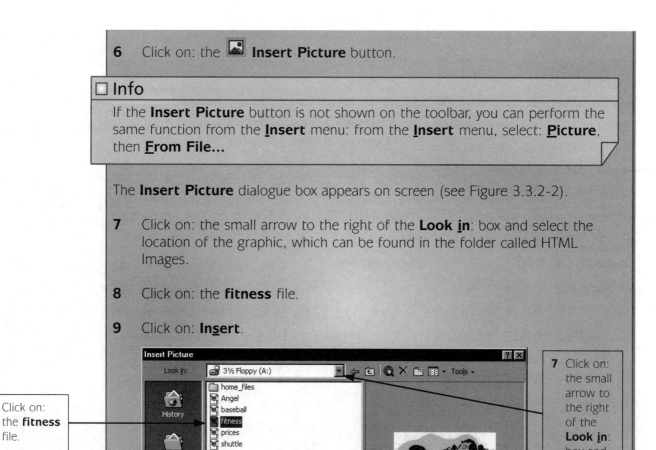 **Insert Picture** button.

The **Insert Picture** dialogue box appears on screen (see Figure 3.3.2-2).

7   Click on: the small arrow to the right of the **Look in:** box and select the location of the graphic, which can be found in the folder called HTML Images.

8   Click on: the **fitness** file.

9   Click on: **Insert**.

8 Click on:
the **fitness**
file.

7 Click on:
the small
arrow to
the right
of the
Look in:
box and
select
the
location
of the
graphic.

9 Click on:
Insert.

Figure 3.3.2-2 *Insert Picture dialogue box*

The fitness image will appear on screen. Sometimes you can click on the image and then on the ≡ **Center** button to centre the image. However, when you try this, you may find that the alignment options are not available (are greyed out).

If the image does not appear centred on the page, then you will need to format the picture properties so that you can centre it.

10   Right-click on the picture.

11   From the drop-down menu, select: **Format Picture...**

The **Format Picture** dialogue box appears on screen. Make sure that the **Layout** tab at the top of the dialogue box is selected. You will see that there are many layout options available for the picture. For this task, the picture needs to be in line with the text.

12   Click on: the **In line with text** box in the **Wrapping style** section. A frame will appear around the selection you have made (see Figure 3.3.2-3).

13 Click on: **OK**.

> Make sure that the **Layout** tab at the top of the dialogue box is selected.

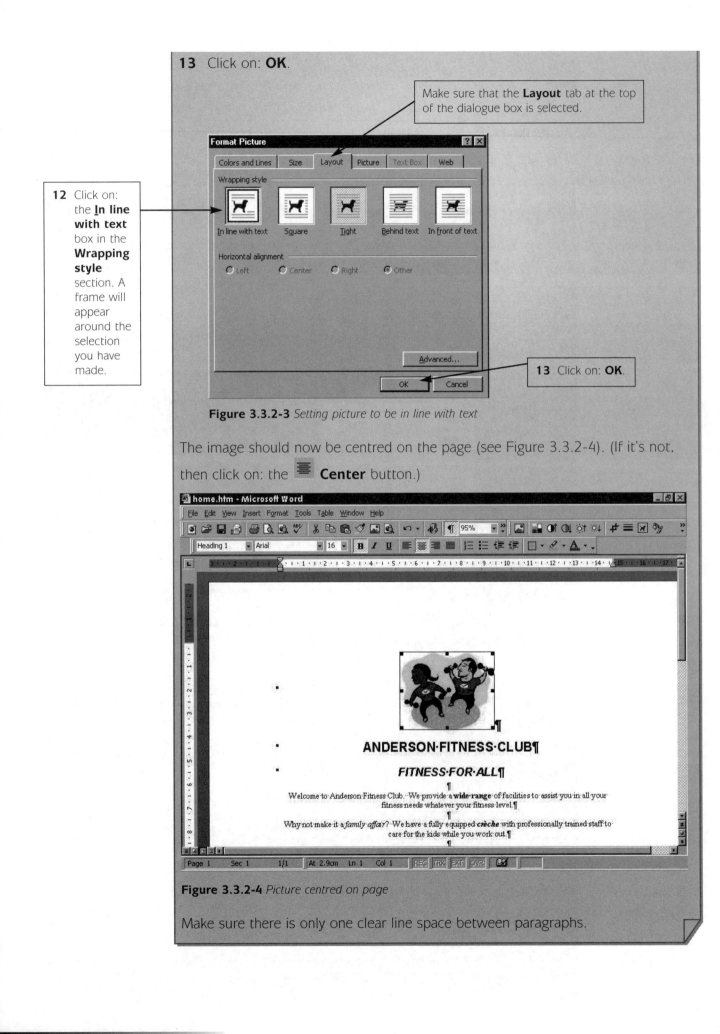

12 Click on: the **In line with text** box in the **Wrapping style** section. A frame will appear around the selection you have made.

13 Click on: **OK**.

Figure 3.3.2-3 *Setting picture to be in line with text*

The image should now be centred on the page (see Figure 3.3.2-4). (If it's not, then click on: the ≡ **Center** button.)

Figure 3.3.2-4 *Picture centred on page*

Make sure there is only one clear line space between paragraphs.

Saving amended web page

It is important to save the changes you make to tasks. This web page already has a name, so it is not necessary to use the **Save As** facility. In the **This web page designed by:** section, change the task number to **2** and change the date if necessary.

☐ Method

1 Click on: the 💾 **Save** button.

Previewing web page in browser

Now that you have inserted the image in the web page you can see how the web page will look if it were loaded on the Internet by previewing the page in the browser.

☐ Method

1 Click on: the 🔍 **Web Page Preview** button.

☐ Hint

If the **Web Page Preview** button is not shown on the toolbar you can perform this function from the **File** menu as well: from the **File** menu, select: **Web Page Preview**.

This will load the web page into the browser (see Figure 3.3.2-5).

☐ Hint

In the example shown, the browser is **Internet Explorer**. If your browser is **Netscape** your web page will be loaded into the **Netscape** browser.

You will know you are in the browser by looking at the buttons on the toolbar – **Back**, **Forward**, **Home**, etc. – these buttons are used for navigating the world wide web.

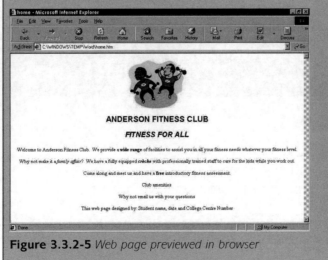

Figure 3.3.2-5 *Web page previewed in browser*

Printing web page from browser

For the OCR Internet Technologies award you are required to print the web page from the browser.

☐ Method

1 Click on: the **Print** button.

Closing browser

To prevent confusion in having different programs open at the same time, it is good practice to close the browser when you have printed the web page.

☐ Method

1 From the **File** menu, select: **Close**.

You will be returned to the web page in Microsoft Word.

Exiting Word and shutting down

If your session is finished, then close the document (from the **File** menu, select: **Close**), exit Word (from the **File** menu, select: **Exit**) and shut down the computer (exit all other applications; click on: the **Start** button, select **Shut Down**; select **Shut Down**; click on: **OK**). Otherwise, move straight on to the next task.

Task 3 — Word

Change background colour

Objectives

- Change background colour
- Save amended web page
- Print web page from browser

In this task, to further enhance the look of the **home** page, you will change the background colour.

Changing background colour

☐ Method

1 If you do not already have Microsoft Word on screen, then load it (*either* click on: the **Microsoft Word** shortcut icon on the desktop, *or* click on the **Start** button and select: **Programs**, **Microsoft Word**).

2 Open the **home** file (click on: the 📂 **Open** button; from the **Look in:** box, select the **home** file; click on: **Open**).

3 From the **Format** menu, select: **Background** and select a colour from the drop-down menu (see Figure 3.3.3-1).

☐ Hint

Select a light colour, as your text is black. If you were to select a dark colour, it would be very difficult to read the text.

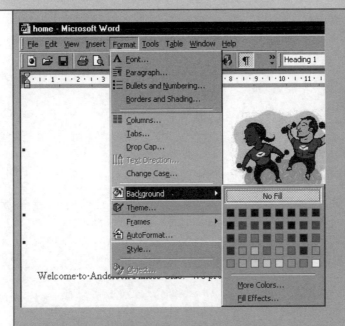

Figure 3.3.3-1 *Selecting background colour*

The background colour of the web page will immediately change to the colour you have chosen.

☐ Hint

If you are not happy with the colour you have chosen, then follow step 3 again and select a different colour.

Saving amended web page

In the **This web page designed by:** section, change the task number to **3** and change the date if necessary.

It is important to save the changes you have made to the web page.

☐ Method

1   Click on: the 🖫 **Save** button.

Printing web page from browser

As mentioned previously, for the OCR Internet Technologies award, you are required to print the web page from the browser.

☐ Method

1   Click on: the 🔍 **Web Page Preview** button (*or* from the **File** menu, select: **We̲b Page Preview**).

This will load the web page into your browser.

2   Click on: the ⧉ Print **Print** button.

Don't worry if, when printed, the web page does not show the background colour. What you must remember is that you are not working on an ordinary document; this is a web page. The background colour you selected will be shown in the HTML code of the web page. It might be useful to write the colour you selected on the printout for your tutor's reference.

3   Exit the browser (from the **File** menu, select: **C̲lose**).

Exiting Word and shutting down

If your session is finished, then close the document (from the **File** menu, select: **Close**), exit Word (from the **File** menu, select: **E̲xit**) and shut down the computer (exit all other applications; click on: the **Start** button, select **Sh̲ut Down**; select **S̲hut Down**; click on: **OK**). Otherwise, move straight on to the next task.

Word

Format text and alignment

Objectives

- Format headings
- Emphasise text
- Align text
- Save amended web page
- Print amended web page from browser

Scenario

Your line manager was very impressed with the web page you designed. So much so, that she has asked if you would design another page to link to the first one. She assures you that your hard work in promoting the club will be rewarded!

In the previous three tasks, you formatted and edited the Anderson Fitness Club **home** page. In this task, you will format the text and alignment in the new Anderson Fitness Club **amenities** web page. The text for this web page has been prepared for you and can be found on the CD-ROM.

Formatting headings

☐ Method

1 If you do not already have Microsoft Word on screen, then load it (*either* click on: the **Microsoft Word** shortcut icon on the desktop, *or* click on the **Start** button and select: **Programs**, **Microsoft Word**).

2 Open the **amenities** file (click on: the 📂 **Open** button; from the **Look in:** box, select the location of the file; click on; the **amenities** file; click on: **OK**).

The Anderson Fitness Club **amenities** web page will be displayed on screen. As mentioned previously, for the OCR Internet Technologies award you are required to use at least three different font sizes when formatting a web page. A reminder of the font styles in Microsoft Word is shown below.

Large font size	Heading 1
Medium font size	Heading 2
Small font size	Heading 3

3 Click at the beginning of the first (main) heading.

4 From the **Style** box, select **Heading 1** (see Figure 3.3.4-1).

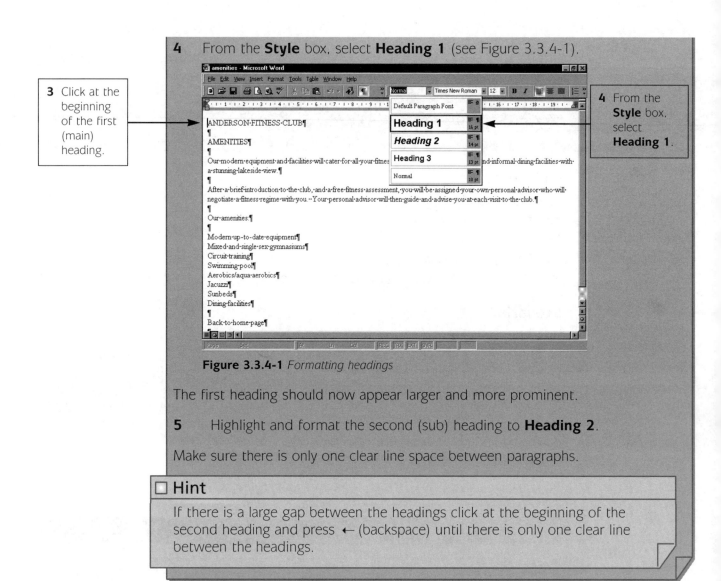

3 Click at the beginning of the first (main) heading.

4 From the **Style** box, select **Heading 1**.

Figure 3.3.4-1 *Formatting headings*

The first heading should now appear larger and more prominent.

5 Highlight and format the second (sub) heading to **Heading 2**.

Make sure there is only one clear line space between paragraphs.

☐ **Hint**

If there is a large gap between the headings click at the beginning of the second heading and press ← (backspace) until there is only one clear line between the headings.

Emphasising text

To make important parts of the text stand out, you can apply further formatting to the web page using **Bold** and *Italic*.

☐ **Method**

1 In the first paragraph, highlight and format the words **modern equipment** to bold (click on: the **B** **Bold** button).

2 In the first paragraph, highlight and format the words **formal** and **informal** to bold (click on: the **B** **Bold** button).

3 In the first paragraph, highlight and format the words **lakeside view** to italic (click on: the *I* **Italic** button).

4 In the second paragraph, highlight and format the words **personal advisor** to bold *and* italic (click on: the **B** **Bold** button, then click on: the *I* **Italic** button).

Aligning text

The text in this web page will be aligned using different alignment options. The web page may not look quite right, but the purpose of this is for you to learn to use the different alignment options available.

☐ Method

The first heading is to be right aligned on the web page.

1 Click at the beginning of the first heading.

2 Click on: the 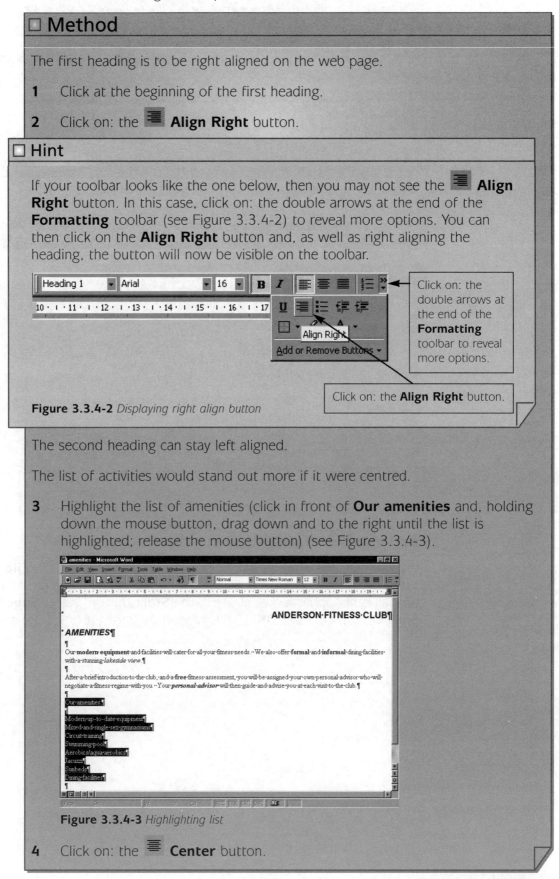 **Align Right** button.

☐ Hint

If your toolbar looks like the one below, then you may not see the ☰ **Align Right** button. In this case, click on: the double arrows at the end of the **Formatting** toolbar (see Figure 3.3.4-2) to reveal more options. You can then click on the **Align Right** button and, as well as right aligning the heading, the button will now be visible on the toolbar.

Click on: the double arrows at the end of the **Formatting** toolbar to reveal more options.

Click on: the **Align Right** button.

Figure 3.3.4-2 *Displaying right align button*

The second heading can stay left aligned.

The list of activities would stand out more if it were centred.

3 Highlight the list of amenities (click in front of **Our amenities** and, holding down the mouse button, drag down and to the right until the list is highlighted; release the mouse button) (see Figure 3.3.4-3).

Figure 3.3.4-3 *Highlighting list*

4 Click on: the ☰ **Center** button.

Saving amended web page

☐ Method

1 At the bottom of the page, key in your name, date, centre number and task number after the text: **This web page designed by:**

2 Click on: the 💾 **Save** button.

☐ Hint

If you opened the file directly from the CD-ROM, then you will need to use the **Save As** facility to save the files to your usual location. *Remember* to keep the same filename.

Printing amended web page from browser

☐ Method

1 Click on: the 🔍 **Web Page Preview** button (*or* from the **File** menu, select **Web Page Preview**).

This will load the web page in the browser.

2 Click on: the 🖨 **Print** button.

3 Close the browser (from the **File** menu, select **Close**).

Exiting Word and shutting down

If your session is finished, then close the document (from the **File** menu, select: **Close**), exit Word (from the **File** menu, select: **Exit**) and shut down the computer (exit all other applications; click on: the **Start** button, select **Shut Down**; select **Shut Down**; click on: **OK**). Otherwise, move straight on to the next task.

Word

Insert graphic image and change background colour

Objectives

- Insert graphic image
- Change background colour
- Save amended web page
- Print amended web page from browser

In this task, you will insert a graphic into the **amenities** page and change the background colour. Refer to instructions in tasks 2 and 3 when necessary.

Inserting graphic image

☐ Method

1   If you do not already have Microsoft Word on screen, then load it (*either* click on: the **Microsoft Word** shortcut icon on the desktop, *or* click on the **Start** button and select: **Programs**, **Microsoft Word**).

2   Open the amenities web page (click on: the 📂 **Open** button; select the location of the file; click on: the **amenities** file; click on: **OK**).

The graphic is to appear centred between the first and second headings. Before you can insert the image you must make space for it.

3   Click at the beginning of the second heading.

4   Press: **Enter**.

5   Click on: the 🖾 **Insert Picture** button (or from the **I**nsert menu, select: **P**icture, **F**rom File).

The **Insert Picture** dialogue box appears on screen. The **fitness** image can be found on the accompanying CD-ROM.

6   From the **Look in**: box, select the location of the graphic image.

7   Click on: the **fitness** image.

8   Click on: **Ins**ert.

You will be returned to the web page with the newly inserted image.

9   Centre the image.

If the image appears like the one shown below (Figure 3.3.5-1), then click on: the ≣ **Center** button to centre the image.

Figure 3.3.5-1 *Image inserted in line with text*

The image should appear centred on the page.

If the image appears with small boxes around it as shown below (Figure 3.3.5-2), then you will need to change the picture properties before you can centre it. (If you look on the toolbar you will see that the alignment options are grey – this means that you will not be able to access them until you change the picture's properties.)

Figure 3.3.5-2 *Image inserted floating over text*

Right-click on the image and select: **Format Picture** from the pop-up menu. Click on: the **In line with text** box in the **Wrapping style** section. A frame will appear around the selection. Click on: **OK**.

Make sure there is still one clear line space between paragraphs.

Changing background colour

To complete the formatting of the **amenities** web page, you will now change the background colour of the page.

☐ Method

1   From the **For̲mat** menu, select **Back̲ground**.

2   From the drop-down menu of colours, select a light colour (choose a different one from the one you chose for the **home** page).

The background colour of the web page will have changed to the colour you chose.

Saving amended web page

☐ Method

1   Change the task number to **5** and the date if necessary.

2   Click on: the 💾 **Save** button.

Printing amended web page from browser

☐ Method

1   Click on: the 🔍 **Web Page Preview** button (*or* from the **F̲ile** menu, select **Web̲ Page Preview**).

This will load the web page in the browser.

2   Click on: the 🖨 Print **Print** button.

3   Close the browser (from the **F̲ile** menu, select **C̲lose**).

Exiting Word and shutting down

If your session is finished, then close the document (from the **F̲ile** menu, select: **Close**), exit Word (from the **F̲ile** menu, select: **E̲xit**) and shut down the computer (exit all other applications; click on: the **Start** button, select **Sh̲ut Down**; select **Sh̲ut Down**; click on: **OK**). Otherwise, move straight on to the next task.

Publish information on a website

Create a web structure using Microsoft Word

Word

Create hyperlink from home page to amenities page

Objectives

- Create hyperlink
- Save amended web page
- Print amended web page from browser

Now that you have formatted the Anderson web pages, in this task you will create a hyperlink that will take you from the **home** page to the **amenities** page.

What is a hyperlink?

A link in a web page can be text or an image. Clicking on a link will take you to another web page. A text link is usually blue and underlined. You will know you have moved to a link when the mouse pointer changes to a hand: 🖑.

Creating a hyperlink

☐ Method

1 If you do not already have Microsoft Word on screen, then load it (*either* click on: the **Microsoft Word** shortcut icon on the desktop, *or* click on the **Start** button and select: **Programs**, **Microsoft Word**).

2 Open the Anderson **home** page click on: the 📂 **Open** button; select the location of the file; click on: the **home** file; click on: **Open**).

To create a hyperlink, you must first highlight the text you are going to use for the link.

3 At the bottom of the page, highlight the words Club amenities (see Figure 3.4.6-1).

> Come·along·and·meet·us·and·have·a·**free**·introductory·fitness·assessment.¶
> ¶
> Club·amenities¶
> ¶

Figure 3.4.6-1 *Highlight Club amenities*

4   Click on: the 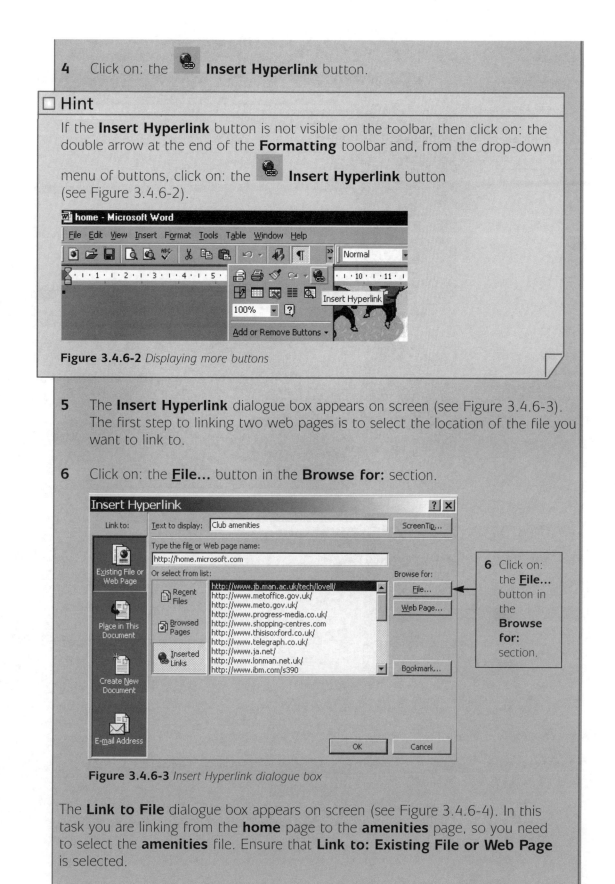 **Insert Hyperlink** button.

☐ Hint

If the **Insert Hyperlink** button is not visible on the toolbar, then click on: the double arrow at the end of the **Formatting** toolbar and, from the drop-down menu of buttons, click on: the **Insert Hyperlink** button (see Figure 3.4.6-2).

Figure 3.4.6-2 *Displaying more buttons*

5   The **Insert Hyperlink** dialogue box appears on screen (see Figure 3.4.6-3). The first step to linking two web pages is to select the location of the file you want to link to.

6   Click on: the **File...** button in the **Browse for:** section.

> **6** Click on: the **File...** button in the **Browse for:** section.

Figure 3.4.6-3 *Insert Hyperlink dialogue box*

The **Link to File** dialogue box appears on screen (see Figure 3.4.6-4). In this task you are linking from the **home** page to the **amenities** page, so you need to select the **amenities** file. Ensure that **Link to: Existing File or Web Page** is selected.

7   Click on: the **amenities** file.

8 Click on: **OK**.

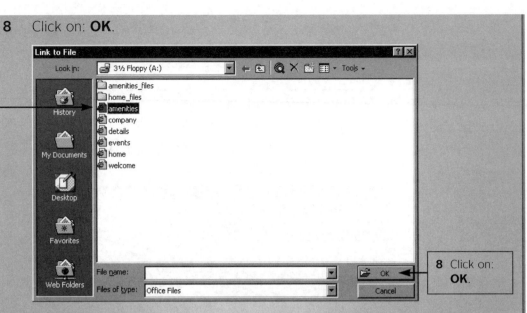

7 Click on: the **amenities** file.

8 Click on: **OK**.

Figure 3.4.6-4 *Link to File dialogue box*

You will be returned to the **Insert Hyperlink** dialogue box. The **amenities** web page you have chosen to link to will now be shown in the white box below **Type the file or web page name:** (see Figure 3.4.6-5).

9 Click on: **OK**.

The **amenities** web page you have chosen to link to will now be shown here.

9 Click on: **OK**.

Figure 3.4.6-5 *Amenities file selected*

You will be returned to the web page.

10 Click in a blank area of the screen to remove the highlight.

You will see that the words **Club amenities** are now a different colour and underlined (see Figure 3.4.6-6) – this is how you know that the text is now a hyperlink. Move the mouse over the hyperlink, but don't click on it. The mouse pointer should change to a [hand icon] hand when you hover over the hyperlink.

Come·along·and·meet·us·and·have·a·**free**·introductory·fitness·assessment.¶
¶
Club·amenities¶
Why·not·email·us·with·your·questions¶

Figure 3.4.6-6 *Club amenities link set*

☐ Hint

If, as in Figure 3.4.6-6, you have lost a space between the hyperlink and the next paragraph, then click at the end of the text **Club amenities** and press: **Enter**.

What you have done in this task is create a hyperlink from the **home** page to take you to the **amenities** page. This means that, when you click the hyperlink you created, the **amenities** page will automatically be loaded onto the screen. This will become clear when you test the hyperlink in Task 8.

Saving amended web page

☐ Method

1   Change the task number to **6** and the date if necessary.

2   Click on: the 💾 **Save** button.

Printing amended web page from browser

☐ Method

1   Click on: the 🔍 **Web Page Preview** button (*or* from the **File** menu, select **Web Page Preview**).

This will load the web page in the browser.

2   Click on: the 🖨️ **Print** **Print** button.

3   Close the browser (from the **File** menu, select **Close**).

Exiting Word and shutting down

If your session is finished, then close the document (from the **File** menu, select: **Close**), exit Word (from the **File** menu, select: **Exit**) and shut down the computer (exit all other applications; click on: the **Start** button, select **Shut Down**; select **Shut Down**; click on: **OK**). Otherwise, move straight on to the next task.

Create hyperlink from amenities page to home page

Objectives

- Create hyperlink
- Save amended web page
- Print amended web page from browser

In this task, you will create a hyperlink that will take you from the **amenities** page back to the **home** page.

Creating hyperlink

☐ Method

1   If you do not already have Microsoft Word on screen, then load it (*either* click on: the **Microsoft Word** shortcut icon on the desktop, *or* click on the **Start** button and select: **Programs**, **Microsoft Word**).

2   Open the Anderson **amenities** web page (click on: the 🖼 **Open** button; select the location of the file; click on: the **amenities** file; click on: **Open**).

To create a hyperlink, you must first highlight the text you want to use as the link.

3   At the bottom of the page, highlight the words **Back to home page** (see Figure 3.4.7-1).

> Back to home page
>
> This web page designed by: Student name, date, Centre Number and task number

Figure 3.4.7-1 *Highlight Back to home page*

4   Click on: the 🌐 **Insert Hyperlink** button or from the **Insert** menu, select: **Hyperlink**.

The **Insert Hyperlink** dialogue box appears on screen. You need to select the location of the page you want to link to.

5   Click on: the **File...** button below **Browse for:**. The **Link to File** dialogue box appears on screen.

In this task you are putting a link on the **amenities** page to take you back to the **home** page.

6   From the **Look in:** box, select the location of the **home** web page.

7   Click on: the **home** file.

8   Click on: **OK**.

You will be returned to the **Insert Hyperlink** dialogue box, where the home web page you have chosen to link to will be shown in the white box below **Type the file or web page name:**.

9 Click on: **OK** to return you to the **amenities** web page.

10 Click in a blank area of the screen to remove the highlight.

You will see that the words **Back to home page** are now a different colour and underlined – this is how you know that the text is now a hyperlink. If you hover the mouse over the hyperlink, the mouse pointer will change to a hand: .

☐ **Hint**

If you have lost a space between the new link and the next paragraph, then click at the end of the link and press: **Enter**. This should give you a clear line space between the paragraphs.

You have now created a hyperlink from the **amenities** web page to take you back to the **home** page. This means that, when you click on the hyperlink you created, the **home** web page will automatically be loaded on to the screen. This might seem quite difficult to understand at this stage, but don't worry, when you test the hyperlinks in the next task, it should all become clear.

Saving amended web page

☐ **Method**

1 Change the task number to **7** and the date if necessary.

2 Click on: the 💾 **Save** button.

Printing amended web page from browser

☐ **Method**

1 Click on: the 🔍 **Web Page Preview** button (*or* from the **File** menu, select **Web Page Preview**).

This will load the web page in the browser.

2 Click on: the 🖨 **Print** button.

3 Close the browser (from the **File** menu, select **Close**).

Exiting Word and shutting down

If your session is finished, then close the document (from the **File** menu, select: **Close**), exit Word (from the **File** menu, select: **Exit**) and shut down the computer (exit all other applications; click on: the **Start** button, select **Shut Down**; select **Shut Down**; click on: **OK**). Otherwise, move straight on to the next task.

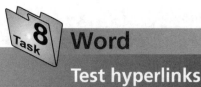

Word

Test hyperlinks

Objectives

- Preview in browser
- Test hyperlinks

Now it's time to see if the links work. In this task, you will test the hyperlinks that you created in the formatted Anderson web pages.

☐ Info

If the hyperlinks don't work, go back to the tasks in which you created the hyperlinks and make sure you followed each step correctly.

Previewing in browser

☐ Method

1   If you do not already have Microsoft Word on screen, then load it (*either* click on: the **Microsoft Word** shortcut icon on the desktop, *or* click on the **Start** button and select: **Programs**, **Microsoft Word**).

2   Open the Anderson **home** page (click on: the 🖆 **Open** button; select the location of the file; click on: the **home** file; click on: **Open**).

3   Click on: the 🔍 **Web Page Preview** button (*or* from the **File** menu, select **Web Page Preview**).

Testing hyperlinks

You should now be looking at the **home** page in the web browser.

☐ Method

1   Click on: the **Club amenities** link that you created.

This should take you to the Anderson Fitness Club **amenities** page.

2   Click on: the **Back to home page** link you created.

This should take you back to the Anderson Fitness Club **home** page.

3   Close the browser (from the **File** menu, select **Close**).

Exiting Word and shutting down

If your session is finished, then close the document (from the **File** menu, select: **Close**), exit Word (from the **File** menu, select: **Exit**) and shut down the computer (exit all other applications; click on: the **Start** button, select **Shut Down**; select **Shut Down**; click on: **OK**). Otherwise, move straight on to the next task.

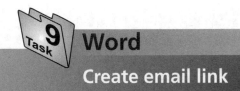

Word

Create email link

Objectives

- Create email hyperlink
- Save amended web page
- Print amended web page from browser
- Test email link

For the OCR Internet Technologies award you are required to create a hyperlink to an email address. Many web pages on the Internet have email links, clicking on which will take you to an email application to compose and send an email message. This will automatically be addressed to a contact at that site.

In this task, you will be loading the **home** web page you worked on previously and creating an email link within the web page.

Creating email hyperlink

☐ Method

1. If you do not already have Microsoft Word on screen, then load it (*either* click on: the **Microsoft Word** shortcut icon on the desktop, *or* click on the **Start** button and select: **Programs**, **Microsoft Word**).

2. Open the Anderson **home** page (click on: the 📂 **Open** button; select the location of the file; click on: the **home** file; click on: **Open**).

3. Highlight the text **Why not email us with your questions.**

4. Click on: the 🌐 **Insert Hyperlink** button or from the **Insert** menu, select: **Hyperlink**.

The **Insert Hyperlink** dialogue box appears on screen (see Figure 3.4.9-1).

In previous tasks you have linked web pages by choosing a file to link to. Creating an email link is different. In some software packages you would key in **mailto:** followed by the email address you are linking to. Microsoft Word has a facility that will enter the **mailto:** part for you.

5 Click on: **E-mail Address** in the **Link to:** section.

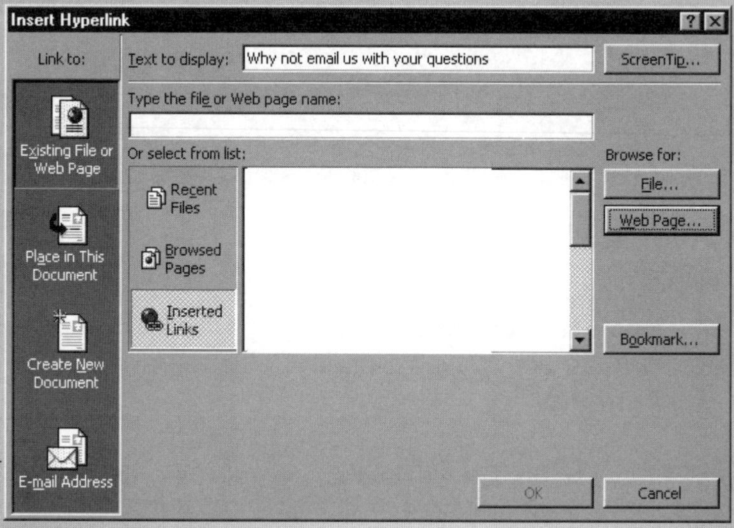

5 Click on: **E-mail Address** in the **Link to:** section.

Figure 3.4.9-1 *Insert Hyperlink dialogue box*

A different **Insert Hyperlink** dialogue box appears on screen (see Figure 3.4.9-2). The flashing cursor will appear in the box below **E-mail address:**.

You now need to key in the email address you want to link to. As soon as you begin keying in, the words **mailto:** will appear.

6 Key in your email address.

☐ **Info**

It is very important that you key in your email address accurately, otherwise the link will not work.

7 Click on: **OK**.

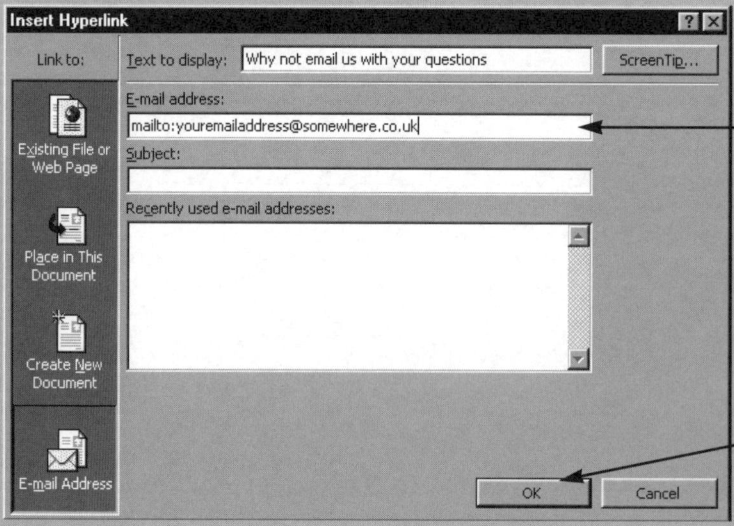

6 Key in your email address.

7 Click on: **OK**.

Figure 3.4.9-2 *Email Insert Hyperlink dialogue box*

You will be returned to the web page with the newly created email link.

8 If necessary, click at the end of the new link and press: **Enter** to make a space between the link and the last paragraph.

The text that you highlighted, **Why not email us...** is now a different colour and underlined. This is now an email hyperlink.

Saving amended web page

☐ Method

1 Change the task number to **9** and the date if necessary.

2 Click on: the 🖫 **Save** button.

Printing amended web page from browser

☐ Method

1 Click on: the 🔍 **Web Page Preview** button (*or* from the **File** menu, select **Web Page Preview**).

This will load the web page in the browser.

2 Click on: the 🖨 **Print** button.

Testing email link

☐ Method

1 Click on: the email link that you have just created.

An email application **Message** window appears on screen (see Figure 3.4.9-3).

☐ Info

In the example below, the Microsoft Outlook **Message** window is displayed. Your email application screen may look different.

2 Click on: the ☒ cross in the top right-hand corner of the **Message** window to close the email application.

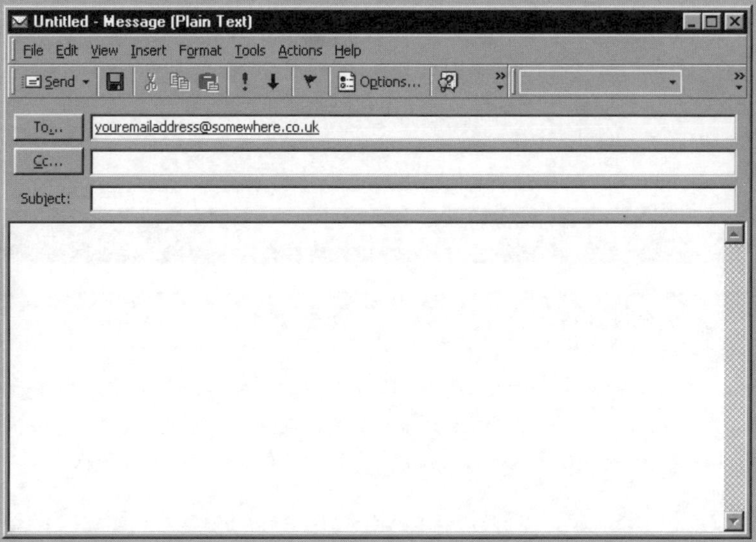

Figure 3.4.9-3 *Message window*

3 If you see the following prompt box (or a similar one), asking if you want to keep the draft of the message, then click on: **No**.

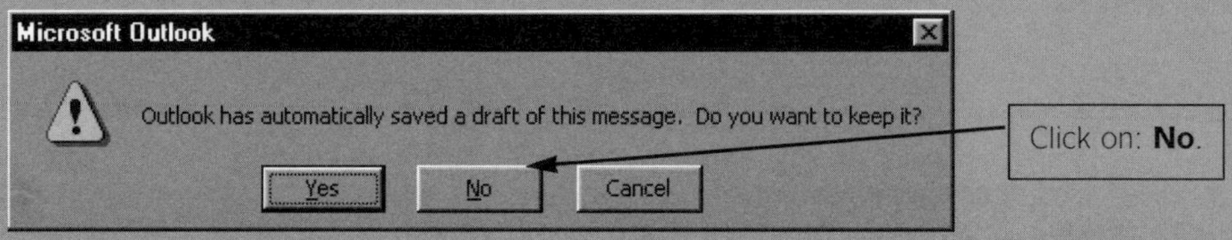

Microsoft Outlook ✕

⚠ Outlook has automatically saved a draft of this message. Do you want to keep it?

Yes　　　No　　　Cancel

Click on: **No**.

Figure 3.4.9-4 *Save draft message prompt box*

4 Close the browser (from the **File** menu, select: **Close**).

Exiting Word and shutting down

If your session is finished, then close the document (from the **File** menu, select: **Close**), exit Word (from the **File** menu, select: **Exit**) and shut down the computer (exit all other applications; click on: the **Start** button, select **Shut Down**; select **Shut Down**; click on: **OK**). Otherwise, move straight on to the next task.

Word

Print HTML source code

Objectives

▶ View HTML source code
▶ Key in personal details
▶ Save source code
▶ Print source code

For the OCR Internet Technologies award you are required to print the HTML codes used to format the web page. When you formatted the alignment, text, changed the background colour, inserted an image and set links, each one of these formatting techniques has an HTML code attached to it. This is called the *source code*. Whilst you do not have to understand this code, it is useful to take some time to look at it.

Viewing HTML source code

☐ Method

1 If you do not already have Microsoft Word on screen, then load it (*either* click on: the **Microsoft Word** shortcut icon on the desktop, *or* click on the **Start** button and select: **Programs**, **Microsoft Word**).

2 Open the Anderson **home** page (click on: the 📂 **Open** button; select the location of the file; click on: the **home** file; click on: **Open**).

To view the HTML source code used in formatting the page, you must first view the web page in the browser.

3 Click on: the 🔍 **Web Page Preview** button.

This will load the web page into the browser.

4 From the **View** menu, select: **Source**.

This will load the HTML code into Windows Notepad (see Figure 3.4.10-1).

Don't panic! A page of text that looks like a foreign language will be on the screen. This page is showing the HTML codes used in formatting the web page. When you produce web pages in Microsoft Word, there is a lot of HTML code produced. However, you do not need to worry about most of this – the important code you need to look at is further down the document.

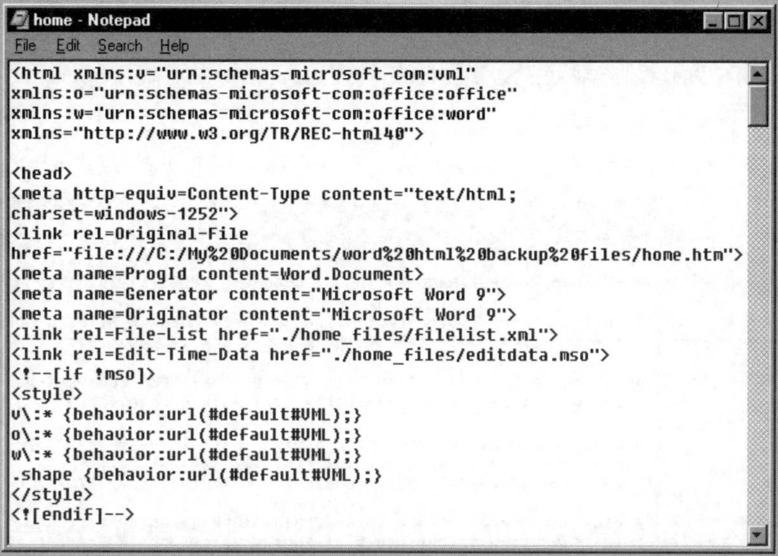

```
🗐 home - Notepad                                          _ □ ×
File  Edit  Search  Help
<html xmlns:v="urn:schemas-microsoft-com:vml"
xmlns:o="urn:schemas-microsoft-com:office:office"
xmlns:w="urn:schemas-microsoft-com:office:word"
xmlns="http://www.w3.org/TR/REC-html40">

<head>
<meta http-equiv=Content-Type content="text/html;
charset=windows-1252">
<link rel=Original-File
href="file:///C:/My%20Documents/word%20html%20backup%20files/home.htm">
<meta name=ProgId content=Word.Document>
<meta name=Generator content="Microsoft Word 9">
<meta name=Originator content="Microsoft Word 9">
<link rel=File-List href="./home_files/filelist.xml">
<link rel=Edit-Time-Data href="./home_files/editdata.mso">
<!--[if !mso]>
<style>
v\:* {behavior:url(#default#VML);}
o\:* {behavior:url(#default#VML);}
w\:* {behavior:url(#default#VML);}
.shape {behavior:url(#default#VML);}
</style>
<![endif]-->
```

Figure 3.4.10-1 *Source code in Notepad*

The first code you need to find is the code that gives the background colour of the web page.

5 Click on: the down arrow on the scrollbar until you see **<body bgcolour=** (see Figure 3.4.10-2).

This code gives the background colour.

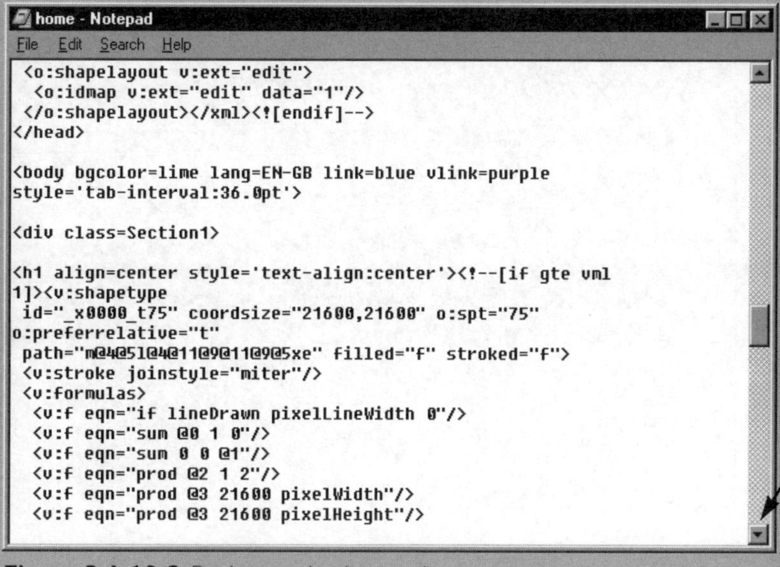

```
🗐 home - Notepad                                          _ □ ×
File  Edit  Search  Help
 <o:shapelayout v:ext="edit">
  <o:idmap v:ext="edit" data="1"/>
 </o:shapelayout></xml><![endif]-->
</head>

<body bgcolor=lime lang=EN-GB link=blue vlink=purple
style='tab-interval:36.0pt'>

<div class=Section1>

<h1 align=center style='text-align:center'><!--[if gte vml
1]><v:shapetype
 id="_x0000_t75" coordsize="21600,21600" o:spt="75"
o:preferrelative="t"
 path="m@4@5l@4@11@9@11@9@5xe" filled="f" stroked="f">
 <v:stroke joinstyle="miter"/>
 <v:formulas>
  <v:f eqn="if lineDrawn pixelLineWidth 0"/>
  <v:f eqn="sum @0 1 0"/>
  <v:f eqn="sum 0 0 @1"/>
  <v:f eqn="prod @2 1 2"/>
  <v:f eqn="prod @3 21600 pixelWidth"/>
  <v:f eqn="prod @3 21600 pixelHeight"/>
```

5 Click on: the down arrow on the scrollbar.

Figure 3.4.10-2 *Background colour code*

This HTML code is giving details about the background colour of the web page. To the right of the text **body bgcolor** you will see that the background colour of the web page is lime (yours may be different if you chose a different colour).

<body bgcolor=lime lang=EN-GB link=blue vlink=purple style='tab-interval:36.0pt'>

6 Now look for this code:

<v:imagedata src="./home_files/image001.jpg" o:title="fitness"

This HTML code gives details of the graphic – the name and size of the image and that the image has been centred on the web page.

□ Hint

Although you choose font sizes for the main heading and subheading, Microsoft Word recognises these as heading styles in the HTML code. You should however still select font sizes rather than apply heading styles.

7 Click on: the down arrow on the scrollbar until you see the line beginning **h1**.

This HTML code gives details of the main heading.

```
home - Notepad
File  Edit  Search  Help
</v:shape><![endif]--><![if !vml]><img width=158 height=126
src="./home_files/image001.jpg" v:shapes="_x0000_i1025"><![endif]></h1>

<h1 align=center style='text-align:center'>ANDERSON FITNESS CLUB<span
style='mso-bidi-font-size:10.0pt'><o:p></o:p></span></h1>

<h2 align=center style='text-align:center'>FITNESS FOR ALL<span
style='mso-bidi-font-size:10.0pt'><o:p></o:p></span></h2>

<p class=MsoNormal align=center style='text-align:center'><span
style='font-size:12.0pt;mso-bidi-font-size:10.0pt'><![if
!supportEmptyParas]> <![endif]><o:p></o:p></span></p>

<p class=MsoNormal align=center style='text-align:center'><span
style='font-size:12.0pt;mso-bidi-font-size:10.0pt'>Welcome to Anderson
Fitness
Club.<span style="mso-spacerun: yes">   </span>We provide a <b>wide
range</b> of
facilities to assist you in all your fitness needs whatever your
fitness level.<o:p></o:p></span></p>

<p class=MsoNormal align=center style='text-align:center'><span
style='font-size:12.0pt;mso-bidi-font-size:10.0pt'><![if
```

7 Click on: the down arrow on the scrollbar until you se the line beginning **h1**.

Figure 3.4.10-3 *Main heading source code*

<h1 align=center style='text-align:center'>ANDERSON FITNESS CLUB <o:p></o:p></h1>

The HTML code used here tells you that the main heading has been formatted to **24 pt font** which in Word is **H1** (large font size) and centred on the web page.

8 Look for this code:

<h2 align=center style='text-align:center'>FITNESS FOR ALL<o:p></o:p></h2>

This HTML code tells you that the second (sub) heading has been formatted to **14 pt font** which in Word is **H2** (medium font size) and centred on the web page.

9 Look for this code:

```
style='font-size:12.0pt;mso-bidi-font-size:10.0pt'>Welcome to
Anderson Fitness Club.<span style="mso-spacerun: yes">
</span>We provide a <b>wide range</b> of facilities to assist you
in all your fitness needs whatever your fitness level.<o:p></o:p>
</span></p>
```

This is the body text of the web page **(12 pt font)**. If you look at the beginning and end of the words **wide range** you will see **** and **** – these are the HTML codes used for **bold**.

10 Look for this code:

```
<p class=MsoNormal align=center style='text-align:center'>
<span style='font-size:12.0pt;mso-bidi-font-size:10.0pt'>Why not
make it a <i>family affair</i>?<span style="mso-spacerun: yes">
</span>We have a fully equipped <b><i>crèche</b></i> with
professionally trained staff to care for the kids while you work
out.<o:p></o:p></span>
```

In the third line of this HTML code, at the beginning and end of the words **family affair** you will see **<i>** and **<i>**. If you remember, you formatted these words to italic in the web page – these are the HTML codes for italic. If you remember, also, you formatted the word **crèche** to bold and italic. Look for the word **crèche** and you will see **<i>** and **</i>** – this is how HTML codes up bold and italic.

11 Look for this code:

```
href="file:///A:/amenities.htm">Club
amenities</a><o:p></o:p></span></p>
```

The **href** in this HTML code tells you that the text **Club amenities** has been linked to the **amenities** web page.

12 Look for this code:

```
href="mailto:otleytutoramb@yahoo.co.uk">Why not email us with
your questions?</a><o:p></o:p></span></p>
```

The **href** in this HTML code tells you that the text **Why not email us...** is an email link to the email address shown.

☐ **Info**

These brief explanations of HTML codes were designed to give you a little background knowledge of HTML. Formatting a web page using HTML code can be quite difficult and time consuming, which is why you have used Microsoft Word 2000. When you produce a web page in Word, the codes are automatically put in for you.

Although there are many HTML editors available, there are still people who prefer to key in the codes in packages such as Windows Notepad. If you inserted the HTML codes using Notepad, the web pages would look the same as the ones you have produced.

Printing source code

☐ Method

1   From the **File** menu, select: **Print**.

2   From the **File** menu, select **Exit** to close Notepad.

☐ Hint

As mentioned previously, you may find that you have pages of code. If you do, then you will find you may only need pages **3** through **6**, which contain the important code for the formatting you performed in the tasks.

Look at the HTML code on the printout. It may be useful to go through and highlight the formatting that you did in the tasks.

3   Look for and highlight the following:
   - the background colour
   - the graphic image you inserted
   - the headings you formatted
   - each time you used bold and italic
   - the links you created.

4   Exit Notepad (from the **File** menu, select: **Exit**).

5   Close the browser (from the **File** menu, select: **Close**).

Exiting Word and shutting down

If your session is finished, then close the document (from the **File** menu, select: **Close**), exit Word (from the **File** menu, select: **Exit**) and shut down the computer (exit all other applications; click on: the **Start** button, select **Shut Down**; select **Shut Down**; click on: **OK**). Otherwise, move straight on to the next task.

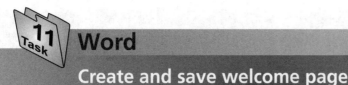
Word

Create and save welcome page

Objectives

- Key in text in new page
- Spellcheck and proof-read
- Save new web page
- Print new web page

Now that you have completed the Anderson Fitness Club tasks, you will create a new website from scratch. In this task and Task 12, you will key in and save text for the two Maryhill Little League Baseball Club web pages in preparation for editing and formatting in later tasks.

Keying in text in new page; spellchecking and proof-reading

☐ Method

1   If you do not already have Microsoft Word on screen, then load it (*either* click on: the **Microsoft Word** shortcut icon on the desktop, *or* click on the **Start** button and select: **Programs**, **Microsoft Word**).

You should have a blank page on screen (if not, from the **File** menu, select: **New**).

☐ Info

Keying-in reminders

The following points are important when keying in new text:

- One space after a comma (,).
- Two spaces after a full stop (.).
- One clear space between paragraphs.

2 Key in the following text, using size 12 font. Retain upper case and lower case as shown. The line endings do not have to be the same as those shown. Add your personal details after the text **This web page designed by:**

> MARYHILL LITTLE LEAGUE BASEBALL CLUB
>
> OPEN DAY
>
> We are having an Open Day on Saturday 11 July to help raise funds for our club. This will be a wonderful opportunity for you to meet the teams and the coaching staff. There will be a short presentation by a member of our twinned American Little League baseball club, Wyndford County, to introduce you to the game of baseball, after which why not try a game or two!
>
> Come along and join us.
>
> The fun starts at 2.30 pm and will finish approximately 4.30 pm.
>
> Click here to see the events planned for the day.
>
> This web page designed by:

3 Spellcheck the document and make any necessary amendments (from the **Tools** menu, select **Spelling and Grammar...**).

4 Proof-read the text carefully for any errors that the spellcheck might have missed.

Saving new web page

☐ Method

1 From the **File** menu, select: **Save as Web Page...**

2 From the **Save in:** box, select the location where you usually save your files. In the **File name:** box, delete the suggested name for the file and key in **welcome**.

3 Click on: **Save**.

Printing new web page

☐ Method

1 Click on: the 🖨 **Print** button.

Exiting Word and shutting down

If your session is finished, then close the document (from the **File** menu, select: **Close**), exit Word (from the **File** menu, select: **Exit**) and shut down the computer (exit all other applications; click on: the **Start** button, select **Shut Down**; select **Shut Down**; click on: **OK**). Otherwise, move straight on to the next task.

Word

Create and save events page

Objectives

- Key in text in new web page
- Spellcheck and proof-read
- Save new web page
- Print new web page

Now that you have created the Maryhill Little League Baseball Club **welcome** web page, in this task, you will key in and create the Maryhill Little League **events** web page.

Keying in text in new web page; spellchecking and proof-reading

☐ Method

1 If you do not already have Microsoft Word on screen, then load it (*either* click on: the **Microsoft Word** shortcut icon on the desktop, *or* click on the **Start** button and select: **Programs**, **Microsoft Word**).

You should have a blank page on screen (if not, from the **File** menu, select: **New**).

Remember to follow the keying-in reminders from Task 11.

2 Key in the following text, using size 12 font. Retain upper case and lower case as shown. The line endings do not have to be the same as those shown. Add your personal details after the text **This web page designed by:**

MARYHILL LITTLE LEAGUE BASEBALL CLUB

OPEN DAY

EVENTS FOR THE DAY

As you can see, we have planned a day of fun for the whole family.
Contributions to the toy and bookstall would be very much appreciated.
The proceeds from the day will help towards uniforms for the teams.
Please come along and support us.

Events

Bouncy Castle, no adults allowed!

Book stall

Toy stall

Hot Dog and Hamburger stall

Cake stall (Bring and Buy of course!)

Treasure Hunt

Children v Parents baseball tournament

AND MUCH MORE!

Back to welcome page

Email us for further information

This web page designed by:

3 Spellcheck the document and make any necessary amendments (from the
   Tools menu, select **Spelling and Grammar...**).

4 Proof-read the text carefully for any errors that the Spellcheck might have
   missed.

Saving new web page

□ Method

1 From the **File** menu, select: **Save as Web Page...**

2 From the **Save in:** box, select the location where you usually save your files.
   In the **File name:** box, delete the suggested name for the file and key in
   events.

3 Click on: **Save**.

Printing new web page

□ Method

1   Click on: the 🖨 **Print** button.

Exiting Word and shutting down

If your session is finished, then close the document (from the **File** menu, select: **Close**), exit Word (from the **File** menu, select: **Exit**) and shut down the computer (exit all other applications; click on: the **Start** button, select **Shut Down**; select **Shut Down**; click on: **OK**). Otherwise, move straight on to the next task.

Word

Format welcome page

Objectives

- 📁 Format headings
- 📁 Format body text
- 📁 Align text
- 📁 Save amended web page
- 📁 Print amended web page

In this task, you will format the Maryhill Little League Baseball Club **welcome** page that you created in Task 11.

Formatting headings

For the OCR Internet Technologies award you are required to format headings and text in three different font sizes.

□ Method

1   If you do not already have Microsoft Word on screen, then load it (*either* click on: the **Microsoft Word** shortcut icon on the desktop, *or* click on the **Start** button and select: **Programs**, **Microsoft Word**).

2   Open the **welcome** page that you created in Task 11 (click on: the 📂 **Open** button; select the location of the file; click on: the **welcome** file; click on: **Open**).

The Maryhill Little League Baseball Club **welcome** page will appear on screen.

3   Highlight the first (main) heading and format it to **24 pt** font size (large font size).

4   Highlight the second (sub) heading and format it to **14 pt** font size (medium font size).

Formatting body text

The main text in the web page is known as the *body text*. You will now emphasise important points in the text using the **bold** and *italic* formatting options.

☐ Method

1   In the first paragraph of the body text, highlight and format the words **Open Day** to bold (click on: the **B** **Bold** button).

2   Highlight and format the words **Saturday 11 July** to bold.

3   Highlight and format the words **short presentation** to bold.

4   Highlight and format the word **twinned** to italic (click on: the *I* **Italic** button).

5   Highlight and format the words **why not try a game or two** to bold and italic.

6   In the third paragraph, highlight and format the words **2.30 pm** and **4.30 pm** to bold.

Aligning text

There are a number of alignment styles available to choose from. In this page, the text will be centred. Text to be aligned must first be highlighted.

☐ Method

1   Centre all of the text on the web page (from the **Edit** menu, select: **Select All**; click on: the ☰ **Center** button).

Saving amended web page

☐ Method

1   Change the task number to **13** and the date if necessary.

2   Click on: the 💾 **Save** button.

Printing amended web page

☐ Method

1   Click on: the 🖶 Print button.

Exiting Word and shutting down

If your session is finished, then close the document (from the **File** menu, select: **Close**), exit Word (from the **File** menu, select: **Exit**) and shut down the computer (exit all other applications; click on: the **Start** button, select **Sh<u>u</u>t Down**; select **<u>S</u>hut Down**; click on: **OK**). Otherwise, move straight on to the next task.

Task 14

Word

Insert graphic image and change background colour

Objectives

- Insert graphic image
- Change background colour
- Save amended web page
- Preview amended web page in browser
- Print amended web page from browser
- Close browser

In this task, to further enhance the look of the web page, you will insert a graphic image and change the background colour of the web page.

Inserting graphic image

The **baseball** image can be found on the accompanying CD-ROM.

☐ Method

1   If you do not already have Microsoft Word on screen, then load it (*either* click on: the **Microsoft Word** shortcut icon on the desktop, *or* click on the **Start** button and select: **Programs**, **Microsoft Word**).

2   Open the Maryhill Little League Baseball Club **welcome** page that you formatted in Task 13 (click on: the 🗁 **Open** button; select the location of the file; click on: the **welcome** file; click on: **Open**).

3   Make a space for the image above the first heading (click at beginning of heading; press: **Enter**).

4   Click in the space you have created and click on: the 🖾 **Insert Picture** button or from the **Insert** menu, select: **Picture From File**.

5   From the **Look in**: box, select the location of the file.

6   Click on: the **baseball** file.

7   Click on: **Insert**.

Changing background colour

□ **Method**

1 From the **Format** menu, select **Background**.

2 Select a light colour from the drop-down menu of colours.

Saving amended web page

□ **Method**

1 Click on: the 🖫 **Save** button.

Previewing amended web page in browser

□ **Method**

1 Click on: the 🔍 **Web Page Preview** button or from the **File** menu, select: **Web Page Preview**.

Printing amended web page from browser

□ **Method**

1 Click on: the 🖨 Print **Print** button.

Closing browser

☐ Method

1 From the **File** menu, select: **Close**.

Exiting Word and shutting down

If your session is finished, then close the document (from the **File** menu, select: **Close**), exit Word (from the **File** menu, select: **Exit**) and shut down the computer (exit all other applications; click on: the **Start** button, select **Shut Down**; select **Shut Down**; click on: **OK**). Otherwise, move straight on to the next task.

Word

Format events page

Objectives

- Open events web page
- Format and align text
- Insert graphic image
- Change background colour
- Save amended web page
- Preview amended web page in browser
- Print amended web page from browser
- Close browser

In this task, you will open the Maryhill Little League Baseball Club **events** page that you created in Task 12.

Opening events web page

☐ Method

1 If you do not already have Microsoft Word on screen, then load it (*either* click on: the **Microsoft Word** shortcut icon on the desktop, *or* click on the **Start** button and select: **Programs**, **Microsoft Word**).

2 Open the Maryhill Little League Baseball Club **events** page that you created in Task 12 (click on: the ☞ **Open** button; select the location of the file; click on: the **events** file; click on: **Open**).

The Maryhill Little League Baseball Club **events** web page will appear on screen.

Formatting and aligning text

For the OCR Internet Technologies award you are required to format headings and text in different font sizes.

☐ Method

1 Format the main heading to a large font size and the subheading to a medium font size and choose two different alignment options.

2 Select important points of the body text and emphasise them using the bold and italic formatting options.

3 Format the body text to alignment options of your choice, using at least two different alignment styles.

Inserting graphic image

☐ Method

1 Insert the **baseball** image in a place of your choice (this is available on the accompanying CD-ROM).

Changing background colour

☐ Method

1 Select a background colour for the web page (choose a different colour to that of the **welcome** page).

Saving amended web page

☐ Method

1 Click on: the 🖫 **Save** button.

Previewing amended web page in browser

☐ Method

1 Click on: the 🔍 **Web Page Preview** button or from the **File** menu, select: **Web Page Preview**.

Printing amended web page from browser

☐ Method

1   Click on: the **Print** button.

Closing browser

☐ Method

1   From the **File** menu, select: **Close**.

Exiting Word and shutting down

If your session is finished, then close the document (from the **File** menu, select: **Close**), exit Word (from the **File** menu, select: **Exit**) and shut down the computer (exit all other applications; click on: the **Start** button, select **Shut Down**; select **Shut Down**; click on: **OK**). Otherwise, move straight on to the next task.

Word

16 Task

Create hyperlinks

Objectives

- Link **welcome** page to **events** page
- Link **events** page to **welcome** page
- Test hyperlinks

In this task, you will create links between the Maryhill Little League Baseball Club web pages and then test them.

Linking welcome page to events page

☐ Method

1   If you do not already have Microsoft Word on screen, then load it (*either* click on: the **Microsoft Word** shortcut icon on the desktop, *or* click on the **Start** button and select: **Programs, Microsoft Word**).

2   Open the **welcome** web page.

3   Highlight the whole of the line: **Click here to see...**

4   Create a hyperlink to the **events** web page. Ensure that **Link to: Existing File or Web Page** is selected.

5   Save the amended web page.

Linking events page to welcome page

☐ Method

1   Open the **events** web page.

2   Highlight the text: **Back to welcome page**.

3   Create a hyperlink to the **welcome** web page.

4   Save the amended web page.

Testing links

☐ Method

1   View the web page in the browser.

2   Print the **events** web page.

3   Click on the link you have just created.

This should take you to the **welcome** web page.

4   Print the **welcome** web page.

5   Click on the link: **Click here to see...**

This should take you to the **events** web page.

☐ Hint

If the links did not work, then check that you have followed the procedure correctly and try again. (Look back at Tasks 6 and 7 if you need a reminder of the steps.)

6   Close the browser.

7   Close the **events** file.

8   Close the **welcome** file.

Exiting Word and shutting down

If your session is finished, then exit Word and shut down the computer following the correct procedures. Otherwise, move straight on to the next task.

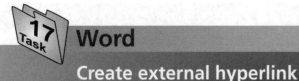

Word

Create external hyperlink

Objectives

- Create external hyperlink
- Save amended web page
- View and print amended web page in browser
- Test hyperlink

For the OCR Internet Technologies award you are required to create an external hyperlink to a published page already on the Internet. This is often done to provide links to other relevant sites on a similar theme. In this task, you will load the Maryhill Little League Baseball Club **welcome** web page, add new text to the web page and link the new text to a page on the Internet.

Creating external hyperlink

☐ Method

1 If you do not already have Microsoft Word on screen, then load it.

2 Open the Maryhill Little League Baseball Club **welcome** web page.

3 Make a space below the text: **Click here to see...**

4 Key in the following text, ensuring there is one clear line space between paragraphs:

   Link to British Baseball Federation

5 Highlight the new text.

6 Click on: the [icon] **Insert Hyperlink** button or from the **Insert** menu, select **Hyperlink**.

The **Insert Hyperlink** dialogue box appears on screen.

7 Click on: **Existing File or Web Page** in the **Link to:** section.

8 Click in the **Type the file or Web page name:** box and key in:

   http://www.bbf.org

9 Click on: **OK**.

Saving amended web page

☐ Method

1 Save the amended web page.

Viewing and printing amended web page in browser

☐ Method

1 View the amended page in the web browser.

2 Print the amended web page from the browser.

Testing hyperlink

☐ Method

1 Click on the link you have just created.

This should take you to the **British Baseball Federation** web page on the Internet.

2 Close the browser.

3 Close the **welcome** file.

Exiting Word and shutting down

If your session is finished, then exit Word and shut down the computer following the correct procedures. Otherwise, move straight on to the next task.

Word

Create new hyperlinks

Objectives

- Link Baseball Club **welcome** page to Anderson Fitness Club **home** page
- Link Anderson Fitness Club **home** page to Baseball Club **welcome** page
- Test new hyperlinks

The Maryhill Little League Baseball Club is being sponsored by nearby Anderson Fitness Club. As a gesture of goodwill it would be nice to link the Baseball Club's website to the Fitness Club's website. In this task, you will create a link from the **welcome** page of the Baseball Club to the **home** page of the Fitness Club and then create another link back from the **home** page of the Fitness Club to the **welcome** page of the Baseball Club.

Linking Baseball Club welcome page to Anderson Fitness Club home page

☐ Method

1   If you do not already have Microsoft Word on screen, then load it.

2   Open the Maryhill Little League Baseball Club **welcome** web page.

3   On a separate line above your personal details, key in the following text:

Sponsored by Anderson Fitness Club

4   Create a link, with this new text, to the Anderson Fitness Club **home** page.

5   Save the amended page.

6   Close the **welcome** page.

Linking Anderson Fitness Club home page to Baseball Club welcome page

☐ Method

1   Open the Anderson Fitness Club **home** web page.

2   On a new line below the text: **Why not email us...** and above your personal details, key in the following text:

We sponsor Maryhill Little League Baseball Club.

3   Create a link, with this new text, to the Maryhill Little League **welcome** page.

4   Save the amended page.

5   Close the **home** page.

Now that the links between the two pages are complete you should test the links in the browser and print the amended web pages.

☐ Method

1 Preview the Anderson Fitness Club **home** page in the browser.

2 Print the amended **home** page from the browser.

3 Click on the new link you created: **We sponsor Maryhill Little League Baseball Club.**.

This will load the Maryhill Little League **welcome** web page.

4 Print the amended Baseball Club **welcome** page.

5 Click on the new link you created: **Sponsored by Anderson Fitness Club**.

This will load the Anderson Fitness Club **home** page.

6 Close the browser.

7 Close the **home** page.

Exiting Word and shutting down

If your session is finished, then exit Word and shut down the computer following the correct procedures. Otherwise, move straight on to the next task.

Word

Task 19

Create demo web page

Objectives

- Key in text
- Format text and alignment
- Insert image
- Create links
- Test links

This task will help consolidate the skills you have learnt in previous tasks. You will create a demo web page which will be formatted using a variety of heading and alignment styles. The links in the page will be to an existing file, an email address and a published web page (a page that exists on the Internet). The **angel** image can be found on the accompanying CD-ROM.

Keying in text

□ Method

1 If you do not already have Microsoft Word on screen, then load it and ensure you have a new blank document on screen.

2 Key in the following text, making sure there is one clear line between paragraphs:

> MAIN HEADING – LARGE FONT AND LEFT ALIGNED
>
> SUBHEADING – MEDIUM FONT AND CENTRE ALIGNED
>
> This text and the image will appear centred on the page.
>
> This is the main body text and this line will appear centred and underlined on the page.
>
> This is a new paragraph and will be italic and bold and right aligned on the page.
>
> This is a link to another file.
>
> This is a link to an email address.
>
> This is a link to a published web page.
>
> This web page designed by:

3 Add your personal details after the text: **This web page designed by:**.

4 Spellcheck the document, making any necessary amendments.

5 Proof-read the document carefully, checking for any errors the spellcheck might have missed.

Formatting text and alignment

□ Method

1 Format the document according to the text – for example, the main heading will be a large font size (24 pt) and left aligned, the subheading will be medium font size (14 pt) and centred, etc.

2 Change the background colour of the page.

Inserting image

☐ Method

1 Insert the **angel** image below the subheading.

2 Centre the image.

3 Save the document as a web page, using the filename: **demohtml**.

4 Print the document.

Creating links

☐ Method

1 With the text: **This is a link to another file.**, create a link to the **amenities** web page.

2 With the text: **This is a link to an email address.**, create a link to your own email address.

3 With the text: **This is a link to a published web page.**, create a link to the following web page:

   http://www.heinemann.co.uk

4 Save the changes.

Testing links

☐ Method

1 Preview the page in the browser.

2 Print the page from the browser.

3 Test all the links that you inserted.

4 Close the browser.

5 Close the **demohtml** file.

Exiting Word and shutting down

If your session is finished, then exit Word and shut down the computer following the correct procedures. Otherwise, move straight on to the next task.

Word

Print HTML source codes

Objectives

📁 View, save and print HTML codes

For the OCR Internet Technologies award you are required to load web pages that you have formatted into the browser and view, save and print the HTML source codes used in formatting the pages. Instructions on how to do this were given in Task 10.

Refer back to these instructions when necessary and view, save and print the HTML codes used for formatting the following web pages:

- Anderson Fitness Club **amenities**
- Maryhill Little League Baseball Club **welcome** and **events**
- **demohtml** web page.

> ### ☐ Info
>
> If your browser is **Internet Explorer**, when you view the HTML source code, it will immediately be loaded into Windows Notepad.
>
> If your browser is **Netscape**, when you view the source code, you will need to highlight the code (**Ctrl + A**); copy the source code (**Ctrl + C**) and paste the code (**Ctrl + V**) into Windows Notepad.

When you have printed the HTML codes, highlight the formatting you used, e.g. font sizes, alignment styles, bold, italic, hyperlinks, etc. Write your name, centre number and task number on each printout.

Publish information on a website

Consolidation

The following tasks will help consolidate the skills you have learnt in the previous tasks.

Word/FrontPage/Netscape Composer

Build-up task 1

In this task, you will create and format a new web page.

1 Load an HTML editing application and key in the following text:

> BROWSING THE WEB
>
> HINTS AND TIPS 1
>
> Find out the off-peak rates of your telephone company. Remember that the modem inside your computer is connected to your phone line. Set yourself a time limit for browsing.
>
> Browsing the web can be expensive during the day. You may find it is less expensive to browse after 6 pm on weekdays. Weekend rates are usually the least expensive.
>
> More hints and tips
>
> Link to my email address
>
> (Your name, date, centre number)

2 Make sure there is only **one clear line** space between paragraphs and spellcheck and proof-read for errors.

3 Save the web page as: **Tips1**.

4 Format the main heading to a large font size, left aligned on the page.

5 Format the second (sub) heading to a medium font size, right aligned on the page.

6 Insert an appropriate image between the two headings to be centred on the page. You can insert an image of your choice or choose an image from the accompanying CD-ROM (the **browsing** image is quite good).

7 In the first paragraph emphasise the following text:

off-peak

modem

phone line

time limit

8 In the second paragraph emphasise the following text:

weekend

least expensive

browse

9 Change the background colour of the web page.

10 Save the amended web page.

11 Preview the page in the browser and print the page.

12 Close the web page.

13 Exit the HTML editing application and shut down the computer, following the correct procedures.

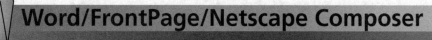

Word/FrontPage/Netscape Composer

Build-up task 2

In this task, you will create and format a new web page.

1 Load an HTML editing application and key in the following text:

BROWSING THE WEB

HINTS AND TIPS 2

If you are searching the web for a particular subject be careful which link you follow from the search results. Read all of the text in the link to see if it contains what you are looking for.

Use more than one search engine. As an example, in Yahoo!, if you cannot find a suitable link for the information you require, scroll down to the bottom of the screen and you will see a list of other search engines. When you click on one of these different search engines, your search will be continued.

Back to Tips 1

Link to a published web page

(Your name, date, centre number)

2 Save the new page as **Tips2**. This time you can choose heading sizes and alignment.

3 Use at least three different font sizes in the web page.

4 Use at least two different alignment styles in the web page.

5 Insert the same graphic image as in **Tips1** – you decide the alignment.

6 Emphasise what you consider to be important points in the body text.

7 Change the background colour of the web page (select a different colour to that of **Tips1**).

8 Save the amended web page.

9 Preview the completed web page in the browser and print a copy.

10 Close the browser.

11 Close the **Tips2** web page.

12 Exit the HTML editing software and shut down the computer, following the correct procedures.

Word/FrontPage/Netscape Composer

Build-up task 3

In this task, you will create links in the web pages that you produced in Build-up tasks 1 and 2.

1 Load an HTML editing application and open the web page saved as **Tips1**.

2 Link the text **More hints and tips** to the **Tips2** web page.

3 Link the text **Link to my email address** to your own email address.

4 Save the amended web page.

5 Close the web page.

6 Load the web page saved as **Tips2**.

7 Link the text **Back to Tips 1** to the **Tips1** web page.

8 Link the text **Link to a published web page** to the Heinemann website at:
http://www.heinemann.co.uk

9 Save the amended web page.

10 Load the page into the browser and test the links.

11 Print the pages in the browser.

12 View, save and print the HTML source code for **Tips1** and **Tips2**.

13 Exit the HTML editing software and shut down the computer, following the correct procedures.

Word/FrontPage/Netscape Composer

Consolidation assignment 1: Freedom Travel Services

Scenario

A major transport company is in the process of announcing a new train service to add to its existing regular scheduled services. You are in charge of design for this project. To promote the new service you have been asked to develop web pages to add to the company website. Although two unlinked web pages already exist (**company.htm** and **details.htm**), you have been asked to produce a third page. (The web pages **company.htm** and **details.htm** and the image **prices.jpg** can be found on the accompanying CD-ROM.)

Company web page design procedures are to be followed:

- Paragraphs must have one clear line space between.

Three different font sizes are to be used for each page. Body text must be shown in a small font size; headings should be in a large font size; subheadings should be in a medium font size.

Each web page must include your personal details (name and centre number).

3.2a 3.2g	**1**	The existing web pages **company.htm** and **details.htm** need to be linked.
3.3a 3.3b		Edit the **company.htm** web page to link the text **Click here for further details** to the **details.htm** web page.
		Key in your personal details after the text: **This web site designed by:**. Save the web page.
3.2a 3.2g	**2**	Edit the **details.htm** web page to link the text **Back to company page** to link to the **company.htm** web page.
3.3b		Key in your personal details after the text: **This web page designed by:**. Save the web page.
3.2f	**3**	It is important to check the links are correct before continuing with the project.
		Load each web page in the browser and check that the links work correctly.

4 You now need to create a new web page showing details of the **Shuttle Prices**.

Create a new document using the text shown below:

FREEDOM TRAVEL SERVICES

Shuttle Service Prices

The prices for the new City Shuttle Service are very competitive. You can pay at your local station, or why not purchase one of our Saver Cards? This is priced at £10.00 and will give you 6 return journeys for the price of 5.

Take the stress out of travelling.

Back to company page

This web page designed by:

Key in your personal details after the text: **This web page designed by:**.

5 Company design procedures must be followed for the formatting of the new web page.

Format the text **Freedom Travel Services** as a heading (large font size).

Format the text **Shuttle Service Prices** as a subheading (medium font size).

The remaining text is to be body text (small font size).

Ensure that each paragraph is separated by one clear line space.

6 Format the first 5 paragraphs to be centred on the web page.

The final paragraph **This web page designed by:** is to be left aligned on the web page.

Embolden the text **City Shuttle Service**.

Embolden the text **£10.00**.

Embolden and italicise the text **Saver Cards**.

7 The web page must show the Freedom Travel Services logo.

Insert the image **prices.jpg** below the text **Freedom Travel Services**, and above the text **Shuttle Service Prices**.

Make sure the graphic is centred on the web page.

3.2b 3.2g	**8**	The newly created web page should link back to the Freedom Travel Services **company** page. Edit the newly created web page and link the text **Back to company page** to link to the **company.htm** page. Save the new page.
3.1f 3.2c 3.3b	**9**	The **company** page needs to link to the new web page. In the **company.htm** page, on a new line below the text **Click here for...** and above the text **This web page...** add the following text: **For Saver Card details click here** This new text is to be centred on the page. Link this new text to your new web page.
3.1f	**10**	Load all of the web pages into the browser and test the new links.
3.1g 3.2g	**11**	A different background colour will enhance the company page. Change the background colour of **company.htm**, making sure that it is not the same as the text colour. Save the amended **company.htm** page.
3.2e 3.2g	**12**	There are links in the web pages that are not yet completed. Edit the **details.htm** to link the text **Freedom Travel Information** to the **Heinemann** website at: **http://www.heinemann.co.uk** Save the amended **details.htm** page.
3.2d 3.2g	**13**	Edit the **details.htm** web page and link the text **Email us with your queries** to be an email link to the following address: (key in your email address) Save the amended page. Load all the pages in the browser and check that the links work correctly.
3.3c 3.3d	**14**	The advertising manager would like to see the changes you have made. Load the **company.htm** page into the browser and print a copy. Load the **details.htm** page into the browser and print a copy. Load the **new page** into the browser and print a copy. Print a copy of the HTML source code used for the three web pages.
3.3e 3.3f	**15**	Close down all applications, following the correct procedures.

Scenario

You work in the busy Personnel department in a large organisation. You have been asked to prepare web pages to promote computer health and safety to be loaded into the staff network system. Two of the web pages already exist. These are **safety.htm** and **reminders.htm**. You have been asked to prepare a third page. (The web pages **safety.htm** and reminders.htm and the image health.jpg can be found on the accompanying CD-ROM.)

Company web page design procedures are to be followed:

● Paragraphs must have one clear line space between.

Three different font sizes are to be used for each page. Body text must be shown in a small font size; headings should be in a large font size; sub headings should be in a medium font size.

Each web page must include your personal details (name and college centre number).

3.2a 3.2g	**1**	The existing web pages **safety.htm** and **reminders.htm** need to be linked.
3.3a 3.3b		Edit the **safety.htm** web page to link the text **More safety reminders** to the **reminders.htm** web page.
		Key in your personal details after the text: **This web site designed by:**.
		Save the web page.
3.2a 3.2g	**2**	Edit the **reminders.htm** web page to link the text **Back to safety** page to link to the **safety.htm** web page.
3.3b		Key in your personal details after the text: **This web page designed by:**.
		Save the web page.
3.2f	**3**	It is important to check the links are correct before continuing with the project.
		Load each web page in the browser and check that the links work correctly.
3.1a 3.3b	**4**	You now need to create a new web page showing details of the **Safety Workshops**.

Create a new document using the text shown below:

> YOU AND YOUR COMPUTER
>
> COMPUTER SAFETY WORKSHOPS
>
> We have planned a series of workshops to give all staff the opportunity to look at good practice techniques when working at your computer. Staff qualified in workstation assessment will supervise the workshops.
>
> It is a requirement for all members of staff to attend a workshop. Workshops will be available on different days and times to suit all members of staff. Your line manager has timetables in which you can book a time to attend a workshop.
>
> Back to safety page
>
> Email a colleague about these tips
>
> This web page designed by:

Key in your personal details after the text: **This web page designed by:**.

3.1c
3.3b

5 Company design procedures must be followed for the formatting of the new web page.

Format the text **You and Your Computer** as a heading (large font size).

Format the text **Computer Safety Workshops** as a subheading (medium font size).

The remaining text is to be body text (small font size).

Ensure that each paragraph is separated by one clear line space.

3.1d
3.1f
3.3e

6 The first 4 paragraphs are to remain left aligned on the web page.

The final 3 paragraphs are to be centred on the web page.

Embolden the text **workshops**.

Embolden the text **good practice**.

Italicise the text **requirement**.

Embolden and italicise the text **timetables**.

3.1d
3.3e
3.1f

7 The web page must show the Health and Safety logo.

Insert the image **health.jpg** above the text **You and Your Computer**.

Make sure the graphic is centred on the web page.

3.2b	**8**	The newly created web page should link back to the Workshops **safety** page.
3.2g		
		Edit the newly created web page and link the text **Back to safety page** to link to the **safety.htm** page.
		Save the new page.
3.1f	**9**	The **safety** page needs to link to the **new** web page.
3.2c		
3.3b		In the **safety.htm** page, on a new line below the text **More safety reminders** and above the text **This web page...** add the following text:
		Computer safety workshops
		This new text is to be left aligned on the page.
		Link this new text to your new web page.
3.1f	**10**	Load all of the web pages into the browser and test the new links.
3.1g	**11**	A different background colour will enhance the **safety** page.
3.2g		
		Change the background colour of **safety.htm**, making sure that it is not the same as the text colour.
		Save the amended **safety.htm** page.
3.2e	**12**	There are links in the web pages not yet completed.
3.2g		
		Edit the **reminders.htm** to link the text **Link to Health and Safety Executive** to the **Health and Safety Executive** website at:
		http://www.hse.gov.uk
		Save the amended **reminders.htm** page.
3.2d	**13**	Edit the **new** web page and link the text **Email a colleague about these tips** to be an email link to the following address:
3.2g		
		(key in your email address)
		Save the amended page.
		Load all the pages in the browser and check that the links work correctly.
3.3c	**14**	The personnel manager would like to see the changes you have made.
3.3d		
		Load the **safety.htm** page into the browser and print a copy.
		Load the **reminders.htm** page into the browser and print a copy.
		Load the **new page** into the browser and print a copy.
		Print a copy of the HTML source code used for the three web pages.
3.3e	**15**	Close down all applications, following the correct procedures.
3.3f		

Glossary

Attachment   A file that can be sent with an email message. On receipt, the addressee is able to open up the attachment (provided they have the necessary software) and save, edit, print or play it, depending on the file type. An attached file could be a word processed file, spreadsheet, image, sound file, video file, etc.

Bookmarks   A feature of browser software that enables you to mark pages you may wish to return to. Also known as Favorites depending on your browser.

Browser   Software that enables you to move around the world wide web. The two most common browsers are Microsoft Internet Explorer and Netscape Navigator.

Domain Name   Part of the naming system used in website and email addresses which reflects the name of an organisation, the type of site and the country. Parts of the address are separated by dots, e.g. john.smith@heinemann.co.uk shows that John Smith is sending a message from Heinemann, which is a commercial organisation in the UK.

Other domain name endings include:

.gov	government
.org	organisation (non-profit-making)
.ac	academic site
.fr	France
.au	Australia
.hk	Hong Kong

For home computer users the domain is likely to be the name of the service provider e.g. john.smith@btinternet.com.

Download   The process of copying a file from a website on to your own computer to store for later use.

Email   Electronic mail messages that are sent over the Internet.

Email Address   A unique address by which other users can contact you. It usually takes the form: Log-in name@domain name, e.g. jane.brown@btinternet.com.

Electronic mail   *see* Email

Favorites   *see* Bookmarks.

Forward   A facility of email software that allows you to redirect an email message you have received, to another party.

Header   Part of an email message that appears automatically at the start of the message and includes information such as name of recipient, sender and date.

Home page   The main page of any website which usually serves as a list of contents leading to other pages within that site. On a home system the home page loaded when you access the Internet would probably be that of your service provider.

HTML   **H**ypertext **M**ark-up **L**anguage is the language used to write web pages. HTML editors such as Microsoft FrontPage or Dreamweaver allow you to create pages without having to understand or write the code.

Hyperlink   By clicking on a hyperlinked word, button or image you jump directly to another place or page which could be on the same site or anywhere on the Internet. Hyperlinks can also feature within electronic documents such as word-processed files. As you move the mouse over a hyperlink, the arrow changes to a hand.

Inbox   Incoming email is stored in the Inbox.

ISP   *see* Internet Service Provider.

Internet   Often known as the Net. A worldwide system of computer networks, large and small – in fact, a network of networks. Information held on these computers in the form of web pages can be accessed by any other in the network so that users, with permission, can also gain access. The Internet has two main features – websites and email access

Internet Service Provider (ISP)   A commercial organisation that offers access to the Internet usually in return for a fee although some are free, e.g. BTInternet, Freeserve, AOL.

Local search engine A facility provided on a web site allowing a search to be made on that site only. *see* Search engine.

Modem **Mod**ulator/**Dem**odulator – the device that converts your computer's digital signals (on/off pulses) into analogue signals (waves) so they can be transferred along the telephone line. The modem is usually inside your computer.

Network A group of computers linked together either by cables over a small area, e.g. within a building or one site, or by telecommunication links over wider geographical areas.

Offline When you are not connected to the Internet your computer is offline. It is cost-effective to compose messages offline and only connect to send and receive them.

Online When you are connected to the Internet your computer is online.

Outbox Messages sent are stored in the Outbox. On a home system they may be stored in the Outbox until you use the Send/Receive option, at which point they will be sent and appear in the Sent Items folder. On a business or college system they are likely to be sent immediately without appearing to pass through the Outbox.

Reply A facility of email software that allows you to reply to an email message you have received, automatically re-addressing it back to the sender.

Search engine Software that searches for web sites matching specific key words or phrases that you have typed in. Examples of search engines are Google, Yahoo!, Alta Vista, Ask Jeeves. *see* Local search engine.

Server A computer that provides a service for other computers that connect to it. In the case of an ISP (Internet Service Provider), the server will give access to the internet to anyone who logs on to it and will receive and forward emails to and from the user.

Service Provider *see* Internet Service Provider.

Site *see* website.

Source code This refers to the readable code used (in the case of HTML) to write web pages. HTML editors generate this code automatically and users do not see it unless they choose to do so.

Subject header The subject should always be entered in this section of an email message to ensure efficient handling of messages when received and thereafter for reference purposes.

Surfing Moving across the world wide web from web page to web page by using hyperlinks or search engines.

Tags The HTML code used to format web pages, e.g. <H1> for Heading 1 size text.

URL A **U**niform **R**esource **L**ocator is the unique address assigned to every page on the Internet. This can be found in the Address box below the toolbar. An address comprises three parts e.g. www.heinemann.co.uk The *www* indicates it is a world wide web site; *Heinemann* is the name of the company; *.co.uk* indicates it is a UK commercial site. URLs are often longer than this as you move on to subsequent pages within a site, showing folders where a page might be stored e.g. www.heinemann.co.uk/vocational/it/, shows the page displayed is IT stored within the vocational folder on the site.

Uniform Resource Locator *see* URL.

Upload To send a file to the Internet, e.g. if you create your own website you would need to upload it to the site of your Internet Service Provider.

Web address *see* URL.

Web site A website usually consists of many linked pages which may contain text, images, sound, animations and video clips. Users access pages via hyperlinks.

World wide web Also known as www, W3 or the Web. This is the part of the Internet that features millions of pages of information (web pages) held on computers all over the world.